STANISLAVSKY DIRECTS

STANISLAVSKY DIRECTS

BY

NIKOLAI M. GORCHAKOV

TRANSLATION BY MIRIAM GOLDINA

VIRGINIA STEVENS
TRANSLATION EDITOR

FOREWORD BY NORRIS HOUGHTON

NEW YORK :: FUNK & WAGNALLS COMPANY

FOREWORD

Opening nights in the theatre have their own kind of excitement, communicable to every member of an audience and behind the curtain to every member of the cast and stage crew. There is, however, another theatrical excitement of which the outside public never knows, and that is the excitement of rehearsal, during the days when, on a bare stage beneath the harsh glare of a white work-light, a play ceases to be words typed on paper and turns into a living experience. To see this happen before your eyes, whether you are author, actor, director, or only a stage manager or assistant looking on, is to participate in the most exhilarating part of stage work. This kind of excitement transcends language and geographic or political barriers.

A number of Americans have read the words of the great Russian stage director, Konstantin Stanislavsky, in books that recount his life and explain his artistic principles. A handful have seen the results of his handiwork here or abroad in the monumental productions of the Moscow Art Theatre that bear the imprint of his direction. A still smaller number saw him, a giant figure with a broad, mobile face, perform in person on the stage. Almost nobody from this part of the world ever had the opportunity of being in on the creative excitement of a Stanislavsky rehearsal. Joshua Logan had such an opportunity in 1932, which he has recalled in the introduction to Stanislavsky's *Building a Character*. I had a similar unforgettable opportunity a couple of years later, which I recorded in *Moscow Rehearsals*.

Now, vicariously, thanks to this book, the doors are open to all. This largely verbatim transcript of the happenings at Stanislavsky's own rehearsals are enthralling—and true. It answers many questions: How can the Russians spend so long rehearsing a play? How did the so-called "method" of Stanislavsky actually work out? Did he practice what he preached?

If the infinite capacity for taking pains is one of the attributes of genius, the Russian master ranks unquestionably near the top. No rehearsal detail is too small to concern him. His imagination never flags. The only regret is that the plays on which he worked as recorded herein should in several instances have been not altogether worthy of his great inventiveness.

Of course, that is one of the tragedies of the Soviet theatre today: The truly creative artist must be subservient to the demands of a state in which art has become a means to an end. For Stanislavsky art was an end in itself. The wonder is that he could exert such theatrical power to the end of a life led in its latter years under these circumstances. But the testimony of this book is that the great artist remains free because his inner power transcends temporary bonds. In this context this becomes a reassuring book. From any point of view it is an incomparable record of the rehearsal—that is to say, the creative—experiences of one of the modern world's great theatre masters.

NORRIS HOUGHTON

TRANSLATOR'S PREFACE

Nikolai Gorchakov, the author of *Stanislavsky Directs* belongs to that group of directors in the Russian theatre whose creative life began in the first years after the October Revolution. He finished Vakhtangov's school in 1922, graduating in the class for directors, and in 1924 he joined the Moscow Art Theatre with a group of other students from Vakhtangov's Studio.

From the first month of his work with the Moscow Art Theatre he was under the direct supervision of Stanislavsky. Thanks to his knowledge of stenography, Gorchakov took detailed notes of everything that was said by Stanislavsky and kept a diary of all his lectures and rehearsals from 1924 to 1936. These notes and the diary are the basic material of the book. The author is today one of the finest directors of the Moscow Art Theatre.

As a former student of Stanislavsky, I experienced his teachings in directing at first hand both theoretically and in practice. And as an actress and director in the American theatre I have come to know how valuable and necessary these teachings are. When the book was brought to my attention, I was tremendously excited and I felt an added connection with it because of having attended some of these same rehearsals which Gorchakov describes in this book.

The volume deals with immutable principles of the art of directing and summarizes the life experience of a great director in the theatre.

MIRIAM GOLDINA

NOTE TO THE READER

An occasional passage of the original Russian text has been omitted in this translation. Most of these omissions have been made because Russian plays or actors, little known in the American theatre, are being discussed or, on the other hand, because they are in a sense digressions by Stanislavsky on topics outside the scope of the play under discussion. The logic and the structure of the original text, however, are retained intact.

As there is no universal method of transliteration of the Russian alphabet, spelling of Russian proper names in this book follows an accepted pattern that differs slightly from the spelling of certain other works on the Moscow Art Theatre.

CONTENTS

ix

STANISLAVSKY DIRECTS

FIRST MEETINGS

INTRODUCTION

I saw Konstantin Sergeyevich Stanislavsky for the first time in person on the stage of the Moscow Art Theatre in 1920, at the dress rehearsal of the play *Cain* by Byron. The auditorium was filled with young people from the studios of the Moscow Art Theatre who had come to study after the Revolution and had been invited for the first time, on this particular day, to see the dress rehearsal of the new production. There was much talk in theatre circles about this production of *Cain*, and of Stanislavsky's daring conception of it and his inexhaustible imagination during rehearsals, and on this day we were invited to be present at the last stages of work on this play.

Acquaintance with the Method

We understood the significance of this dress rehearsal and probably were no less excited than the actors behind the footlights. The mood of those in the auditorium gave this impression. Suddenly the auditorium became silent. Stanislavsky appeared at one of the doors and approached his director's table. One could see that he was also very nervous. He looked attentively at the faces smiling at him

3

and at the enthusiastic eyes turned to him, and it seemed as though he was absorbing the sincere, warm feeling of the audience. He stopped by his table and looked over the auditorium once more, gazing into the farthest corner. At that moment each one of us had the feeling that Stanislavsky was looking directly at him. Then he clasped his amazingly expressive hands in a friendly shake, raised them high and with one wide gesture of welcome greeted the audience. The audience rose enthusiastically to its feet and responded to his greeting with thunderous applause. Stanislavsky bowed, gestured his thanks at the ovation, and then asked us all to be seated. When silence had been restored, he spoke a few words, telling us that this was his first meeting with the audience as a director after the Revotion. He said that the performance was not ready yet, that the "Angel" did not even have his costume; he would appear in some sort of a sheet. But he found it necessary to test the play before an audience at this particular stage in its development. He was silent for a moment and then he sat down in his armchair. He was very serious, even tense. From my seat in the auditorium I could observe Stanislavsky and at the same time watch the performance on the stage. On the stage I saw the scenes of Byron's tragedy *Cain* as they were played one after another, and I also saw how every move and every word of the actors was reflected on Stanislavsky's face. I have never seen a more mobile, a more expressive, or a more impressionable face. What childish joy it reflected when the actors worked well! When they did not, his hands wrote rapidly on the paper in front of him and his lips moved impatiently, whispering something. The change in expression on his face was instantaneous. It was alive every minute, either nervous or happy or sad, reflecting whatever experience the actors on the stage were going through.

Sometime later Vakhtangov told me that he had asked Stanislavsky to include a group of his young students with others to hear Stanislavsky lecture on his method. Vakhtangov appointed me as representative of his group and told me that Stanislavsky wanted to see the representatives in order to get an idea of the young people with whom he would meet.

"Here is your chance to get acquainted with Konstantin Sergeyevich," Vakhtangov said to me. "I know that you have been waiting for such an opportunity for a long time. Do not try to ingratiate yourself. Be relaxed, natural; don't try to win him all at once. His charm is enormous but he is not as trusting as he gives the impression of being. Oh, how difficult he can be!"

With this advice I set out for Leontiev Street. I was terribly nervous and scared. Stanislavsky received me simply, with reserve, in an almost businesslike manner. He looked at me intently, as though trying to detect from my answers to his questions something more that was important and necessary to him. His questions were clear and their purpose understandable to me.

"How many students will there be from the Vakhtangov Studio? When did they begin to study at Vakhtangov's? What kind of an examination did they have to pass in order to be accepted? How old are they? Have any of them been in the theatre before? Who taught them the method?"

He asked me if I knew anything of the students from the other groups. He asked what we expected from his lectures. Did we realize that even if he lectured for a whole year this would not make actors out of us?

"The method is only the road to the actor's self-education," he said. "It is only a path which must be followed during one's whole life toward the goal one has chosen."

He said he had no recipes for playing this or that role and had no intention of giving any. "The method is only a number of exercises which must be repeated every day in order to play any role."

He said he would like all who were to attend these lectures to be told this before they began. They should not expect some miraculous revelation from him and should not be disappointed at the simple exercises that he would offer them instead. Would I please gather the three other representatives and tell them, and each in turn should inform his group of the plan of work. Perhaps after learning of the plan some of the students would not be interested in attending. He would like to have a well-organized, well-prepared group. His introductory speech would be very short. He would start the very first lecture with exercises.

"The method is study through practice, not theoretical dissertations." If things developed in the right way he would take a play very soon and introduce the elements of the method while working on the play. Would I please repeat his remarks so that he could be sure I had understood him correctly.

I tried to repeat all that I had heard as precisely as possible and endeavored not to give my own interpretation to his thoughts. I felt that he was pleased. Then we parted. Our meeting lasted only twenty-five minutes but it seemed to me that I had been in his study for hours, because of the intense concentration with which I had listened to him. I told Vakhtangov of my impression of this meeting that same evening.

Vakhtangov asked me finally, "Well, what do you think he's like?"

"Severe and very efficient," I answered after thinking it over.

"That is because he was afraid of you," the unexpected answer came from Vakhtangov. "Along with an absolute conviction that his conception of art is correct, Konstantin Sergeyevich has an astounding modesty. To him each

meeting with anyone—no matter how old or young, or
what his position in the theatre may be—is another test of
his ideas of art and of his method, made on that particular
person. He doesn't so much expect contradictory opinions
from the person with whom he is talking, but rather he
checks the impression that his words and his assertions
make. He is afraid, or rather he worries, that his words will
not make the kind of impression that he feels is necessary.
You were the representative of the new youth whom he
doesn't know, about whom he knows nothing. That is why
he was nervous. Now don't you worry. You made a satisfac-
tory impression on him," Vakhtangov added, quite unexpectedly. "Immediately after you left him, he telephoned
and told me that. You've just had an example to remember
all your life: of how concerned a great artist is for young
people.

"His sense of responsibility for his work equals his mod-
esty. But he is just as demanding of others as of himself.
Remember this too when he scolds you, as he surely will,"
Vakhtangov finished with amusement.

Stanislavsky proceeded to work with the combined student groups in the way he had outlined at our first meeting. At his first lesson he spoke of the difference between
the art of living one's part and representing it. And then
he started the exercises on relaxation of muscles, attention,
and the rest of the elements of the method.

It was my privilege to call for him at his home and then
bring him back after the lectures. On his way to the lectures Stanislavsky was silent, preoccupied with the coming
lecture, and I dared not talk to him. On the way home he
was very tired and seemed to rest as we drove in the carriage. His health that winter was not good. He also was
worried about the future of the Moscow Art Theatre, the
lack of a new repertoire, and the lack of clarity in the general trend of theatrical art at this time. He kept to his plan

of work with the group, and six weeks later we began rehearsing *The Merchant of Venice*. He worked on the material of the play and its separate beats (2), demonstrating to us the principles of his method in working with actors. Summer and the traditional end of the theatrical season interrupted our meetings. The following fall his physical health was worse and our studies with him did not continue.

Fathers and Children

In the summer of 1923, after Vakhtangov's studio had become the third studio of the Moscow Art Theatre, we toured Sweden and Germany. Our tour was very successful, but because of the currency crisis in Germany and the catastrophic daily fall in the German mark, when the tickets had to be sold in advance, our actual receipts when the day of the performances came were one fifth of the box-office receipts. This meant financial failure for us. We had no means to proceed to Prague and Bucharest as we had planned. Our conscience did not allow us to ask for help again from the Soviet Embassy. On leaving Moscow we had been given a substantial sum in foreign currency. In Stockholm we had again received a large sum from the Trade Delegation of the U.S.S.R. for our transportation to Germany. And it was our own fault that we did not secure the right contract for our performances in Germany. We were ashamed of our overconfidence, of our lack of business sense, of our inexperience which had brought us to such a sad end on a tour which otherwise had been very successful. After exhausting every possible resource, the management of our studio decided to approach the touring company of the Moscow Art Theatre for help. They were having their summer vacation in Germany after a year's tour of America.

The majority of the company headed by Stanislavsky and Nemirovich-Danchenko, who had arrived from Moscow, were staying on Lake Varien, within an hour and a half of Berlin. I was sent with Ruslanov on this mission. When we reached Varien, we didn't know where the artists of the Theatre lived. We inquired where we could find the leading actor of the company—meaning Stanislavsky—but instead we were brought to Luzhsky. It turned out that Luzhsky was in charge of the Moscow Art Theatre's business affairs. He had brought the company to Varien, hired summer cottages, organized a communal dining-room and taken care of the bills with the local shopkeepers. Because of this the Germans considered him the leading member of the company.

I knew Luzhsky well. Vakhtangov had invited him to direct the play *Georges Dandin* by Molière for our studio and since then in Moscow I had been invited to his beautiful garden on Arbat Square. It was a lucky break for us to meet Luzhsky first. If we had talked first to Stanislavsky of our misfortunes, the result might have been very sad. Luzhsky was disturbed by our story, but he went immediately to see Podgorny, Stanislavsky, Vishnevsky, and Nemirovich-Danchenko. These actors, together with Luzhsky, constituted the management of the tour. Luzhsky told us that a problem as important as ours could only be decided by the entire management of the tour. He suggested that we return in two hours, and named some reasonable places where we could eat lunch. He asked if we had money for food. We lied, saying yes. Two hours later we returned to Luzhsky's cottage, and, to our amazement, found the table set for three. Obviously we had not convinced him that we had money for lunch. Luzhsky had prepared "relief," as he called it, and he invited us to the table.

"You will need a lot of strength to take all Konstantin

Sergeyevich is planning to give you so you better fortify yourselves," he joked. Then he told us seriously that they would give us the money but the continuation of our tour to Prague and Bucharest was out of the question. We must return to Moscow immediately, accompanied by a member of the management of the Moscow Art Theatre. During the coming year we must pay back the debt. He also said that we were severely criticized for our behavior, but the fact that we first approached the Moscow Art Theatre for help touched the management. It made them feel that there was an inner tie between the Theatre and our studio. Stanislavsky had ordered us to come to see him that evening at five o'clock. Luzhsky warned us that Stanislavsky did not want a word of gratitude but that he had something to tell us. We thanked Luzhsky for the lunch, which had been a real dinner, and for his aid to the studio.

"Now come, I'll take you to 'Himself,' " Luzhsky said.

We were at Stanislavsky's apartment exactly at five. He occupied two rooms on the second floor of a small summer cottage, the downstairs rooms being occupied by Podgorny. Stanislavsky met us sternly. He was silent for a long time. He was nervous and chose his words carefully.

"Pass on to your colleagues in the studio whatever you think necessary. I will say to you everything that is on my mind," he began. His voice broke.

"Please don't get excited, Konstantin Sergeyevich," Luzhsky said. "It is all taken care of."

"I can't help being excited," Stanislavsky answered him. "They think that this tour, whether successful or not, is their personal affair. They forget that they are not only under the auspices of the Moscow Art Theatre but, what is more important, they represent the young Soviet Art. They don't realize how carefully one must protect these young shoots from everything that might hurt their growth. Berlin is full of white guards who are looking for any kind of failure from Soviet artists. They take advantage of every rumor, every bit of gossip about us, and here the best young theatre of Moscow, under the protection of the Moscow Art Theatre, drowned because of their financial stupidity! Luckily they came to us. It is also lucky that we are able to send them home like erring school children. Suppose we were not here, what then? The theatre is not just a few good productions, it is not only a good acting company; it is an irreproachable artistic working body in all its parts, including finances. I am sure that your productions are kept at just as high a standard as when Vakhtangov was alive and your actors undoubtedly have developed. You have many talented people. But your management is no good, no good at all, if it could not secure a modest but steady material success! You have not yet learned about the organization of the theatre and you have undertaken hazardous travel. This is thoughtlessness and lack of responsibility to your government. What am I to say to Lunacharsky if he asks me to explain your attitude? You did not write me for advice or permission for your tour either. Now you are asking for our help like spoiled children."

"Who doesn't have spoiled children?" Luzhsky utilized Stanislavsky's pause to say.

"That's right," Stanislavsky continued, "we all have children. You, Luzhsky, have two sons. I have a son and a daughter (he looked at us sternly but suddenly softened, we looked so desperate) and they, too, are the children of the Moscow Art Theatre. You are putting down everything I have said," he addressed me. "That's good. I have nothing against it. But I repeat, tell your colleagues only what you think is necessary. Send me a copy of what I have said. I am very excited now and might say unnecessary things, but it is because I love the theatre and I am very uneasy about the fate of our new art. I want you to understand me correctly. The theatre is not only a director, and an acting company with well-produced plays: it is the entire ensemble of the theatre—director, administrator, and wardrobe mistress included. Only in this way can the new theatre develop and bring its culture to the audience. He who breaks this rule pays dearly. The theatre is not a game of darts. It is a serious occupation and now it is the concern of the people's government. Write to me from Moscow about your plans for new productions. Thank Luzhsky. Some of the members of our management wanted to take the support of the Moscow Art Theatre away from you, but others fought for you, and we decided to extend our support for one more year, until we return to Moscow. When we are back we will talk over your future."

We got up and took leave of Stanislavsky, and in the garden we met Podgorny and Nemirovich-Danchenko. "Well, did you get it?" Nemirovich-Danchenko asked. "You didn't listen to my advice and got into a mess. Traveling in Europe is not as simple as it seemed, is it? Well, all will work out. Return to Moscow immediately and come to see me in the fall. We will talk over everything." He shook hands with us firmly.

What Is a Director?

In the spring of 1922, when Vakhtangov was still alive but had been bedridden for a number of months, Stanislavsky came to us unexpectedly one Sunday matinée. We were giving one-act plays by Chekhov. I don't remember exactly the reason for his visit. Probably he felt for us, because we were so deeply upset by Vakhtangov's serious and prolonged illness, or perhaps he wanted to see one of our performances in its general run, as our theatre bore the name of The Third Studio of the Moscow Art Theatre, which meant that the Theatre carried the responsibility for the standard of our work.

He told us after the performance that he liked it. He remained for awhile in the theatre getting acquainted with us and when he was ready to leave I asked permission to see him home. That year I graduated from our theatre school and at Vakhtangov's suggestion, I was about to work on my directorial assignment for graduation, Dickens' story, *The Battle of Life*. It was very tempting to me to spend an extra half-hour with Stanislavsky.

He said, "I'm on my way to Isadora Duncan's to say good-by to her. She is leaving for France. You can walk with me to her house if you wish."

Isadora Duncan had a house on Kropotkin Street where she lived and also had her studio. We entered her house. I witnessed the parting of Isadora Duncan and Stanislavsky, which took fifteen minutes. They conversed in French. Their parting was very warm and friendly.

After leaving her house, we walked along Gogol Boulevard. Stanislavsky inquired about the affairs of our theatre, what our plans for work were, and what were our personal plans. He suggested that we sit on one of the benches along the boulevard. It was a beautiful spring evening. He asked me, with his invariable politeness, if I were not in a hurry to go somewhere. How could I rush away from him? I asked his permission to put the question to him that was most important to me, "What is a director?"

He answered my question with a question, "What you are really anxious to know is, are you a director? You want to know if I consider you a director. Well, let me examine you."

This wasn't exactly what I had anticipated but I couldn't get out of it very well.

"Here we are sitting on a bench on the boulevard. We

are looking at life as through an open window. People pass by us, incidents take place in front of our eyes. Now tell me all you see."

I made an attempt and told him what seemed to me important and interesting that had attracted my attention. I must confess that it wasn't very much. I was embarrassed by being examined and by this question suddenly put to me. I was not satisfied with my account, and neither was Stanislavsky.

"You have skipped a lot." He named a number of things I had missed. He told me about the coachman who drove up, whose passenger was a woman who was obviously bringing a sick child home. He noticed tears in the woman's eyes. He spoke of other incidents that occurred. He pointed out that I had missed all the sounds that he could hear around us. Then he said, "Tell me, what kind of a man is that one walking toward us?" I looked at the man.

"I think he's a bookkeeper of some kind. He looks very neat and has a pencil in his upper pocket. His portfolio is clean and he is so preoccupied."

"Your description fits a bookkeeper," he said, "but it could be characteristic of a number of other professions. And who do you think this one is?" He pointed to another. I looked at the man and said; "I think he's a messenger of some kind. He doesn't seem in a hurry. He has a kind of loose walk. There's an envelope under his arm. Suddenly he decided to sit down, then he jumped up and walked faster, then he waved his hand and sat on another bench and took out a cigarette. I take him for a messenger sent with an urgent message."

Stanislavsky liked this better. He said on the basis of this observation one could build a character and a dramatic situation.

"What are those two on that bench talking about?" he asked.

"They are in love," I answered.

"What makes you think so?"

"Because they are so attentive to each other even in small things. They speak more with their eyes than their lips. Besides, their glances at each other are abrupt and so are their gestures."

Stanislavsky agreed that they might be.

"Now, what do you know about this boulevard?" he asked me.

I know very little about it.

"What do you know about today? What is its importance to Moscow and even to the whole world?"

My bad luck! I had not even read the newspaper that day. Stanislavsky had, very carefully.

"What did you notice at Isadora Duncan's?"

"I was so excited," I answered, embarrassed by my failure to answer the previous question, "seeing the two of you, watching you say good-by to each other; all I was aware of was that I was in the presence of two famous people and I have nothing else to report."

"You noticed the most essential element—we were playing at being two world celebrities—but you did not understand for whom we were acting. You didn't notice a short gentleman who was sitting in the corner of the room? This man is Duncan's special secretary who was taking notes on all he saw and heard. He is going to write a book on her life. She was playing a role and so was I. Do you remember that we spoke French? How good did you think our French was?"

"It seemed to me it was very good," I replied.

"We spoke very poor French, pretending it was exceptionally good. When we were in the hall she shook my hand so hard I still feel it. Did you notice this? I think she likes me and I like her very much. You could have observed this too. You saw only the result of our acting but you did not see what we were acting and why. What do you know about Miss Duncan?"

"All I know is that she dances barefoot," I replied.

The next question was the most difficult for me. "What do you know about me?" he asked.

To this question as well I had nothing sensible to say.

"We have just reviewed the course in directing," he said. "The director must not only know how to analyze the play, how to advise the actors on playing, how to use the sets the scenic designer gives him, but the director must know how to observe life. He should be equipped with the maximum possible knowledge of other fields. Sometimes this knowledge comes as an immediate result of the needs of a particular play, but it is better to store it up. One can accumulate one's observations specifically for the play, but one should really train oneself to observe life and to put one's observations on the shelf of the subconscious. Later on they will stand the director in good stead.

"You are not the first to ask me what a director is. I used to answer that a director is a matchmaker who brings together the playwright and the theatre and when the play is successful he brings happiness to both. Later on I used to say that the director is a midwife who brings to birth the performance, the new creation of art. As the midwife gets older she sometimes becomes a sorceress who knows a great deal. By the way, midwives are very observing in life. But now I think the role of a director is becoming more and more complex. Politics is an integral part of our lives now. This means that the director's horizon includes the government's structure, the problems of our society. It means that we, the directors of the theatre, have much more responsibility and must develop a broader way of thinking. A director cannot limit his role to being a medium between author and audience. He cannot be just a midwife, merely assisting at the birth of the performance. The director must be independent in his thinking and must arouse with his work the ideas necessary to contemporary society. I tried to work with that approach in *Cain*. I gave myself the task of making the audience ponder the ideas of the play."

And with his usual self-criticism he added, "It seems to me I did not succeed."

The qualities which Stanislavsky enumerated for me on that spring evening in 1922 as so necessary for a director— the ability to observe, to think and to build one's work so that it will arouse in the audience the thoughts needed for our contemporary society—these were all distinctive traits of Stanislavsky himself, the director and leader of the theatre, and, as I understood later, they were also the characteristic problems of the Soviet director.

In the Moscow Art Theatre

In the winter of 1923 Nemirovich-Danchenko and Stanislavsky decided to fill their acting company with young actors. Nemirovich-Danchenko began negotiations with the management of the Moscow Art Theatre studios to merge them into one theatre organism. But the First Studio believed that they would find their way to a better theatre more easily if they remained independent, and so they refused his offer to merge with the Moscow Art Theatre. The Second Studio accepted the offer and in 1924 entered as the nucleus of the young company. From the Third Studio a number of actors joined. I entered too. Early in the fall of 1924, Stanislavsky gathered all the new members of the theatre and addressed us with the following words:

"You are entering the life of the Moscow Art Theatre at a difficult moment. We have just returned from America. We have no new repertoire and we don't even know where we will get it. Our old repertoire is too old and hardly suitable to the demands of the new Soviet theatre. There is a proverb, 'Don't pour new wine into old skins.' The skin of the Moscow Art Theatre is undoubtedly old, twenty-five years old to be exact. But I believe it can still do a good turn for the new art, for the new theatrical generation. We are very sturdy yet. You are the new wine. You will ferment, become more aromatic and firmer. Absorb from the old skin of our tradition adherence to the best ideals of the Russian Theatre.

"The tradition of the Moscow Art Theatre had its roots in that of Shchepkin and Gogol. Gogol saw the theatre as an institution capable of influencing the spiritual needs of the audience, of educating it toward a higher morality and ethics. He gave the theatre a task of a social character: to educate society through the dramatist's words embodied in the artistic image and the scenic action. The Moscow Art Theatre adheres to the Gogol precept and dedicates itself to the service of society. Shchepkin demanded that Gogol's precepts be embodied on the stage in realistic, artistic images. He was the greatest Russian artist-realist. He did not accept situations which could not be justified, which were not taken from life itself. He demanded knowledge of life from the actor, a complete artistic reflection of it in his work on the stage. The Moscow Art Theatre adheres to the precepts of Shchepkin and demands that an actor create a living human being in all the complexity of his character and behavior. When you enter the Moscow Art Theatre, you dedicate your life to serve these great precepts of Russian genius. Realize them every day and hour in your work in the theatre and outside it. I know it is very difficult. I promise you my help, but I warn you that I will be very particular and very demanding. The theatre begins not from the moment you make-up or from the moment of your entrance on stage. The theatre begins from the minute you awaken in the morning. You must ask yourself what you should do this day to earn the right to come to the theatre, to rehearse, to perform, or to take a lesson with a clear conscience.

"You are in the theatre when you greet the doorman on the way to your dressing-room, when you ask Fyodor for a pass, and when you put your rubbers in the hall stand. You are in the theatre when you talk about it to your acquaintances, to the clerk in a bookshop, to a friend, to another actor, or to the barber who cuts your hair. From now on, the theatre is your life, totally dedicated to one goal: the creation of great works of art which ennoble and elevate the soul of a human being, works which develop in man the great ideas of freedom, justice, love for the people, and love of country.

"We need new blood in our company. We will begin immediately to work. Lessons will be held every day in the school. I want to draw your attention especially to the lessons on speech, voice, rhythm, movement, and plastics. They are saying that we in the Moscow Art Theatre do not pay attention to these qualities in our actors. It is such nonsense and such idle gossip!

"Those of you who have graduated from the acting school will take roles in our old repertoire. We are going to revive the productions of *Czar Fyodor*, *The Cherry Orchard*, *The Bluebird*, *Much Woe from Wisdom*, and *The Lower Depths*. All these plays have large group scenes. The group scenes are the best school for a young actor. Each character in a group scene contains the elements of the scenic image and the action. We will rehearse these scenes with great care and I hope you will be convinced how useful it is for you to participate in them. We have lost a large number of actors and the First Studio has separated from us. We will distribute a number of small parts for which we have no actors among those of you who are suitable for them.

It is a great honor for an actor to play a speaking role in the old plays in his first month in our theatre. Don't let it turn your heads. It is not a reward for work but a cruel necessity. Let us do it so that you young actors benefit by it."

This was Stanislavsky's introductory speech to us. His actions followed his words. An hour later he watched the lesson in rhythm which his brother conducted in the same upper foyer. This was the exercise of the graduating class of the Moscow Art Theatre School. While observing these young men and women he asked Sudakov and me about them in an undertone. He looked them over and right away marked them for certain roles in forthcoming productions, expressing his estimation of them brilliantly and accurately. During the year he gave his careful attention to the school, giving lessons in his method, criticizing scenes from the plays; he was constantly in close touch with all the studies of the school. He was an extraordinarily sensitive artist with a love for every talent, no matter how young and undeveloped. He was teacher and educator, a man of big heart and pure soul.

"Czar Fyodor" by Alexei Tolstoy

We became acquainted with how Stanislavsky worked as a director on a major production during the revival of *Czar Fyodor*. He gathered us together and told us in detail the history of its production. He demonstrated how the boyar's fur coat should be worn, how one should gird himself in the long wide boyar belt, how to "play" the rich embroidered shawl or the caftan stitched with gold. His memory retained all the incidents connected with this production from the day of its opening until the meeting with us, the future cast. The rehearsals were a combination of marvelous lessons in acting skill and a living history of the

Moscow Art Theatre, its staging, and its special theatre ethics.

"I have never been completely satisfied with the way the scene in Mstislavsky's garden was played," Stanislavsky said. "I would like to try once more to solve this staging problem with you. We have never succeeded in giving a picture of that large complex political conspiracy of the boyars against Fyodor and Boris Godunov. We used to shout too much in it. The result was not justified. It was not a true revolt. It was unbelievable. Then sometimes we would do just the opposite—fall asleep in this scene, causing it to lose its sharpness. The scene is the key to the rest of the play. Without its correct realization, the following scenes are less dramatic, less comprehensive. Alexei Tolstoy wrote it exceedingly well. The text is not great but the structure is sharp and colorful. I would like to suggest that you play an étude on this scene, not today but at the dress rehearsal. From now on our rehearsals will be in preparation for this étude."

It is easy to imagine with what interest we listened to this unusual suggestion. We were entrusted to play, impromptu at the dress rehearsal, a scene of real importance in this magnificent production!

"I'll explain to you what I have in mind when I talk about the étude, our preparation for it, and its direct execution on stage. I came to this idea in the following way. I started to think what a conspiracy is. It is a gradual accumulation of events in pursuit of one problem. But the people who participate in the conspiracy often do not even know each other, do not know all the threads of the conspiracy, do not even know the date for its execution. I suggest that all of you become conspirators in relation to the étude I have proposed, which we will play in a week at the dress rehearsal. Our aim and our problem is to prove to the theatre that this scene can be played so that the audience will applaud. Our judge will be Nemirovich-Danchenko, who will watch the dress rehearsal. But we will promise, as true conspirators, that no one will tell him our special plan which we will follow in preparing for the dress rehearsal. Now, do I have your word?"

A harmonious chorus of voices answered Stanislavsky's challenge. That very moment he had planted in us, the participants in the scene, the seed of conspiracy, transforming us into conspirators. Of course at that time we didn't realize all this. We were simply engrossed in the problem he had put to us and excited at his personal participation in the étude.

"Now, let us talk it over," Stanislavsky continued. "What does it mean for each one of you to prepare himself for the conspiracy against Boris and Fyodor? First, you must know the life of that period in Russia well, its chaos and distress, the structure of its government. You must know the system of succession to the throne, know what sort of place Uglitch was, how things were done there, why the successor to the throne lived there and how old he was. You must visualize exactly and clearly what would happen in Russia if the young boy Dimitri occupied the throne. You must know the political significance of the actions of the Shuiskys and of their opponents. Let's not lose any time. Let's talk it over right now. For tomorrow's rehearsal each one of you must prepare answers to the following questions:

1. Who turned out to be right after the reconciliation, Boris or Ivan Shuisky?

2. How long have I been a supporter of the Shuiskys?

3. My opinion of the reconciliation.

4. What do I think must be done now after reconciliation?

5. What must Ivan Shuisky take upon himself and how is he to share power with Boris?

6. What position am I after and who is my competitor?

7. What political perspectives do I picture as a result of reconciliation?

8. What do I welcome and of what am I afraid?

9. Was I present at the reconciliation yesterday and how do I feel about being invited to the palace? Was I in disfavor before or not?

10. If I was not at the palace when the reconciliation took place, where was I then?

11. Who told me about the reconciliation and what did I plan to do about it after I heard?

12. Who brought me to Ivan Shuisky?

"In order for you to answer these questions, you must answer all those concerning the biography of your own character, such as:

1. Who am I? How old am I? My profession? Members of my family? What is my disposition?

2. Where do I live in Moscow? (You must be able to draw the plan of your apartment and the furniture in the rooms.)

3. How did I spend yesterday? How did I spend today until this evening?

4. Whom do I know among those present and what is my relationship to them?

"After you have answered all these questions for yourself, we will read and analyze the whole scene in the garden according to the text of the play. Then each one of you get together with two or three others and talk over your group's relationship to the rest of us. Thus, within the general group scene there will be small groups. I will work with each small group separately. I will establish the trend of thought of each member in each group, and the relationship of this little group to the lines of the principal characters and the turning point of the conspiracy. We will establish the mise en scène for each small group. But each group will not know what I have told the other groups, for this is typical of the way a conspiracy operates. Then each group will have to follow not only its own plan of action but will have to be very attentive to its neighbors. This is so each group doesn't put its foot in it, but will be on the watch so that it won't make a wrong move in relation to another group. This is also typical of a conspirator. He doesn't lag behind the others, nor at the same time is he among the initiators, for he isn't the leader of the decisive action. I, alone, as the director of the conspiracy, will know the thoughts and actions of all of you. At the dress rehearsal we will act simultaneously. Of course we will devote one of our preparatory rehearsals to the lines of the principal characters.

"Do you want to experiment with such a method of work on the group scene, the one we have never succeeded in getting right before?"

Our enthusiastic answer was a unanimous yes. Stanislavsky asked Luzhsky, an authority on Russian history, to conduct the next rehearsal, which would be a discussion of the historical-political situation in Russia during Ivan the Terrible's epoch. He entrusted me with the collection of all the questionnaires and a discussion of the biographies. He himself began to work with us on the reading and analysis of the scene in the garden.

The following days he kept strictly to his plan. He questioned Luzhsky and me about our meetings with the actors. He looked through some of the questionnaires and was satisfied with the result. I remarked that all our actors showed great persistence and efficiency in their work. In these three days the actors had widened their knowledge of the epoch and of the characters, and they had tried, to the best of their ability, to penetrate the depths of the play. Stanislavsky held his discussions with each separate small group. I was present at almost all his sessions and was amazed by his patience in talking to each group about the same actions separately. With what endless imagination, with what variety and richness of nuance he invented individual problems for each group of conspirators that were all to be merged in one main action!

He assigned me the technical rehearsal—that is, the rehearsal in which the lines of the principals were to be coordinated. The actors in the group scene participated, but Stanislavsky's instruction to them was, "Hide your reaction to the text." They were only allowed to whisper and exchange glances; because of this treatment the scene became very expressive, and Stanislavsky was satisfied with all the preparations for the étude.

At the dress rehearsal the success of the garden scene was tremendous. All the accumulated, previously restrained passions of the conspirators burst forth and created an exciting, brilliant performance. The audience applauded. Nemirovich-Danchenko was sincerely amazed and Stanislavsky was delighted.

"The Marriage of Figaro" by Pierre-Augustin Caron de Beaumarchais

I was also fortunate enough to see a few rehearsals of *The Marriage of Figaro*, each one of them an object lesson in directorial skill.

The first scene was remarkably staged. Regardless of the tradition and Beaumarchais' own directions that Susanna's room should be between the Countess' bedroom and the Count's study, Stanislavsky put it in a round, isolated tower, with one door and a steep staircase leading up to it. In this unexpected set he brilliantly discovered the line of inner life of the characters and the line of the mise en scène.

Perhaps the most striking scene was the marriage of Figaro and Susanna. I knew that Stanislavsky had made

Golovin, the designer, change the sketch three times before the first rehearsal. Count Almaviva, angry at being forced to give his permission to the marriage and furious at many of Figaro's pranks, gave orders to hold the ceremony in the "backyard" of the castle, as Stanislavsky put it. This order was very typical of the wilful artistocrat, who on the one hand was afraid of antagonizing his servant too severely and on the other did not want to give up his ancient privileges.

The scene is usually staged as a luxurious affair, in rich colors and with much splendor. But Stanislavsky had been returning Golovin's sketches. He insisted that they were too elaborate and too brilliant in color, and he declared that they didn't give the feeling of petty revenge which was the seed of the scene. At last Golovin brought a very simple sketch. It showed a narrow triangle consisting of three walls of white plaster, slightly sloping diagonally and covered with reddish tile along the upper edge. A blue southern sky was above. In the left side wall, simple wooden gates. In the right corner, a great number of barrels, boxes, broken benches—in other words, a heap of wooden junk. Stanislavsky was delighted with this sketch.

"Bravo, Golovin!" he said. "Now you've got it! It is exactly what this scene needs."

"Konstantin Sergeyevich, how will we place the crowd?" I asked. "There are over forty people in this scene."

"They will find places by themselves," he answered. "This time don't worry about mise en scène for them. Just see that this pile in the corner has all the barrels, boxes, benches, and ladders that we need."

"Where will the Count sit? You don't expect to put him in a barrel?" Zavadsky asked. He was playing the Count.

"It's your own fault that you have no place to sit. You shouldn't have been so capricious, exhibiting your foolish character," Stanislavsky answered, as though he were actually talking to Count Almaviva.

"When the set is ready," Stanislavsky continued, "have the actors in costume, ready to go on. Until then, test the lines of the scene along the inner action and the relationships. Do not bother about the mise en scène."

The simple set was ready very soon, and in a few days we all saw the first rehearsal on stage of this scene. As usual, upon entering the auditorium, Stanislavsky began to examine the set. It looked very well, in spite of the simplicity of color and line. The dark blue shadows from the brilliant sun, the dazzling white walls, the tile and the deep blue sky created a perfect atmosphere of evening on a hot summer day.

"Is everyone in costume?" Stanislavsky asked.

"They are all ready and waiting on stage to know where to go," the directors answered, hinting their desire to receive the mise en scène.

"Let them all come to me in the auditorium," he replied.

When the group in colorful costumes (Golovin was a master of theatrical costumes) came from the stage to the auditorium, those of us sitting there could appreciate the effectiveness of the artist's conception: the brilliant costumes against the white walls in the rays of the setting sun, all the colors shining like precious stones.

Stanislavsky addressed the actors: "Do you remember that the Count, angered by Figaro, gave orders to Basilio to celebrate the marriage in the 'backyard' of his castle?" There was no such order in the play but Stanislavsky had become so used to his own conception that he was certain it was Beaumarchais' direction. "Well, here in front of you is the backyard. Look at it carefully. The inhabitants of the castle know it well, but you actors are seeing it for the first time. This is where the servants and friends of

Susanna and Figaro bring all the broken objects no longer needed in the castle. (Something like the sheds on our estates, where all the junk is kept and for some reason never burned: sometimes something might be needed from that rubbish.) Naturally Susanna feels insulted to have her wedding here. Figaro is only concerned to have it take place; nothing else bothers him. The Count gloats. The rest of you know that you must fight for pieces of junk to stand on so that you can see the ceremony. Everyone wants to get as close as possible.

"Everyone on stage, please. All of you stay in the far corner near the organ. When the stage manager gives you a signal, rush in through the gates and grab the best box or barrel or old chair you can find. Before your entrance, play the scene by the organ, where you are waiting for the Count and the Countess. I must hear talk, exclamations, laughter, whatever the crowd would be doing while awaiting the arrival of their superiors." Then he said to the stage manager: "When the curtain goes up, count ten, then signal the crowd. Is everything clear?"

"Yes, Konstantin Sergeyevich."

"All right, on stage!"

The curtain was closed. In a few seconds it swung open smoothly. The familiar set was before us, but how different it looked! How alive it was, with the songs and laughter and talk of the crowd behind the walls! The crowd rushed in; someone stumbled, caught in the gates; some fell; someone got hold of the ladder in order to see from the highest point. In this way a very interesting mise en scène was created, full of life, brilliant in action, expressive of the purpose of the scene, and filled with temperament.

After the first group rushed through the gates, another group came through, and so forth. Gaiety, laughter, loud talk broke out among them, not ordered by the director but springing spontaneously from their clear desire to find the best place to watch the ceremony. No one knew or could even guess where Count Almaviva and his wife would sit. The crowd was in perpetual motion, carrying benches or chairs or other objects around, until the lords of the manor arrived. When the Count entered, the people cheered him, shouting, "Long live the Count!" But because of these objects in their hands it sounded more like the shouts of discontented people than a festive greeting. The bewildered Almaviva and his wife stood arm in arm, not knowing where to move, until the ingenious Basilio put two large planks on four barrels and on top of them put two gilded armchairs dragged from the junk pile. But the moment the Count sat down, one of the legs of his chair gave way, and, when he struggled for balance, his feet were flung up in such a comical fashion that no one, on stage or off, could control his laughter. Stanislavsky joined all of us in our laughter. It seemed to me that he wanted to show the unexpected happening. He solidified this mise en scène immediately and made his actors and directors find a basis in the logic of the characters' behavior to justify the way in which such an accident could arise. Only after they were justified did he include such spontaneous mise en scènes in the design and conception of the play or the role.

There were many great rehearsals with Stanislavsky that were not such creative holidays, especially those which he called "actors' rehearsals," when the problem of the production as a whole was put off for a time and he concentrated all his attention on some individual actor's problem. It might have been work on the dialog or on the specific quality of the character or the development of the main trait of the role. These were long hard hours for Stanislavsky and the actors. He was strict, demanding, patient. Nothing could be hidden from his eyes. His demands covered all aspects of the actor's skill. An actor might rehearse with genuine temperament but be stopped by: "Your hands, what are your hands doing? Why do you wave them like a windmill? Please begin again."

The actor begins to think of his hands, cuts out his gestures. Then another remark comes from Stanislavsky: "Empty, nerveless! You have forgotten the connecting links of your relationships. Your temperament is asleep. Begin again."

There were often tears, but they did not soften Stanislavsky. "Cry all you want, it doesn't disturb my rehearsal."

There were also naïve actors' revolts, which made no impression on him either, and when an actor began to plead, "Please take the part away from me if you don't like what I'm doing," the answer came, "When it is necessary, we will. Meanwhile rehearse." And the demands on the rebel grew stricter.

But there was no greater joy for the actor and for Stanislavsky himself when, after very long work and persistent search for a deep and true feeling or for a physical action or a new trait of the character, new qualities of the actor's individuality were revealed, new forms of expression discovered, and the thoughts and words were filled with truth and inner power. The actor's transformation into the character in those happy moments took place before our eyes and the actor created the life on the stage which Stanislavsky had been struggling to bring out.

Stanislavsky was very strict and demanding both as teacher and director. He never tired of telling us again and again that the inner technique of an actor is of first importance, but that almost as important are diction, voice placement, breath control, and knowledge of the laws of speech. I saved the pages on which Stanislavsky outlined graphically the laws of phonetics in theatre speech. He gave to plastic movement just as much significance. Stanislavsky considered rhythm in all its manifestations a necessary inner control of the actor's behavior on stage.

We were very fortunate not only to learn directly from him his great ideas of the art of the theatre but also to hear the intonations he used when speaking of art and of the significance of ethics in the life of the theatre. His voice was fiery and impassioned, and sometimes was filled with compassion for those who did not want or were not capable of absorbing his teaching. Stanislavsky's thoughts and intonations will stay with me forever.

ROMANTIC DRAMA

CHAPTER ONE

THE BATTLE OF LIFE

BY Charles Dickens

The action of the Charles Dickens' story, *The Battle of Life*, takes place in a small town near London in the middle of the eighteenth century. The family of Dr. Jeddler lives in the town.

SYNOPSIS OF THE PLAY
The dramatization of the story begins with the celebration of the birthday of Dr. Jeddler's youngest daughter, Marion. On the same day the doctor's ward, Alfred Gottfeld, leaves for the continent to complete his education. He and Marion are in love and are planning to get married as soon as Alfred returns. But on this day, Marion, who is happy because of her birthday and yet sad because Alfred is leaving, suddenly realizes that her older sister, Grace, is also in love with Alfred and has been hiding her affection in order not to upset Marion. Alfred guesses Grace's love for him. During the farewell dinner in his honor, he gives a speech about the greatness of modest, inconspicuous, heroic deeds performed in the great battle of life by modest, inconspicuous people who often sacrifice their own happiness for the happiness of those they love. That speech makes a very strong impression on Marion. She begins to doubt whether she has the right to accept Grace's sacrifice and begins to question the depth of her own love for Alfred.

A few years pass. A new admirer of Marion appears on the scene, Michael Warden, a dissipated young man who leads a fast life. Two months before, he had been thrown from his horse

33

in front of Dr. Jeddler's garden and had been brought into the house with a broken leg. Dr. Jeddler kept the patient in his house while he was convalescing and during that time the young libertine fell in love with Marion. He is convinced that his feeling is reciprocated, but, as he is sure that Dr. Jeddler will not give his blessing, he plans to elope with Marion.

The first scene of the second act takes place in the office of the local lawyers, Mr. Snitchey and Mr. Craggs. The two lawyers represent both Dr. Jeddler and Michael Warden. In this scene Michael tells them of his intention to elope with Marion and asks them the state of his finances. Snitchey and Craggs inform him that he is completely ruined. They advise him to leave Marion alone and also to leave London in order to escape his creditors. The two lawyers are sure that Marion is very much in love with her fiancé, Alfred, and that she would never consent to elope with Michael.

In the second scene of the same act, Dr. Jeddler, his two daughters, and Clemency and Britain, the devoted servants of his household, are spending an evening by the fire in the living-room. Marion is reading aloud an old ballad about a certain Jenny who is compelled to leave her parents' home because of her love for an unworthy man. Marion's excitement and tears prevent her from finishing the reading, and on top of this a letter from Alfred arrives telling of the completion of his education and his arrival home in another month at Christmas time. Seeing Grace's tremendous joy at the news, Marion is embarrassed and runs to her room. Soon the doctor and Grace also go to bed. The servants remain by the fireplace talking. Clemency speaks of her longing to get married, but the phlegmatic Britain tells her she hasn't a chance. A strange noise in the garden interrupts their conversation. Britain goes to the garden to see what it is. In his absence Marion comes into the room and insists that Clemency go with her to her rendezvous in the garden. "Who are you having a rendezvous with?" the devoted servant asks. But before Marion has a chance to answer, the somber figure of Michael Warden appears in the garden door.

A month goes by. Dr. Jeddler invites his friends to his home to celebrate Alfred's return. The same evening Michael Warden is supposed to leave England for six years, according to his agreement with the lawyers. In their turn they promise to send Michael six hundred pounds a year from the income they receive from his estate. Also this same evening Marion plans to elope. And when Alfred, so happy to be home, finally appears at Dr. Jeddler's he is met by the embarrassed guests, and Grace faints in his arms.

"What has happened?" the young Alfred asks, bewildered by this welcome. "Is Marion dead?"

"She has eloped," one of the lawyers answers.

"She has run away from home." Dr. Jeddler confirms the sad news, handing him the letter Marion has written to Alfred, which Clemency has given the doctor a few minutes ago.

"The world aged six more years," Charles Dickens writes in his story. The first scene of the fourth act is in the tavern at the city gates. The tavern is owned by Clemency and Britain, who have been married since they left Dr. Jeddler's house. From their conversation we learn that Dr. Jeddler took Marion's elopement very hard at first but later on not only got over it but seemed to be quite happy. This happened soon after Grace and Alfred were married. Their conversation attracts the attention of a gloomy stranger who has dropped in for a glass of beer.

"Has there been any news about his younger daughter since then?" the stranger asks Clemency suddenly. And she recognizes his voice. It is Michael Warden.

"Where is she? What has happened to her? Do you know anything about her? Where, where is she, sir? Why isn't she with you?" Clemency bombards him with questions, terribly excited. But Warden only turns away silently.

"Oh, she is dead!" the devoted servant exclaims.

Mr. Snitchey enters. His meeting with Michael is very sad. "Yes, many have left us during these past six years." His partner Mr. Craggs had died, as have many others in the town. "And still one should never despair," Snitchey consoles Clemency. "One should always wait and hope for tomorrow, Clemency."

At last that tomorrow comes. The scene is Dr. Jeddler's garden, where the first act took place. Grace and Alfred are reminiscing about the occasional letters that come from Marion, especially the last one, in which Marion hinted that everything would soon be explained. Suddenly we see Dr. Jeddler and Marion enter arm in arm. Marion holds out her hands to Grace. We learn from Marion's speech that she loved Alfred six years ago but felt that Grace's love for him was deeper, so she had to make them believe that she had eloped with Michael Warden. The truth is that she spent all these six years at the home of her aunt, her father's sister. As soon as she learned of Alfred and Grace's marriage, she wrote her father the truth. She is sure that if she had not pretended to love Michael Warden six years before, Alfred and Grace would never have accepted her sacrifice. At that moment Michael Warden enters. All these years he has been thinking of Marion's noble deed. He has completely changed his mode of life. He is here to thank Dr. Jeddler and Marion for all they have done for him. Clemency enters. She sees Marion alive and is convinced now of the truth of Mr. Snitchey's words that one should never lose hope for tomorrow.

O N SEPTEMBER 4, 1924, we showed Konstantin Stanislavsky our production of the play *The Battle of Life* as I had directed it in Vakhtangov's studio, where we had played it for some time. After the performance that day I was left alone with Stanislavsky in the auditorium.

"Would you like to talk with me privately about the play, as one director to another or—if you are not afraid to hear my criticism—in the presence of your cast?" Stanislavsky asked me.

"I think I can take your criticism in the presence of my cast, Konstantin Sergeyevich," I answered. "But if you think it's more in order for me to hear you privately, I am at your disposal."

"No, I don't think that," Stanislavsky replied. "When, after this kind of showing, the two directors lock themselves in their study to discuss it and then bring their verdict to the cast, the actors feel cheated. They are left with the feeling that the directors are hiding something from them and are conspiring against them. Actors like to hear their directors' criticism immediately after the performance. Like all artists, they trust the first spontaneous impression. So let's wait, if you have no objection, until your cast joins us here."

The "Idea" of the Play

After the actors had taken off their make-up, they gathered around Stanislavsky in the auditorium. He looked at them with great interest, trying to recognize traces of the characters they had portrayed that had not disappeared with the removal of the make-up and wigs. His searching look rested on each actor for a few seconds with an intense curiosity, examining them always with the same unspoken question, which, when he liked the actor very much, he would say out loud, "How do you do it?"

I always had a feeling that in those first minutes after the actor had taken off his make-up Stanislavsky was trying to solve that always exciting question, "How does it happen that one artist creates a character under circumstances given him by another artist?"

"In order for me to speak to you frankly," Stanislavsky said, "you must answer the following question: how many times would you like to do this play?"

His question surprised all of us and we didn't know how to answer.

"I know that you love the play," he continued, "because you have played it many times with success. I like it too. Your director has analyzed the play correctly. There are many sincere and touching moments in your individual performances. You deserve the right to play it. But I'm interested to know how many times you would like to do it? How many years? Do you want us to keep it in the permanent repertoire of the Moscow Art Theatre?"

We were embarrassed. Some of us were even laughing from embarrassment. Our dreams hadn't reached this far.

"We were only hoping for one season," I said.

"That's bad," Stanislavsky answered. "The artist must work so that his creation will live. Now tell me, would you like to play this play two hundred times?"

"Certainly we would, Konstantin Sergeyevich."

"And would you make certain sacrifices for that?"

Though the question was put to us in a warm, kindly tone, we realized its seriousness and we instinctively kept silent. Even the youngest and most inexperienced actor knows how fatal his answer may be. But being the oldest in the company and also because I knew the "sacrifices" were meant for me as the director, I felt I had to speak.

"Please don't be angry with us for not answering your question immediately, Konstantin Sergeyevich," I said. "You probably understand us better than we do ourselves. Please tell us what we need to do to improve our performance and keep it in the repertoire as long as possible."

"Do you all agree with Gorchakov?" Stanislavsky asked. He continued: "I don't know you very well. We're meeting around the work table for the first time and I don't want to spoil the beginning of your career as artists. I promise you that the play will be presented and you will be in it, but not immediately."

We answered unanimously that we would do whatever he thought we should do.

"See that you don't regret this decision an hour from now," he replied half-jokingly.

Then he continued: "I will spend very little time in analyzing the merits of your production. Please don't hold it against me. The time is short until the date the play should be presented again. You all understood the author well, and your director guided your work in creating Dickens' characters correctly. You followed the theme of the play and, because of that, the plot and its idea was clear to the audience. Working with your director, you found the right rhythm and you carried out your acting problems sincerely and enthusiastically. Your performance was inspired with a youthful devotion. This reaches the audience, charms it, and makes it overlook your defects. Do you have them? I think you do. But you aren't aware of them. You don't feel them—not yet. My task is to point them out to you, to convince you to fight them, to get rid of some of them and turn others into assets. Your chief defect is your youthfulness. You are amazed at my saying this? You don't follow my thought? I will explain.

"Youthfulness is a splendid thing if you can keep it forever, but that is very difficult to do. Of course I'm talking of inner youthfulness. There isn't one middle-aged lady among you. In your play even the old men are played by young actors. If such a lady were sitting among us, we would hear her sigh loudly and sympathetically in answer to my words.

"Now, let us analyze what it means to be young on the stage. It has nothing to do with make-up or costumes. We know many examples in which the most colorful costume and the youngest make-up only tended to emphasize the actor's age. At the same time, we know that an older actor or actress can play a young part very convincingly without any make-up or vivid costume, if he or she knows the secret of theatrical youthfulness. You must be wondering now what sense there is in telling you this when you are so young and I have just been praising you for the freshness of your performance. I'm telling you this now because you have no idea how quickly you and your performance may age without your even being aware of it.

"The first essential to retain a youthful performance," he continued, "is to keep the *idea* of the play alive. That is why the dramatist wrote it and that is why you decided to produce it. One should not be on the stage, one should not put on a play for the sake of acting or producing only. Yes, you must be excited about your profession. You must love it devotedly and passionately, but not for itself, not for its laurels, not for the pleasure and delight it brings to you as artists. You must love your chosen profession because it gives you the opportunity to communicate ideas that are important and necessary to your audience. Because it gives you the opportunity, through the ideas that you dramatize on the stage and through your characterizations, to educate your audience and to make them better, finer, wiser, and more useful members of society. This is an enormous problem in the theatre—especially in our time, when a great number of people come to the theatre for the first time in their lives. If the new audience sees and hears the answers to their problems, they will learn to love the theatre and accept it as their own. Therefore, the first way to retain your theatrical youthfulness is to answer clearly for yourself the question: Why are you working in the theatre as an actor, why are you performing this play?

"Today you knew the purpose of your performance. You wanted to impress me as actors. You have accomplished this purpose. When you gave your performance at Vakhtangov's school you also knew the purpose: you wanted to be acknowledged grown-up actors who have graduated. You accomplished this purpose too. But what was enough for yesterday and today will not be sufficient for tomorrow when you present your performance to the public. It is important to the audience that its own thoughts and life excite you and that the thoughts that fill your stage life excite it. The audience is concerned with the author's idea and with your presentation and interpretation of it as theatre artists. The idea should be always vital and important to today's audience and it is necessary for you to recreate it truly. You must keep the idea alive and be inspired by it at each performance. This is the only way to retain youthfulness in performance and your own youthfulness as actors. The true recreation of the play's idea— I emphasize the word *true*—demands from the artist wide and varied knowledge, constant self-discipline, the subordination of his personal tastes and habits to the demands of the idea, and sometimes even definite sacrifices.

"Now let's discuss your play. Has it an important, a vital idea for the contemporary audience? I think so. The idea of your play is one of self-sacrifice for a high purpose—that

is, for the happiness of another human being. This idea
will excite today's audience. Great changes in the life of
the people always demand personal sacrifice for the good
of the country. All of us must suffer privations today for
the better life of all in the future. Do you recognize the
idea of your play? Certainly you do. Your director has undoubtedly spoken of this idea more than once.

"The director cannot begin to work on a play without
knowing the idea, the basic theme. But, in the process of
work, you were preoccupied with immediate rehearsal
problems and pushed your feeling for the idea into a secondary place. Now you must bring back your first enthusiasm for the idea. You must broaden your understanding
of it. You must establish the accents and the high points
which will help you bring it out most expressively and
which will convey its fullest meaning. You must do everything in your power to make the idea exciting, colorful,
strong, and important to the audience. This is what will
give your performance lasting youthfulness—or if not
everlasting, then at least useful to the audience as long as
the play's idea is vital.

"Now what never fails to excite an audience? What it
sees around it in life. In your play, *The Battle of Life*, the
two sisters are in love with the same man. One sister thinks
that she is sacrificing her life for the other. But the other
doesn't just think she is, she actually is sacrificing her feelings for the happiness of the other. This is self-sacrifice.
Sometimes this self-sacrifice takes place for the sake of
duty, sometimes for love of one's country, sometimes for a
high ideal, or sometimes for the happiness of the majority
of the people—in order to diminish misery or injustice. A
human being's capacity of feeling for self-sacrifice is great,
deep, and complicated. The audience knows that feeling
from life itself. The audience must recognize this quality
in the acting on the stage; they must see people who are

helping others even at the cost of their own happiness. The audience knows, through personal observation, that to sacrifice one's own happiness for the sake of another is not easy or simple. It is a tremendous and complicated process of inner conflict within one's self. In *The Battle of Life*, you show two girls, Marion and Grace. You are 'telling' the audience what the girls' thoughts are and what they intend to do for each other. The audience listens with pleasure because you are young, and because you have theatrical charm, beautiful voices, and beautiful faces and figures. You are 'telling' in person the events that took place a hundred years ago as Charles Dickens described them. You don't show the audience self-sacrifice as an inner action in the hearts and minds of your characters taking place before their eyes.

"Let me illustrate what I think is the difference between 'telling' about feelings, thoughts, the plot, and the idea of the play, and finding hidden in text and situation the deep, inner life of human beings which is familiar to us all. I'll show you how to bring this inner life to the audience.

"I remember a scene in the first act between Marion and Grace on the swing. They are talking about Marion's birthday; the swing is moving slowly. This mise en scène is correct and good. In the distance we hear street musicians playing. (Their presence is justified by the text: the orchestra was hired to celebrate Marion's birthday.)

"The girls are talking about Marion's wedding. Soon their father joins them. He says something carelessly and Marion runs off in tears. Grace follows her. I understood from that scene that the two girls love each other and the father loves his daughters very much and they, in turn, are devoted to him. I could see clearly what their home atmosphere was, but I didn't understand what had actually *happened* in the scene.

"Now I remember still another scene: the meeting of the two sisters with Alfred, Marion's fiancé. This scene also ends with Marion's running off—and I couldn't understand why. During the scene when the family is having dinner in the garden, Alfred gives a speech on the greatness of self-sacrifice. He hints that he understands Grace's love for him, and he promises for himself and his fiancée, Marion, that they'll remember Grace's generosity in sacrificing her own feeling for her sister's happiness. And, for the third time, Marion runs off in tears seemingly very moved by Alfred's speech. And when Alfred is parting from the girls in the last scene of the first act, Grace says good-by to him with great warmth and sincerity, while Marion, on the other hand, seems reserved—in fact, quite cool. Now this is the end of the first act as I saw it. Can you get the feeling from hearing me tell you what I remember that Marion had the idea of self-sacrifice, of giving up Alfred for Grace's sake? I don't think so. All you could conclude is that Marion is a very capricious girl and that her older sister, Grace, is much more positive and profound in her emotions. Now I'll try to describe the same act, not changing in the slightest the plot or even the director's design.

"Let's begin again from the scene of the girls in the swing. The same talk about Marion's wedding . . . but how would the scene feel and look if I suggest to Marion that she change her acting problem, that she seem not to enjoy herself capriciously, but that she think seriously and watch Grace carefully when the latter talks about Alfred's love for Marion? Let us suppose that exactly at this moment—not somewhere else, but right here on the stage before the audience—Marion understands for the first time how deeply Grace loves Alfred. Don't you think the scene will be stronger, more expressive, and more dramatic than the mere expository scene which you played? Can't

you remember from your own life experience how it feels
when suddenly the feeling of someone very close and dear
to you is involuntarily revealed? You listen, holding your
breath, afraid to make a wrong move, afraid of meeting
her eyes. Isn't that how Marion would act in this situation?
Then the audience will be excited because they will recognize a familiar moment which they, too, have experienced,
and they will whole-heartedly take part with Marion in
the scene. They will experience the same feeling that
Marion does, and her thoughts, as she struggles to solve
this predicament, will be theirs.

"When their father joins the girls and Grace begins to
talk about how little Marion appreciates Alfred, Marion
once more will verify her suspicion that Grace is also in
love with Alfred. Naturally this will bring the tears to her
eyes, tears of love for her modest and devoted sister. (And
let the audience see your tears. You shouldn't hide from the
audience but from your father and Grace.) That is why
Marion runs off. The audience should understand this
clearly. This is not a young girl's whim, but the reaction
of a young heart. It is the first really serious feeling of a
human being entering adult life and becoming conscious
of her relationships and her own reactions. Every human
being has gone through such a moment. Every human being remembers the day and hour in which the thread of
his careless childhood was broken. The first serious anxiety, or emotion, or sorrow makes him suddenly older. It
starts to form his consciousness and his emotions in relation
to life.

"Imagine how attentively the spectator will watch
Marion, now that he has understood and lived with her
through this moment of birth, this moment of true adult
understanding.

"Here is the next scene: both sisters for the first time
meet Alfred in front of the audience. What will Marion's

behavior be like? How will she look at her sister now? Will she be jealous? What feelings will spontaneously come to her as she watches Alfred and Grace? Now she knows Grace's secret. You'll tell me that Marion is too fine a person to be jealous of her sister. Nonsense! Fiddlesticks! Only cold-hearted people with blood like fish who are indifferent to life fail to know the terrible, fiery feeling of that 'monster with the green eyes.'

"Marion has the feelings of any normal young girl. She must go through all that is natural for a human being and not try to be an exception to the rule. This is the worst form of sentimentalism. Dickens is guilty of this trait. Our time does not encourage it. Let us improve upon Dickens in this respect.

"Marion must be jealous of Grace at that moment. She is just like all the young girls in the audience. They will understand her and sympathize with her. Let Marion leave Alfred and Grace alone in this scene, because today, now, she doesn't yet know how to fight to overcome all these natural feelings aroused so suddenly in herself. The audience will understand why she leaves the scene at that time. And then when Alfred talks about the wonderful feeling of self-sacrifice in the next scene at the dinner table, for the first time Marion will have the idea of sacrificing her love. She will know the feeling of joy at doing something truly heroic. Let her forget everyone at the table. She doesn't hear anyone or see anything; she is absorbed in her idea. Her imagination overpowers her now. She sees deeds of self-sacrifice which she has either read or heard about. The house she lives in is built on a former battlefield where fierce fighting took place. How many legends has she heard in her childhood about this great battle! Here she sees her older brother, an experienced soldier bravely defending young recruits. She sees an officer give up his own horse to his commander when the latter's horse is killed. The battle is not yet finished. The cannon balls are still exploding and a few women in rough gray dress move from one wounded soldier to another. These women are hurrying to bandage their wounds, to help them to stand up or lie down more comfortably. They exhort the dying with words of hope. Here one of these women is hit by a shell splinter. With soft moans she sinks down close by the one she was about to help. Marion sees that this woman is still very young. What made her give her life to save a strange soldier who meant nothing to her?

"Marion is so absorbed in all these imaginary fantasies that, when she suddenly realizes that everyone at the table is looking at her, she gives Grace and Alfred a loving, tender glance of understanding. Her decision is made. Slowly she leaves the table and walks away. This scene should last only a few seconds, but the audience will understand Marion. Again it will sympathize with her and be moved by her emotion. And in the last scene of the first act—where the two sisters part from Alfred, who is on his way to Europe to finish his education—Grace can no longer control her emotion. She cries, not realizing that she is revealing her feeling. She remains in Alfred's arms, clinging to him. He is embarrassed. Marion, filled with sadness and deep excitement, looks at him. She will never see him again. She has made this decision. Now this is the line which your first act should develop and follow. If the idea of self-sacrifice is developed in this way, the idea will be alive in the play as long as it lives and the play will retain youth and vitality.

"What did I do to make the idea come alive so powerfully and strongly in the play? First, I moved all the events and the beats of your performances from the 'telling about' to inner action and, where it was necessary, to external action. And I made this action take place in front of the audience. I designed it for you through Marion's role. You must design the action for the other roles in the same way, including them in the main line that expresses the idea of the play. The action of some characters will supplement Marion's and the play's idea (for example, the lawyers' and servants'), while other characters, according to their qualifications, will be in constrast to the idea—for example, counteracting it with a pose of skepticism, as Marion's father, Dr. Jeddler does.

"Second, I discovered and defined the starting point, the rudimentary stage, in the development of the play's idea—the seed of the play. (It is fortunate when the idea is born in one of the play's characters before the audience in a scene like this.) Then I began logically to develop from scene to scene the growth of action based on the development and solidification of the idea. This growth must continue through the following acts until it reaches its culmination at the end of the play.

"In directors' terminology we call this process the correct distribution of the plot's dramatic highlights within the theme of the play. You did plan them, but weakly, without emphasis, without real development. I showed you the dramatic conflict. I told you clearly how to emphasize the dramatic character of the text but I said nothing about the lyrical atmosphere in which you created your performance. One should never be that obvious about a play's *genre*. One should not make people laugh constantly in comedy; in a lyrical play such as your *The Battle of Life*, one should not use a light poetic tone in telling about the past. When playing comedy on the stage, the more serious you are, the funnier the comedy will be, and it will be funny where the author meant it to be funny but not where the actor decides to make his audience laugh.

"I also changed many of the problems in Marion's role, striving to make them active. I mean problems that force an actor to make a decision here and now in front of the audience, rather than somewhere off stage before the rehearsal or in the intermission between acts. I made her role more difficult and complex. You must work on all the parts in exactly this way. One needs a developed technique for this. One needs temperament and the ability to communicate, to 'come across' to the audience. That is why some of you must give up your parts to more talented young actors in our company. These are the sacrifices of which I spoke at the beginning. When the play is done perfectly, when it stands on strong, solid ground, then it will be safe to bring all of you who now sacrifice your parts back into it. I want to give a chance to everyone in your group. During rehearsals it is most helpful to young actors to learn what it means to find the idea, to make it exciting and important. Your work will always be alive when you do this; it will always have youthfulness.

"Now let me say good-by. (It was 2 A.M.!) Gorchakov, Luzhsky, and I will stay a few minutes longer. We must outline the plan of future work and set the opening date for the play. I think we can reopen it within a month. But it is impossible to work without a precise plan."

The actors thanked Stanislavsky and left us.

The Inner Monologue

The next day Stanislavsky asked me to come to his home. With a copy of the play in his hand, he marked all the rehearsals, meetings, and discussions which he felt were necessary. He asked me about the natural talent and technique of each actor. After arranging the time for the daily rehearsal, he suggested that I prepare the first rehearsal. He warned me that he would establish only the scenic design and define the actors' problems. I would have to get them accomplished.

Stanislavsky decided that rehearsals should be on stage.

with sets and costumes but no make-up. Any supplementary work that the actors needed must be done between rehearsals.

As usual, Stanislavsky was prompt. The actors were on stage, the curtain was down, and everything was ready for the first act.

"Raise the curtain," Stanislavsky said, "but don't start yet."

He examined the stage carefully. The backdrop represented an orchard. On both sides of the stage there were screens covered with monks-cloth. The tops of old apple trees could be seen above the screens. Ladders stood by the trees. The act begins with peasants picking the apples in Dr. Jeddler's orchard. Stage right was the swing. The young peasants stood on the ladders picking apples. Grace and Marion led the four-man orchestra upstage. When the orchestra began to play, the peasants danced. Then the maid, Clemency, entered and the dancing stopped. The peasants returned to picking apples. Grace and Marion sat down in the swing and there began between them the dialogue which Stanislavsky had criticized in detail at our first meeting. Now he asked us to repeat this first little scene. He seemed to like it. Then he stopped the scene between Grace and Marion.

"Did you think about the criticism I gave you, Angelina Osipovna?" he asked the young actress named Stepanova who was playing Marion.

"Yes, but I don't know . . . how I can make the audience see and understand my thoughts about Grace without her realizing my state of mind. I have nothing in my text to show that I guess her love for Alfred."

"Perfectly true," he answered. "There's no text to that effect and this is good. Our eyes and our facial expressions are often much stronger than words. In order for you to believe this, let's do an étude. You two begin the scene again.

Sophia Nikolaevna (who played Grace) will keep to her text, but, you, Angelina Osipovna, speak not only your text but also all the thoughts that come into your mind during the scene—about Grace, about her love for Alfred . . . This second text, made up of your thoughts, may sometimes coincide with Grace's words. You may both speak simultaneously. Don't let this confuse you. It's only a short exercise.

"Angelina Osipovna, you must use two tones—one for the text of your part and one for your thoughts. Very likely the second tone will be much lower and more expressive. But I want to hear both clearly. We will have an understanding with Grace that she won't react to your thoughts. As an actress she doesn't hear them. I suppose if Marion were really talking to herself in such a situation, muttering half aloud as one sometimes does in life, Grace would pay no attention, as she would be preoccupied with Alfred. But don't take me literally, Angelina Osipovna. Don't mutter because I must hear you. I must see that your thoughts about Grace—or, as we call it, your inner monologue—is correct. All you young actors must realize that when we listen to someone in life, this kind of inner monologue goes on. Actors very often think that listening to one's partner on stage means staring at him and not thinking. How many actors *rest* during the long speeches of other actors and come alive only for their cues! Now is this clear?"

"Very clear," the actors answered.

Luzhsky said, "Konstantin Sergeyevich, I taught one of the actors the technique of the inner monologue, but no matter who tells him what to do now, he mimics, gesticulates, exclaims, and mutters during the scene on stage— constantly reacting, he calls it. The company is complaining. Nobody wants to act with him. I tried to reason with this actor, but his answer is always, 'Well, you taught me the inner monologue; now you'll have to endure it.' "

"Any fool can act that way," Stanislavsky said. "This amusing example is typical of applying the method of the inner technique in a general way, taking the terminology literally. Besides the method, actors must have all the qualities that constitute a real artist: inspiration, intelligence, taste, the ability to communicate, charm, temperament, fine speech and movement, quick excitability and an expressive appearance. One cannot go very far with just the method. Now, let's continue the rehearsal."

The dialogue began again.

"Where did the minstrels come from?" their father asked, pointing to the musicians.

"Alfred sent the music," his daughter Grace replied. "This morning I got up very early. I went to the garden. I wanted to meet Marion with flowers in my hands. Today is Marion's birthday. But Alfred got ahead of me. He met me with flowers. How wonderful they smelled! Dew was still shining on the petals of the roses. When he held out the bouquet, Alfred's hands seemed to me covered with diamond rings . . ."

Then we heard Marion's voice, much lower than Grace's. But, perhaps because of this, or because we felt Marion's excitement as an actress, trying for the first time the method that Stanislavsky had shown her, her low voice excited our attention.

"I did not receive the bouquet . . ." Marion said unexpectedly in a soft but clear voice. Her glance fixed on Grace, who was looking obviously toward the spot at the far corner of the garden where she had met Alfred that morning.

Grace said: "Alfred asked me whether I would have any objections to his bringing minstrels to serenade you. His eyes looked at me with such tenderness."

Marion said softly, "With such tenderness." There was a new expression in her voice.

"Oh, Marion, it seems to me sometimes that you don't love Alfred as much as he deserves," Grace continued.

"Is it possible that my tender, modest Grace is in love with Alfred too?" Marion spoke her thoughts aloud, and then she said the actual lines of her part: "I don't really know, Grace. I'm tired of always hearing about his perfection."

There was a new, totally unexpected quality in Marion's voice, and we watched her carefully. We saw that her eyes were constantly on Grace.

And the light-hearted appearance of Dr. Jeddler, swinging with his daughters, emphasized Marion's inner drama.

"How can you talk like that about your fiancé?" Grace continued. "Is there any man in the world who is better, nobler, more splendid than Alfred? How can one help loving him?"

"And you, Grace, you love him too?" said Marion in a deeply dramatic voice during Grace's tirade. Then she answered in her normal voice. "I'm tired of hearing only praise of him! And just because he's my fiancé, he doesn't have to think himself the best in the whole world!"

Grace said: "Stop it, stop it, Marion! How can you speak that way about a heart which belongs to you so completely?"

Marion spoke *sotto voce*: "What am I to do? Does she really love him that much?" Tears filled her eyes.

Grace went on: "Don't say things like that even in fun. There is no one more devoted, more splendid than Alfred. His love means your happiness for life."

Marion softly again: "And I would deprive you of that happiness, my sweet, kind Grace!" She spoke through tears, jumping from the swing, but then she said the words of the text capriciously: "I don't want him to be that devoted. I never asked for it."

"Marion, Marion, come to your senses. What are you

saying?" Grace said, as she looked at Marion with sincere horror. Never before had she heard Marion speak in such a manner.

Stepanova continued, "Yes, yes, yes!" The tears in her voice could be interpreted simply as those of a capricious child. "It doesn't mean anything that he's my fiancé!" Marion threw a long glance at Grace, impulsively hugged her sister, kissed her passionately, and rushed off the stage.

We had not planned this move for her in the acting production, so the perplexed Grace looked around desperately, as though seeking an answer or looking for help, and then she rushed off screaming, "Marion, Marion what's happening to you?"

"Does it really pay to upset oneself like that for love?" their self-assured, cynical father spoke, putting an excellent end to the sisters' scene.

"Bravo! Wonderful! Good girls!" Stanislavsky said in a happy, excited voice. "Only don't pay any attention to my words. Don't lose the state you are in now. You touched the source. Listen, but stay in the same mood and keep the same relationships. Your excitement and sincerity of feeling must now be deepened, developed, and solidified. Go back immediately to the swing and repeat the scene from the beginning. Stepanova, your spoken thoughts are correct. Go over them once more when you do the scene, but you can whisper them now because I know them. Of course you can change them within the limit of the logic set by your feelings and thoughts. Take your places quickly," Stanislavsky said with such excitement that the actors and even we in the auditorium were infected by it. We all felt part of the creative process of this rehearsal.

Grace, Marion, and Dr. Jeddler immediately took their places on the stage. The last bars of the traveling orchestra died away and the scene on the swing began again. This time the scene sounded much more intense, sincere, and profound. Grace spoke with much more enthusiasm, Marion was more excited, more stirred, and Dr. Jeddler was more skeptical. After the girls rushed off stage, Stanislavsky praised them. "Excellent! Now, once more."

"First listen to me, but retain your creative mood. Stepanova, this time don't even whisper your inner monologue. Say all that you have accumulated with your eyes only; the thought will be reflected naturally in your face. Don't wrinkle up your forehead; don't raise your eyebrows; don't blink your eyelashes in exaggerated fashion. Trust yourself. Your inner world has been created correctly by your thought and feeling. Pronounce everything you think about Grace soundlessly; express it only with your eyes. You have a most expressive face and magnificent eyes. They will tell us everything. The text which the play gives you will be filled now with all that you are not allowed to say. Find a position for yourself on the swing so that you can watch Grace comfortably without her seeing you. The audience must be able to see you easily, though."

Bewitched by Stanislavsky's temperament, we saw the scene again for the third time. This time not a word was added to the play's text, but how much more profound it sounded! The movements and intonations were so much richer. Now the fact that Marion understood Grace's love for Alfred was perfectly clear. It was also clear that Marion was faced with a crucial problem if she loved Grace so much. The actors seemed so full of inner excitement that they could hardly finish the scene. Stanislavsky applauded when it was over.

After a short intermission we rehearsed the remaining scenes of the first act in the same way. In the scene in which the girls meet Alfred, it was Grace's turn to speak the inner monologue at the point when she saw how adoringly Alfred looked at his fiancée, Marion. In the Dinner Scene inner monologues had to be created by all the characters, including the servants who waited on table—although they had only a few words in the text. But each character's inner life took on fresh interest through his monologue.

For example, when Alfred said, "In spite of the light-mindedness and contradictions of people's behavior in the great battle of life, there are victories and heroic acts of self-sacrifice so much more noble because they are not known to others; there are no legends told about them and perhaps there never will be any told," the servant Britain thought out loud: "You won't talk me into any nonsense. I'm not going to clean the stove for Clemency. Let her get all black doing it, maybe then she'll soften and knit a sweater for me."

And Clemency spoke her thoughts: "He'll drive me to tears again. I think I do all I have to do, but, when I listen to Mr. Alfred talk, I immediately remember that I did hurt someone's feelings or I neglected some work I should have done."

"I'm curious to know how far he can get with all these idealistic notions. I bet he'll lose every cent he has, or he'll lose his aunt's money, if he succeeds in hypnotizing her with this kind of talk," Craggs, the lawyer, thought aloud.

"As far as I'm concerned," Snitchey echoed his partner's thought, "I cannot afford the luxury of self-sacrifice. Much too expensive. No, that occupation is either for the very rich or those who have nothing to lose anyway."

"How far removed from reality Alfred is! How naïve. He doesn't know the futility of people's striving to make life have meaning," the self-contented Dr. Jeddler muttered aloud.

All these spoken thoughts reached us in the auditorium, sometimes all at once and sometimes separately. They created such a true, vivid background for the actor who was actually speaking the text that the Dinner Scene sounded most interesting. For once the director didn't have to plead: "Listen to your partner! Please! Find the right reaction to your partner's words. What are you thinking about during this conversation?" It was all because of the inner monologue technique that Stanislavsky had suggested. The actors couldn't help listening to their partners, answering what they said, and reacting correctly to all that was happening. And suddenly all the roles became colorful, and the speeches were filled with new expression.

By the time we had gone through all the scenes of the first act it was very late, but the tireless Stanislavsky said, "Take five minutes and then do the first act without stopping."

The act went perfectly: it was sincere, colorful, and exciting in a most infectious way. "How many times can you repeat the act now?" Stanislavsky abruptly asked the question as he approached the stage.

"As many times as you want us to," the actors answered.

"I believe you," Stanislavsky said watching their excited faces. "I believe you because now you know the secret of keeping a scene youthful. The whole play must be worked out in the same way as we have worked out the first act. And now, good night."

Justification of the Mise en Scène

Stanislavsky asked me to prepare the first scene of the second act for the next rehearsal. This takes place in the lawyers' office between Michael Warden and the two lawyers, Snitchey and Craggs. We didn't feel that this scene would be redirected too much because it was one of our best.

After watching the scene on the stage—it lasted only eighteen minutes—Stanislavsky asked all the performers to gather around him in the auditorium.

"I want you all to help me make the decision," he said,

addressing them and staring at me. "Listen carefully to what I'm going to tell you. In every director's work, and especially in the work of a Senior Director like myself, there are moments when he hesitates about what decision to make in relation to some scenes. It often happens that the scene in question is particularly well rehearsed. It is almost certain that the audience will accept it as it is, but the Senior Director sees a finer, more complicated problem in the scene that has been overlooked by the director and actors, a problem that demands a lot of work from the actors and a complete break with what they have achieved up until then. The answer seems to be very simple. If the Senior Director knows of a better way to do the scene, a way which is more correct, he must immediately work toward it and must ignore completely the aggravation and disappointment it may cause the young director and his actors.

"When some of our leading directors see the possibility of the deeper and more colorful staging of a scene, they like to show off and to command their actors, 'All this has to be changed! Everything is wrong!' They destroy, categorically and in daring fashion, what has been worked out already, and they don't always accomplish what they had expected. I don't think this is the best way for the more experienced director to work with his actors and his assistant directors. To destroy is always easier than to build. Besides, one has to know how to save each grain of artistic truth that has been discovered after long and persistent toil, especially if this grain of truth relates to a character which has been planned correctly, and also relates to the 'red thread' and the idea of the play. You will notice that in our conversation today I introduced a new person, a new participant—the Senior Director. Now sometimes the Senior Director is the director and producer. Sometimes he is the director-coach supervising the work of his assistant in the

theatre school. Sometimes he is the head director of the theatre—as I am. In each case, it is very important that the
relationship between the Senior Director on the one hand
and the director and the actors on the other be irreproachable. You are the newcomers to our theatre and I want the
relationship between you and me to be one of true understanding in all phases of our theatre work. I wish you to
follow my instructions consciously and with creative desire
and not because I am the oldest, the most experienced, and
most important person among you.

"I want to put a very important question to you, Gorchakov. And to you, my young performers, I want to put a
question of principle. The decision I leave to you, Gorchakov, as the director. And I ask you actors to test with your
intuition everything I'm going to say to him. You,
Gorchakov, interpreted the scene in the lawyers' office as
a kind of conspiracy scene. The form you gave it and the
inner problems you gave the actors made me come to this
conclusion. I agree with you that the seed of the scene is
some kind of conspiracy: three shady characters against
Dr. Jeddler's family. I see why you play the scene on a
practically bare stage. You've placed on the stage only the
lawyers' two desks, the stools on which they sit, and an armchair used by Michael Warden. The two top hats hang on
screens at either side of the stage and the scene is lit only by
one candle on a desk.

"This is a very precise and graphic picture of the kind of
place it is. In my imagination it creates a picture of a provincial lawyer's office in England. My guess is that you
are trying to make the audience feel concern for the fate
of Marion, Grace, and Alfred. There is little movement in
the scene. Everything seems to be planned correctly. Why
is it, then, that the scene creates a pleasant feeling at the
moment the curtain goes up and also at the last moment,
when both lawyers take their top hats and say their final

words as they blow out the candle and leave? This finale is correct and the audience will probably applaud, but why isn't the audience interested or concerned during the whole middle section? Real interest and real feeling are your most important concerns. The actor and director must always strive toward this. It is much more valuable than laughter or the loudest applause.

"Now let me try to explain why the audience is not excited by the middle section. At the curtain's rise, you show to your audience a severe but expressive picture of the lawyers' office. The audience listens attentively—for the first five minutes. The correct mise en scène will always hold them for the first five to eight minutes. This is a stage law. The following three or four minutes they wait quietly to see what will happen next. Then ten minutes after the scene's begun, the end approaches and, since the audience realizes this, it consents to listen to the remaining three or four minutes. It is always intrigued by an interesting and clever finale, and it is excited by seeing the true form for the given content. That's why they applaud. Here is the simple arithmetic of the response to your lawyers' scene. This satisfies you. But, as your Senior Director, as the more experienced theatre artist, I am not satisfied. I know what has to be done to that scene so that it will really excite the audience. Yet I hesitate. I admit this to you. The Board of Directors gave me only one month to improve your play."

"But, Konstantin Sergeyevich, if you ask for more time," Luzhsky said, "the Board will certainly give it to you."

"I myself realize the necessity of having a new production as quickly as possible," Stanislavsky said. "Because of that, I am searching for a creative approach for you young actors which will enable me to make the greatest accomplishment in the shortest time. I think we must change the form of this scene, simplify it, and clarify it not only from the point of view of scenic effectiveness but also from the point of view of creating more profound inner problems for the actors. To be precise, I suggest changing the basic design of this scene."

I was shocked by this suggestion because I had had so much praise for my own design.

"Why do I find it necessary to simplify the external form —to be precise, the basic design of this scene? I was satisfied with it, as I told you before, but when I considered how much attention it will draw from the audience I came to the conclusion that I must ask you to give it up."

Stanislavsky stopped, and took a long pause—intentionally, I think. There was a tense silence in the auditorium. We had never expected Stanislavsky to ask us to give up our most cherished mise en scène. How much we, and especially I, as the director, had been praised for it! How many flattering adjectives we remembered in those seconds of silence! It seemed to me that even Luzhsky's face expressed a certain surprise. For a moment an idea flashed across my mind: perhaps Stanislavsky intended to create an even more colorful mise en scène than ours, but in the same direction, on the same plane.

"What will you substitute?" I burst out.

"Nothing, nothing," was the surprising answer that followed. "I suggest that you get rid of your effective desks and high stools," he continued. "I further suggest that instead of it you use an ordinary square table, with three armchairs and a candle on the table. That's all."

I was completely confused. I had a feeling that I was being robbed of something so near and dear to me that I could never be compensated. As I was the center of attention at that moment, I felt I had to say something. I gathered all my courage and began to speak.

"Konstantin Sergeyevich, you told us that you wanted the change in design coordinated with the new problems you are going to give the actors." It seemed to me that I had found something to hold onto. "Perhaps you can discuss these now and that will make it easier for us to think about the new form."

"You're afraid to tell me honestly and directly how painful it is for you to part with your effective design," he said. "And you want to influence the actors to side with you in case I give them equally difficult and complicated problems." Stanislavsky had immediately guessed my intention.

"First allow me to ease your position as a director who is the author of a good and colorful mise en scène. Let me explain to the actors why I'm so cruel to you. Gorchakov, you remember, and perhaps a few of the actors do, and no doubt Luzhsky does, that twenty years ago I was nicknamed 'The Despot.' I admit I was a despot then, because I thought my chief merit as a director was to demand the unquestionable subordination of everyone to myself and to demand the absolute right to use my power. But now when I hear a number of actors and young directors complaining that after they've worked very hard on a play I come and change it all according to my personal point of view, I feel very hurt and angry at those who accuse me of despotism. Strange as it may seem, I am often told for the purpose of flattery, in order to get into my good graces, 'Stanislavsky, you have such a remarkable imagination! You love to do everything in your own way!' This from some of my women admirers! It is terrible to be taken for such a fool, especially when you are not twenty but fifty and no longer 'the darling'!" It hurts when you realize how important it is to share the knowledge that you have gained during thirty years of experience with your young colleagues.

"Gorchakov, beware of the compliments that your friends give you so generously. Don't ever completely trust a compliment. I can hear them say, 'Oh, how expressive

the scene is! How well you grasp the spirit of the epoch!
What a picture! Like sculpture, Gorchakov!' Now, confess,
those were praises you heard. I'm not trying to say that
those things are wrong, but there's something much more
valuable more profoundly expressive which our art theatre
has striven for over the past thirty years. I feel that I
achieve much more when I hear people say how splendid
the officers are in *Three Sisters*, or, 'If all the people in
Russia were like that!' or, 'Konstantin Sergeyevich, you
know my uncle is just like your Andrey in *Three Sisters*.'
The human being and his inner spiritual life—these are
what must be shown on the stage of our theatre. These are
what the actors must reveal. That is why I ask you a direct
question, Gorchakov: Do you want the audience seeing
your production to be interested in the lives of human
beings or in an excellent likeness to the prints of that
period?"

"Can't we combine them?" I tried once more to save my
lawyers' office.

"One should always strive for such a combination," he
answered, "but in order to do this, one has to be a very experienced director, a master who has had much experience
working with actors and scenic designers. I could have
tried to do this, but we don't have time."

"Konstantin Sergeyevich, I feel bitter and heavy at heart
of course," I said. "My head understands everything you're
saying and what you're demanding of me, but my heart
protests violently against you and your suggestions. Perhaps this is my primitive director's jealousy, but I feel like
crying when I think that I will never see my scene as I
conceived it, as I created it and as I am so accustomed to
seeing it. Please leave at least something as it was. It will
be easier for me to accept your suggestion. But of course
do what you think is necessary for the success of the
work as a whole. Tell us, as you did at our first meeting

with you, what is necessary to preserve the youthfulness of our performance and the life of our play in the theatre repertory. If you grant me my request I promise you I will try to control my bad feelings and cooperate in everything you want me to do."

I was probably very nervous and almost on the verge of tears when I spoke. To my regret, I have always been inclined to sentimentality, but I could see no anger in Stanislavsky's eyes because of what I had said.

"I praise you for your sincerity and your persistence, Gorchakov," Stanislavsky answered very softly and kindly, after a short pause.

"The director must fight for what he feels is right, especially in the presence of his actors," Stanislavsky continued. "The director is responsible for his performance to his chief director, to the board of directors of his theatre, to the critics, and to the audience. If he gives up his stand only because his opponent has more artistic and administrative power, he will lose his authority over his actors. Your behavior deserves special praise because your opponent is the chief director in the theatre where you are a newcomer. Your request to leave some moments in the lawyer's scene unchanged is fair. It will help you as a director to accept the new design. It will help you to keep your taste for the play. Which moment would you like to keep as it was?"

"The finale of the scene after Michael Warden's exit," I said, inwardly relinquishing everything that had gone before.

"Fine," Stanislavsky answered. "I planned to leave it anyway. I'm very glad our tastes coincide."

While the desks were being removed from the stage and the correct square table was being found, Stanislavsky addressed us in the following words:

"We have spent almost two hours on the discussion between the directors. Some of you might think the time wasted, although I'm sure those two hours have been fruitful. First, because during the time that Gorchakov and I were discussing our problems, the actors were inwardly adjusting themselves to the new setting. Is that right?"

Gribov, who was playing Craggs, said, "Perfectly right."

Orlov (Michael Warden) agreed, "Yes, yes, Konstantin Sergeyevich."

Stepun (Snitchey) said, "That is what I have been doing."

Stanislavsky continued: "You see that the actors in their imagination worked with us directors. The second reason why I allowed myself to spend two hours on our discussion is that I want all of you sitting in this auditorium, all you young newcomers to our theatre, to learn the main links in the chain of our theatre organism.

"The first link is the repertoire. The members of the theatre responsible for its selection choose the ideas which they consider are important for the playwrights and the theatre organization to communicate. And as far as our repertoire is concerned all my compliments go to Nemirovich-Danchenko. His word in this aspect of our theatre has always been law to me and to the other members of the Moscow Art Theatre. He discovered Chekhov and he brought Gorky to us. Because of him we produced plays by Tolstoy. And without these great authors the Moscow Art Theatre would not be as you know it today.

"Before I saw your performance, Nemirovich-Danchenko told me: 'I took a group of young actors from Vakhtangov's Studio. I think they are talented. They have their own director and they put on a fine play adapted from Dickens' story. I think it would be right for our little stage, as Dickens is a humanist and a romanticist. After you see their *Battle of Life* perhaps you will want to work on it with them. It doesn't need much work. The play is in good solid shape. You'll just have to sprinkle it with a little of the *aqua vitae* of the Moscow Art Theatre.'

"After seeing your performance, I agree with Nemirovich-Danchenko. He has almost perfect judgment in the selection of plays; a great love of fine literature which is the foundation of our theatre. If the directors had no taste or no love for fine plays—for great literature in the theatre —then there would be no theatre as we understand it: a great school whose function is to give the audience a true sense of life, of 'man in the most important moments of his existence,' as Gogol said. If a theatre does not answer this requirement, then it is only a commercial enterprise.

"The second link is the stage direction: the chief director, staff directors, the young directors who should be constantly trained for the theatre's future, assistant directors, and production crew. All must work together in friendly cooperation regardless of their respective rank in the theatre. The chief director must be especially attentive and sensitive to the work of the staff directors and young directors and to his assistants and the production crew.

"The third link, the Administrative Board, is the most important link in the theatre organism. It coordinates the work of the writers, directors, and production crew. In its hands lies the regulation of time and money. Its work must be above suspicion and understandable to all the theatre workers. We all must subject our tastes and plans to the Administrative Board. I have sinned many times in this respect and have been punished accordingly. My most recent sin was to demand that the backdrop of the play *Cain* be made entirely of brocade. The Administrative Board suggested covering only part of the stage, in order to test the effect, but I insisted on having my way, only to find, after it was all done, that I had made a mistake. The brocade backdrop had to be taken down, and I felt ashamed and disgusted with myself. Finances are a very important element of theatre. Theatre does not exist for money-making. Its true profit lies in revealing to the audience the true purpose of the play through the performance. But if there is no audience, there is nobody to communicate to, nobody to perform for—in short, there is no theatre. The administrative board should know why the theatre has or has not an audience and give its analysis to the artistic heads of the theatre.

"If these three links of the theatre—repertoire, direction, and administration—work in coordination with complete respect and understanding, then the theatre as a whole lives in full-blooded and purposeful fashion.

"If the company, both venerable elders and young actors, has confidence in those three links—and recognizes their mutual independence, their trust in each other, and their sincerity—then everyone works with enthusiasm, happy in the theatre's successes and bravely enduring its failures—which, you must realize, are plentiful in the theatre. There is no true creative work, no advancement without failures.

"But if the company does not have that confidence in the unity of the three links, its actors live in a constant fever of uncertainty, and the various members run from the administrative board to the chief director, from the chief director to the manager of the repertoire. Each one is striving to affirm his position through personal contact with whichever one of the links seems to him to have the most power. But in reality there is no affirmation of anybody's position, and the disintegration of the theatre begins because no one of the three links, taken separately, has any meaning or strength.

"We remember a theatre that had a genius for a director, or a theatre of high literary caliber, or one with a great administrator, but each eventually failed because theatre is a form of art in which each must fulfill the work entrusted to him, and the summation of all gives birth to the performance. Theatre is like a bee hive: some of the bees build honeycombs, some gather the flowers, and some educate the young; and the result is a marvelous aromatic product—honey."

At that point the stage manager informed Stanislavsky that the stage was ready for the rehearsal. The curtain was raised on the lawyers' office. In the middle of the stage was a plain square table covered with a dark table cloth. On the table was an inkstand, a few books, and one candle. There were three armchairs around the table, one of which had a higher back; this was for Michael Warden.

"The set is fine. Now I want to talk to the actors," Stanislavsky said. "You directed this scene so that the two lawyers who had been handling Michael Warden's affairs, Mr. Snitchey and Mr. Craggs, are the masters of the situation. The scene was naturally theirs. Michael Warden's financial situation is desperate; he has squandered his wealth and now he is in the hands of his lawyers. He needs money to live in Europe with Marion. He is trying to make some deal with them. He argues and quarrels with them, but in the end he is forced to accept their advice.

"You have chosen an appropriate mise en scène for your interpretation. The two lawyers, like two ravens, were placed on their high stools above Michael Warden and held their consultation over his head. But the text of the scene suggests quite a different solution for the scene and the relationship of the three characters. Everyone who has experienced any kind of a law process knows how helpless he feels in dealing with the rules and regulations of the law. How lost he is when told that this or that was illegal from the legal point of view. That is why anyone involved in any kind of legal affair is anxious to have his personal representative who knows the law and also knows his personal position. I think this is called selling one's soul to the devil, because God help you if you quarrel with your own lawyer or if you think of changing him for another! Your own lawyer knows all the manipulations of your affairs as no one else and you are in his power. Of course I have in mind the lawyers of the old days; I don't yet know the contemporary lawyers, and I gladly believe that they treat their clients differently. But the lawyers we are discussing now are of the old school, and I think that my impressions and observations are perfectly suited to them. So from that point of view your approach was correct: we do see Michael Warden at a critical moment in the power of his lawyers.

"But I reread the Charles Dickens story most carefully. The peculiarity of both the lawyers' speeches and the author's description of the scene led me to think that the crux of the situation has a different character from the one you gave it. When you analyzed the text, you undoubtedly noticed, as I did, that Snitchey and Craggs address Michael in the third person. After Warden has confessed his intention to elope with Marion the dialogue goes as follows:

" 'He can't, Mr. Craggs,' said Snitchey evidently anxious and discomfited. 'He cannot do it, Sir, she dotes on Mr. Alfred.' "

" 'She dotes on him, Sir,' said Mr. Craggs."

" 'I did not live for six weeks, some few months ago, in the doctor's house for nothing; and I doubted that soon,' observed the client. 'She would have doted on him if her sister could have brought it about; but I watched them. Marion avoided his name and avoided the subject; she shrank from the least allusion to it with evident distress.' "

" 'Why should she, Mr. Craggs? Why should she, Sir?' inquired Snitchey."

" 'I don't know why she should, though there are many likely reasons,' said the client. 'She may have fallen in love with me, as I have fallen in love with her.' "

" 'I think it will be better not to hear this, Mr. Craggs,' said Snitchey, looking at his partner across the client."

" 'I think not,' said Craggs—both listening attentively."

"As you see," Stanislavsky continued, "in the beginning of the scene the two lawyers talk to Mr. Warden in the third person, quite obviously avoiding addressing him directly. Why? Because they are tactless? I don't think so. Because they are aware of their power over Michael Warden? I doubt it. Your director justified the behavior of the lawyers by placing them in such a manner as to force them to talk to each other over Michael Warden's head. But the actors did not justify this in their acting. For the actors it was never clear why they talk to Warden as though they were trying to ignore his presence. It is not clear what inner impulse calls for that kind of talk on the part of the lawyers. Your mise en scène is for the sake of an effect only. The clash between the lawyers' interests and Warden's plans is formal. In the original story of Charles Dickens I found the following remarks related to that scene:

" 'All kind feelings of the respective office of Snitchey and Craggs were toward their old client, Dr. Jeddler. But their professional ethics did not allow them to neglect the interests of their more recent but much more profitable client, Mr. Michael Warden.' "There is not much earnings for you from your honest and honorable client," Michael's eyes were saying as he shifted his gaze from one to another, realizing that his neglect of his fortune in the past is his power in the present. Because of that the conversation between them has the air of a meeting of diplomats. The two parties are extremely polite to each other on the surface, but in their hearts they curse each other.' "

"Doesn't this give you the right clue to the seed of the

scene? The lawyers avoid addressing Michael directly because it makes it easier for them to hide their real feelings toward him. Michael Warden is the master of the situation and that fact makes the lawyers uncomfortable and angry."

"Because of this undercurrent to the scene, I suggested the change of the mise en scène. Michael Warden should be placed in the center as master of the situation, and around him the two lawyers turn and twist, dodge and squirm. I ask the actors to go over their texts in their minds now and tell me what change there will have to be in their roles because of the new problem—that Michael is the master of the situation. The lawyers, frightened and angered by Warden's plan to elope with Marion, will have to manipulate to protect Dr. Jeddler's family on the one hand and on the other try not to lose a convenient client in Michael Warden. In other words, who will outsmart whom? This is the character of the scene."

Orlov (Michael Warden) said: "I'll behave completely differently now. I will not dwell on the morbid thought that I am ruined, as I did before. The lawyers are lying to me! Crooks! But I'm not a fool. I still have an estate. I owe something on it, but the estate is still mine, and if those two scoundrels cannot get me a decent sum of money for it, I will get other lawyers. They took enough advantage of my carelessness before, damn them! I need money now. They are scared to death that I will kidnap Marion from Dr. Jeddler's stuffy, virtuous home. I will give countenance to their fear. But Marion understands me and my intentions and will trust me. All I need is money."

Stanislavsky replied: "Excellent thoughts for such a rake. But don't you think it's *too* ungentlemanly?"

"Konstantin Sergeyevich, I think this is why there was no conflict in my scene with the lawyers. I was trying to be a gentleman. Because of this, Warden came out a fishlike character. Let me go in the other direction for a while. You and Gorchakov will take out what seems to you too rough."

Stanislavsky answered: "Very likely you are right. It is always easier to take away the superfluous than to add teaspoon by teaspoon to the thoughts and actions of an actor's role. Go ahead and act according to your conception. What thoughts do you have, Craggs?"

Gribov (Craggs) said: "I think that we have met all kinds among our clients. If we're such loyal friends of Dr. Jeddler, we should let Michael go with the wind. But Marion has fallen in love with him. One can expect anything from such a wilful young lady. Of course, the scoundrel Michael deserves to be 'put away,' but we must learn more about the circumstances."

Stepun (Snitchey) put in: "We must try to trick Michael. We will promise him some money on condition that he leave England immediately and stay away for several years. Then we will warn Dr. Jeddler to keep a watchful eye on Marion. We must try to separate those two, and, for all the irritation that Michael causes us, we will add a round sum to our 'office expenses.'"

Stanislavsky laughed: "A very proper method of revenge from the lawyers' point of view. I am completely satisfied with your analysis. And now we can continue the rehearsal."

Luzhsky made an aside, with a slight note of sarcasm: "Especially after having spent three hours talking and with one hour left to rehearse. . . . The plan was to finish the whole scene in one day."

Stanislavsky accepted the challenge: "Perfectly correct. The scene must be finished today. How long does it last?"

"Between sixteen and eighteen minutes," I answered.

Stanislavsky looked at his watch: "Fine. For the next hour I will ask you to do the following: Begin to rehearse the scene immediately. Don't stop, no matter what happens. The scene will take twenty minutes. Then come down to the auditorium and I'll give you the notes five minutes later. All together it will take twenty-five minutes. Then we will repeat the scene on stage without stopping. I will give you eighteen minutes for that. My remarks will take three minutes and the third run-through of the scene fifteen minutes." He addressed Luzhsky: "So it will take one hour and one minute. We are allowed to finish the rehearsal at four thirty-five?"

Luzhsky answered: "Even at four forty-five, Konstantin Sergeyevich."

"Go on the stage!" Stanislavsky said to us.

It was very interesting during the next hour to watch Stanislavsky working with the actors. In the first place, he himself worked with great concentration and attention. The tempo of the rehearsal made the actors work with great clarity of purpose. One of the actors when on his way to the stage asked Stanislavsky what the new movements were.

Stanislavsky replied: "There are only two movements in the whole scene. Until Warden leaves the office all three sit around the table. From the moment Warden rises from his chair, ready to leave the office, we go back to the original ending as Gorchakov set it. Go ahead. The stage must be lit by the candle on the table. Now raise the curtain."

The two lawyers were sitting around a fairly solid-looking, square table with their heavy books, a counting board and a bulk of legal documents in front of them. The upstage side of the table facing the audience was occupied by Michael Warden, carelessly dressed and sprawling in his chair. The lawyers grumbled under their breath; Mr. Snitchey looked over each document, examining every paper separately. He shook his head and handed them to Mr. Craggs. Mr. Craggs looked them over, also shook his head, and laid them down. Sometimes they stopped and shook their heads as they both looked toward their abstracted client.

In the corner of the stage, in profile to the audience, two old-fashioned black top hats hung. The candle on the table crackled and sputtered. Mr. Warden impatiently whistled some melody, lashing his leg with a whip.

For a few minutes the new setting seemed to me much less interesting. But from the first word of dialogue, as soon as the actors began to act according to their new relationship to each other established by Stanislavsky, our attention was switched to the excitement of their feelings and thoughts. How maliciously in the first beat Mr. Snitchey and Mr. Craggs counted up the profits and losses of Warden! And how indifferent the latter seemed to it! How angry his indifference made them! With what malignant joy Snitchey spoke in the third person: "A few years of nursing Mr. Warden's estate by myself and Craggs would bring it around. But to enable us to make terms, Mr. Warden must go away and live abroad."

"To hell with nursing my estate!" exclaimed Warden.

Because this dialogue of the lawyers took place literally in front of Warden's nose (Mr. Snitchey sat on one side of him and Mr. Craggs on the other), it was obvious that after being insulted by Warden to their faces they could not address him directly, and the form in which Dickens wrote the following speeches was perfectly justified.

Stanislavsky proved to us how a plain table (which I as the director thought to be the most inexpressive object on the stage) could become a very expressive object when the circumstances and the relationships between the people sitting around it were correctly planned and truly realized. When in the second part of the scene Warden told the lawyers he was in love with Marion, Mr. Craggs and Mr. Snitchey simultaneously jumped from their seats; but at that moment Stanislavsky practically shouted at them,

"Back to your seats! Nobody told you to change your mise en scène. Be as excited as you please, strike any pose you wish, but don't leave your seats. Don't stop the rehearsal. Continue the text."

We had never heard him give his directions in such a sharp tone, but to our surprise the actors' attention increased and they played more seriously and with more enthusiasm. During the next beat of the scene the lawyers laughed and mocked their client, and it was only when Warden unexpectedly got up and gloomily said, "I did not live for six weeks, some few months ago, in Dr. Jeddler's house for nothing," that the lawyers stopped their mockery.

The actor playing Warden got up at that point. We in the auditorium liked that. It seemed to us it was the right way to change the mood of the scene and to break the lawyers' mockery. But in a few seconds we were convinced how little we knew Stanislavsky, the director.

"Who gave you permission to get up to say that effective phrase?" Stanislavsky addressed Warden in a sharp tone. "I will remind you once more. Up to Warden's exit use any form of adjustment you like but don't leave your chair. In the old days the actor would jump from his seat in order to pronounce an effective phrase of the text. That was the rule of cheap provincial theatre. In the old days the actor used the expression, 'Ah, what a candle I will give to that phrase!'—meaning that he would jump so that the whole audience would gasp. So they jumped on the stage like grasshoppers, one higher than the other. But this is not appropriate within the walls of the Moscow Art Theatre. Continue the scene."

The embarrassed actor sank quickly into his chair and the scene soon ended as it had been planned in my original design. After finishing the scene the three actors came down to the director's table as he had requested.

Stanislavsky began to speak: "The scene is going well.

You played the first part of it colorfully and convincingly in the new circumstances. My first remark didn't throw you off because it referred not to the inner content of the beat but to its external expression. My second remark upset Orlov (Warden) because he thought that getting up and shouting at the lawyers from his handsome height would be the right form for his inner content. He could not substitute anything else, so the second part of the scene had no inspiration. If I had more time, Orlov, I would show you how to discover for yourself the right form for the transition from one beat to another. But because our time is figured to the second I'll only give you a hint. Let the lawyers laugh and ridicule you all they want. Don't pay any attention to their mockery until they get tired of it—until they themselves will begin to wonder why this fellow sits there so indifferent and unconcerned. And when you feel that they are ready for this question, and all their mockery has been exhausted, take a short pause and then say casually and calmly, as though you have already had six children by Marion:

" 'I did not live for six weeks, some few months ago, in Dr. Jeddler's house for nothing.' "

"It should come out as if you'd had a child a week," Stanislavsky added, joining us in an hilarious outburst of laughter. "Now back on the stage quickly and repeat the scene from the beginning. We have just forty minutes left to finish the rehearsal. And remember, according to our agreement in this run-through, the scene must be two minutes shorter. To cut two minutes out of twenty is not so easy. And, besides, I gave you a 'playing pause.' Remember that you will play the scene faster not by hurrying the text but by carrying out each of your inner problems more energetically."

The second run-through went much better. It was clearer, and none of the actors made any attempts to change the mise en scène. The pause after the lawyers' mockery was very convincing. And the following scene, in which Warden attacked the lawyers and then forced them to capitulate to his plan, Orlov played with real temperament, fire, and perfect tempo. When the actors finished, Stanislavsky approached the footlights.

"Please repeat the scene once more. Keep the same problems, the same physical actions, the same relationship to each other, and the same mise en scène. Why? The way the scene is played now, the audience, I think, will watch the conflict between the lawyers and Warden and will be anxious about Marion's fate, the lawyers' conspiracy, and Warden's sinister intention. But the law of theatrical art decrees: discover the correct conception in the scenic action, in your role, and in the beats of the play; and then make the correct habitual and the habitual beautiful. So far, we have only the correct interpretation and actions in this scene. Let us try to make the correct habitual by repeating the scene today and every day without stopping, using our 'under the pencil' method—which means getting the corrections put down by the director during the run-through and then giving them to the actors in the scene after each rehearsal. I plan to meet with you seven or eight times before opening night. During this time we will try to make the correct habitual. Perhaps after ten or fifteen performances the habitual will become beautiful. This will happen if we are concentrating and are strict and demanding with ourselves at each rehearsal and performance. But it is the only path to the beautiful. Nobody has discovered another. Now, if you agree with me, please repeat the scene for the last time today."

This time the scene went even more smoothly and was even more convincing. Stanislavsky praised the actors, then showed his watch to Luzhsky. "Four forty-two. The rehearsal is finished, the scene is ready. What will the

Board of Directors say to that?" he asked Luzhsky with a childish, almost naïve, triumph.

"Please forgive an old fool," Luzhsky said. "I was hurt at the beginning of the rehearsal when you called me a member of the administrative board and continued to address me in this way. What kind of a member of the administrative board am I? I am here to learn from you just as these youngsters. I think I have no less right than they, maybe more, but you suddenly promoted me to 'director of the administrative board.' "

Stanislavsky answered: "You know how I feel about the Board of Directors, Luzhsky. You heard me emphasize in my explanation to the group today how important the coordination of all three links in our theatre organism is. You are the most energetic member of the Board and I don't know how we could get along without you."

"Here you go again! I want to be an actor and your assistant stage director; today you showed me how the director should work for a definite opening date for the play and this lesson is more precious to me than your compliments on my membership on the Board of Directors."

"I wasn't fair to you today, Luzhsky. I often take advantage of my independent position in the theatre. This is wrong of me. Probably you felt it today but didn't want to bring it to my attention in front of the youngsters."

"No, Konstantin Sergeyevich, it is because it's been so long since I have worked as an actor and director; I was envious of your work with the youngsters and not happy at having only the administrative part of the work left to me."

"The good administrator is very important to the theatre, as important as a good actor, but, besides all your many talents, you are a great actor, Luzhsky. I want to make it clear to everybody in our theatre that by working on *The Battle of Life* I am bringing this new young group into the Moscow Art Theatre, and I ask you, Luzhsky, to help me in doing this; and please explain to all the members of our theatre, beginning with Nemirovich-Danchenko, that I am not just directing the play, but that I am using these meetings with the young actors and directors to educate them and prepare them to take our places in the future life of the theatre when you and I will be no more. This is why I go to such lengths in discussing the general principles of actors' and directors' work. At this point it is much more important for me to prepare the new young group who will eventually replace us older people than to put on another play. I want to pass on my knowledge, my achievements, and my power to the youngest group in our theatre. Perhaps I am working with them also because I'm somewhat crafty. I am interested in learning from the new generation. What are they like? This question intrigues me and occupies my thoughts constantly. Who are they? What are those who will take our place like? But I think that this craftiness of mine will be forgiven me, because, actually, it's just healthy curiosity."

"You are the youngest and most inquisitive among us. I hurt your feelings today. Please forgive me, Konstantin Sergeyevich," Luzhsky said.

"On the contrary, allow me to thank you, Luzhsky. You showed the youngsters how important it is to plan rehearsal time, for meeting the date set for the next play on the schedule directly affects the over-all planning of our theatre work. I have the weakness, I must admit, of prolonging and extending my sessions. Until the next session then . . ."

The Nature of Emotions

The next day we played the two following scenes for Stanislavsky in costumes and sets. The first scene took place in Dr. Jeddler's room. The two sisters and their father were in this scene. The second scene was between Clemency and Britain. The set for this scene had a door leading to the garden, near which the end of the scene took place—the secret rendezvous between Marion and Michael Warden.

The first scene opened with Marion sitting by the fire reading a ballad aloud. The content of the ballad suggested Marion's own thoughts and experiences, and she was much moved but tried to hide her emotion from her father and her sister Grace.

Stanislavsky said: "I approve of your performance in this scene except for two moments. First, at the very beginning, the actress reads only three sentences of the ballad and you, Gorchakov, expect her not only to express in this beat all the feelings that excite Marion but also to project the idea to the audience that the fate of a certain Jenny leaving her home, as the ballad describes it, is Marion's own fate in the near future. I think you made the actress' problem more complicated by giving her the usual directorial warning for this kind of situation: 'Accumulate all the necessary feelings but restrain them. Don't show them to the audience. This will make the scene stronger.' Confess, isn't that what you told Stepanova (Marion)?"

"Yes, that's what I told her," I replied.

Stanislavsky continued, "Well, I thought so when I heard her. Now, according to the general rule, your advice was correct. But you must remember that this rule applies only to the type of scene in which the character's feelings are deep and have a universal significance, as in Joan of Arc's farewell speech to her beloved fields and woods. Here the dramatist creates the situation to reveal these feelings and he writes enough words to express them fully and colorfully. In our modest play neither the situation nor the text gives that strong a motive nor is there a great depth of emotion. Marion's problem is noble and dramatic to herself and the people involved. But this is not a tragedy; the theme is not common to all mankind. If the actress hides Marion's feelings, we will have nothing to excite the audience. Therefore the actress must reveal freely the emotion that surges up in her when she reads the ballad. Without falling into sentimentality, cry all you want to, Stepanova, while you read the ballad and we will correct you if you snivel. Do the scene again from the beginning."

The curtain went up and again we saw the scene by the fireplace. Stepanova read the lines of the ballad with more agitation. She had tears in her voice.

Grace interrupted her: "What's the matter, Marion? Please, dear, don't read anymore tonight."

Here Stanislavsky stopped her: "I don't understand a thing. Why shouldn't Marion read anymore tonight?"

Grace replied, "She is getting terribly upset, Konstantin Sergeyevich."

Stanislavsky said: "I don't see it. She is simply sniveling. Perhaps Marion caught cold. But there was certainly nothing in her behavior to demand such a strong reaction from Grace and her father. Please begin the scene again."

The curtain went up again. But this time Stanislavsky did not interrupt the scene. The actors were about to go into the next scene when his voice came from the audience:

"Everything is wrong. You didn't understand what I said. Stepanova, in your reading I get no sense of the similarity between Jenny's fate and your own plan to run away from home. Nothing gives me an idea of the impending drama in this house. I asked you to cry when you read the ballad."

Stepanova answered, "I have tried, Konstantin Sergeyevich. But I don't seem to be able to do it. I have no real tears now. I don't know how to pretend that I have them. I don't know how it's done."

Stanislavsky said, "In the first place, you know very well how it's done. You have seen many actors do it. Perhaps you don't want to fake tears, but don't try to convince me that you are such a true, one-hundred-percent honest Moscow Art Theatre actress that you don't even know how to simulate tears on the stage. I don't need that pretense of innocence.

"Everyone of you knew very well how to simulate sorrow, joy, fear, surprise, and so forth when preparing for your entrance examination to the dramatic school. And this is only natural, because you have been going to the theatre since you were ten or twelve years old, so that when you are ready to enter the dramatic school you have quite a collection of clichés, as well as true expressions of feeling and action. All this evasiveness! 'Today somehow it doesn't come out' or 'I don't have real tears now' or 'I don't know how it's done.' Please leave this for arguments with a younger director. If you are an actress, especially a Moscow Art Theatre actress, and, in my opinion, you are a very gifted one, you must know how to command your willpower. You must know how to bring out the feelings called for by the situation in the play. You must know the theatre laws and the actor's techniques through which these feelings do come to an actor."

Stanislavsky's voice was so severe that Stepanova, without knowing all those laws, started to cry. Of course Stanislavsky immediately noticed it and said: "Here now you have tears in your eyes, tears of insult and offense. You're crying because I spoke harshly to you when you have heard nothing but praise from me for the last three days. Now you can read your ballad with the tears caused by my lecture. These are the tears you need when playing the scene. But I cannot come to your dressing-room to insult and scold you. One must know the law by which an actor can arouse the necessary emotion in himself without such outside help."

"You didn't offend me, Konstantin Sergeyevich," Stepanova answered. "It's just that it's difficult for me to start crying suddenly."

"First, don't argue with me but try to understand what I am saying. When the director talks to an actress sharply, it's a natural reflex to take offense. If you were not offended by my sharp remarks, I would think you an insensitive, indifferent artist without nerves and temperament.

"Second, you did not listen to me attentively when I asked you to cry. Yes, cry; but don't hold the tears back when you are reading the ballad. You have rehearsed this beat twice now and each time you've tried to increase your agitation as you read the ballad, but you did not cry. I know definitely that when Marion reads the ballad she cries bitterly. You were not attentive to my direction and that is why you didn't fulfill the problem I asked you to."

"But I wanted . . ."

"Please don't interrupt me and don't get so excited," Stanislavsky said. "This 'talking out' that you and I are doing now is an excellent illustration for all young actors and directors of how a director should 'talk out' with an actor the design of every part of his role—his acting problems and their justification. Before you interrupted me I wanted to tell you that no one asked you to start crying suddenly as you put it. The secret of this moment in Marion's role consists of the fact that her tears don't come to her during the reading of the ballad nor in those few seconds that follow the rise of the curtain. Marion has been reading to her father and sister half an hour before the curtain goes up and she cries then. In those days and even in mine, it was the accepted thing for a young girl to read poetry out loud and to cry over it without being embarrassed in front of her listeners. 'She is so sensitive,' the family would say. You have a scene like that in Tolstoy's *War and Peace* between Sonya, Nicholas, Boris, and Natasha when they were very young. So I see nothing unusual in the design of this beat in our play and in Marion's adjustment to it."

"You mean that I sob over the ballad even before the curtain goes up?" Stepanova asked.

"That's right."

"But how can I get myself to really cry in the intermission before the scene?"

Stanislavsky smiled contentedly: "This question is an essential one. You as an actress must work out a full score of inner and outer actions for this, and then you can be certain real tears will come to you. Let us establish the problems of this beat now, together. Subsequently you will do this alone. Let's first define exactly what tears in real life mean. They are a reflex of both inner and outer action. We all know them from childhood as a reflex of outer action. The reflex is a result of physical pain striking the nerves that control the tear ducts.

"I know a great number of actresses who used to put drops in their eyes before an emotional scene. These drops irritated the tear ducts, and their tears were supposed to make you think the actress was overcome with emotion. A true feeling, brought forth by the use of inner psychological technique applied to a physical action, needs no such vulgar mechanical trick. Let me tell you that the main cause of any feeling is the thought process by which an actor finds the inner vision of the actions which his character in the play has performed or is about to perform in the given circumstances of the play. In order for an actor to have that inner vision he must be able to put himself into the given circumstances. An actor must ask himself, 'How would I behave if it happened to me in real life?' He must never say about the given action of his role, 'It could never happen to me or it could never happen in life,' but he must naïvely believe in that magic 'if' and freely and easily imagine what he would do 'if' he were to find himself in these circumstances—as, for example, Marion does.

"For this, an actor must know the biography of the character he is creating, the plot of the play, and the theme. It is especially important to recall your own observations of people and events from life, those which will be useful as associations for widening the range of your knowledge of the thought, behavior, and situation of the character. All this work on the psycho-physical world of thought and action will bring you nearer the correct state of mind for your role. Yet this is not enough. This is absolutely necessary, but it's only preparatory work to enable you to arouse the feelings which the character in the play must have. This is only a well-prepared, well-masked trap for the feeling, because the real feeling is very sensitive and easily frightened away. It cannot be caught with bare hands. An actor must know how to lure it to him and, when he does, the trap should be closed. Then the feeling will begin to rush about and to live in the situation that has been prepared for it in the heart and mind of the actor.

"I know from your expressions what you are thinking. 'This is all clever and right. All this that Konstantin Sergeyevich is telling us is undoubtedly necessary for us to know and to do, but all of it is theory, "round and about," and we have heard it numerous times. But how do we really find the true emotion? Tell us that.'

"I will try to answer your question and also teach you the secret of our profession. First of all, you must know the nature of the emotion you are trying to arouse. And because an actor has to create varied parts that call for a great variety of emotions, he should know the nature of every emotion. Today we are analyzing a beat in Marion's role. According to our conception of this beat, she must cry as a result of certain feelings that overwhelm her. Let's name the feelings that make people cry."

"Offense, injustice," came the answer.

"More," Stanislavsky said.

"Sorrow."

"Joy."

Stanislavsky mused: "Weep with joy . . . well, I will confess that I often tell an actor, 'In this spot you simply weep with joy,' but as soon as I finish saying it, I am ashamed of myself; it really happens so seldom in life. What other feelings make you cry?"

Everyone was silent.

Finally I said: "Konstantin Sergeyevich, tears are a kind of result, a form of expression of so many feelings. You have always taught us that only actions are the cause of feeling. Why do you ask us then what kind of feelings arouse tears?"

"I was trying to provoke you. I wanted to know which of you expect a recipe for playing this or that feeling. I could catch only two or three of you."

Luzhsky broke in, "They are wiser now, Konstantin Sergeyevich, not like we used to be—guilty professionals, as you called us."

Stanislavsky continued: "Professionalism is a necessary and healthy beginning in every work and every field of art—that is, professionalism in contrast to dilettantism. But it depends whom the profession is serving and what problems it solves. The fact that these youngsters are educated in the right sense of the word pleases me very much. It proves that the great number of studios we started are bearing fruit. Now let's go back to the rehearsal. Angelina

Osipovna, what is the nature of the emotion that you feel when you read the ballad?"

"I am sorry for my father and my sister," Stepanova responded. "I don't want to leave home or the town where I've lived all my life. I love Alfred; it is terrible to think that I will never see him again and it is even more terrible to think what his reaction will be when he learns that I have betrayed him."

"Select the most important of these sensations and thoughts."

"Pity. I pity my father, my sister, and Alfred as I imagine them without me, not finding me in my room at home in our native town. When I think of their receiving a letter from me from France where Michael and I have eloped, I feel such pity for them that I am ready to cry."

Stanislavsky replied: "Of course, it is very noble of you to love and pity them all, but very often it happens differently in life. Who do you pity most? I don't want you to have too many objects of pity. Choose one."

Stepanova thought for a while. "Father."

Stanislavsky tapped on the table with his pencil, almost triumphantly, "I don't believe it!"

How often we had heard about this expression of Stanislavsky's. How we feared to hear it! The auditorium was silent. We knew from what we had been told by older actors that now he would begin to pursue the actor with this famous phrase, "I don't believe it!"

Everyone was silent, including the embarrassed Stepanova.

Stanislavsky continued: "I don't believe that you are pitying your father more than the others. I don't believe that you will miss your father, that rather dry philosophical babbler, more than the others in your exile. This is sentimentalism of a pure literary and theatrical order. Ask your heart once more, seriously and honestly, whom you pity most of all."

Stepanova said with unexpected joy, obviously quite easily sacrificing her father, "Alfred!"

"I don't believe it, although this is closer to the true nature of Marion's mood."

Stepanova said rather hesitantly, "My home!"

Stanislavsky remarked sarcastically, "I see you passed from an animate object to an inanimate one."

"Nothing else is left," Stepanova said, completely lost.

"You are mistaken. The strongest object of your pity is left, the one which will make you cry bitterly."

Stepanova said with a last hope: "Oh, my God! How could I miss it! It is my dearest Grace, my beloved sister who is the reason for my sacrifice."

"No, I don't believe it," Stanislavsky replied. "It is not Grace. You're sliding over the surface. You're not looking in the depth of your heart. You do not answer my question as an artist would when he penetrates into the nature of the human heart and character. You do not want to confess to us and even to yourself what secret spring very often controls the feelings of a human being."

"I can't think of anything more, Konstantin Sergeyevich, forgive me." Stepanova covered her face with her handkerchief, trying to hide her tears.

Stanislavsky said: "Answer me immediately and honestly. Why are you crying now? Think, think. Penetrate the innermost recesses of your heart, the heart of an actress and a human being. Don't hurry to answer and don't get frightened if at the bottom of your conscience now there is not a very noble thought. Reveal it to us bravely."

"I'm terribly ashamed of myself, Konstantin Sergeyevich, but now when you pounced on me like that I had such pity for myself." And Stepanova burst into bitter tears, turning away from us.

"Bravo, bravo!" Stanislavsky exclaimed. "Good girl! At last you confessed that you discovered in yourself the strong spring which so very often defines the nature of pity. Don't be ashamed that you are crying now. Cry all you like. You made a significant discovery for us and for yourself: that at the bottom of that noble emotion very often a not very noble one lies. I am speaking of egotism. You can cry now with the happy tears of an artist who has reached the truth in a hard and painful way."

It seemed to us that Stanislavsky's eyes shone even more than usual. He continued: "So we have established the nature of the emotion that excites you when you read the ballad. It is self-pity."

"But, Konstantin Sergeyevich, isn't this an ugly feeling for a person to have who is supposed to be inspired by the great idea of sacrifice for another's happiness?" Stepanova asked.

"True. I said it before and I'm ready to repeat it. I told you that it is not easy to accomplish an heroic deed. One has to go through a terrible struggle with himself, and you, as an actress who, in the final analysis, are portraying an heroic role, want every beat of your part to be only noble and heroic. Where will the struggle with yourself take place? This is the most interesting, the most complicated, and yet the most familiar feeling. Do you think Marion would accept the decision without any hesitation or without any faint-heartedness? Do you think she is a heroine all the time? Play it all that way, in the heroic style, and the audience will say, 'Well perhaps this strong nature gets everything in life easily but I know real people and how difficult it is for them to accomplish even a small thing.' Remember that the audience loves to see how a human being fights and overcomes his weaknesses."

"You didn't understand me . . ."

Stanislavsky answered: "I understood you perfectly.

Why is it that I, a beautiful young actress, in a beautiful heroic role should show my waverings, my egotism, and my self-pity by crying over myself? These are negative traits in any character."

"But the idea of *The Battle of Life* . . ."

"Oh, how actors love to clutch at the idea of the play to rescue them when they don't want to play some beat of a part in a certain way that it seems disadvantageous to them! Marion doesn't like these traits in herself either. She doesn't like to see her own egotism, and she cries because she is fighting it. But she can't overcome it too soon —to be precise, she certainly can't do it at the beginning of the second act. Are you worrying for fear the audience won't like Marion? Let's watch Marion through the play and then decide whether the audience will love her or not. And if we love her, then, why do we? For which of her actions and thoughts? Perhaps we will love her for her weakness and not for her heroism. Remember, Charles Dickens wrote about simple, ordinary people with the romantic and sentimental flavor of the last generation. He did not write about heroes."

"You have convinced me, Konstantin Sergeyevich," Stepanova said. "I am ready to curse myself for this egotism. I will fight it. And I will cry because I am furious with myself."

"That's splendid. Now let's find out what Marion's actions should be to create this self-pity."

Stepanova involuntarily adopted almost a capricious tone: "I want nothing today! I don't want to read the ballad! I don't want to leave my home! Why did I make myself that stupid promise to sacrifice my love for Grace's happiness? I don't want to elope with Warden."

"Bravo! Bravo!" Stanislavsky said. "Already you have a number of colorful 'I wants' and 'I don't wants.' Go and act right now, being guided by them. Catch them by the tail. Protest with all your heart against the decision that you made in the first act. Begin! Read the ballad right here to us and to your partners. Don't lose any time in going back on the stage."

Stepanova began to read the ballad. Almost from the first sentence her eyes filled with tears, and then she cried quite openly. Because of the intonations with which she read the ballad and answered Grace's request to stop reading, we could feel her tears were not noble but of quite a different character, and the dramatic intensity of the scene became much stronger.

Stanislavsky did not stop the rehearsal in the auditorium once. It was only after the scene was over that he said to Stepanova, "You played the scene beautifully, and your partners picked up your tone and your rhythm perfectly, though they didn't know what problem you took for yourself before the beginning of the scene. Now you don't have to tell me if you don't want to, although I'm terribly curious to know what helped you to catch the right feeling."

"I wanted my father and Grace to guess my decision, to force me to tell them my plan and talk me into staying home and not to run away. But they are so stupid they don't see my suffering and they don't guess my plan—even when Jenny describes word for word in the ballad everything I plan to do. And I feel such pity for myself. I am poor Marion, abandoned by everybody."

As she finished telling us her problem, Stepanova sobbed bitterly.

Stanislavsky was in ecstasy: "Splendid! Wonderful! You found the most important element for yourself. You found that bait which your feeling will always bite. Just say to yourself before the scene begins: 'What an unhappy, miserable girl I am. Nobody wants to help me. Nobody understands me. Nobody tries to make me stay home.'"

Stepanova burst in tearfully, "Now I can cry all you want me to."

"Marvelous! I want you all to see that Stepanova cries without forcing tears, and without any influence from me this time, and without any hysteria. Stepanova, can you cry less if you want to?"

"Yes," she said and began to weep softly.

"And now can you really sob as if your heart would break?"

Stepanova said through her tears, "Yes, Konstantin Sergeyevich." And in five seconds she was weeping bitterly.

Stanislavsky asked, "How do you do it, Stepanova?"

She replied: "I use what strength I have to make you understand why I, as Marion, am crying. I use my tears as complete phrases. I am even angry at you that you don't understand me, that you don't understand that I don't want to leave home or go anywhere! Please try to understand!"

Stanislavsky said: "As you pity yourself in this way, you are acting; you are protesting; you are revolting; you are fighting our lack of understanding. And as Marion, by the same process, you are fighting yourself. This is the true design: birth, development, and flow of feeling."

"The servant scene is going well," he continued. "It is alive. The relationships between partners are correct and the mise en scène is good. We won't rehearse it now. Let's take the end of the first act, the secret rendezvous between Marion and Warden. The preceding scenes prepare us for a strong and dramatic moment. But you're afraid to play it for all it's worth. Gorchakov, please remind me of the design for this last scene."

I answered: "At the end of the servants' scene a rustle is heard in the garden. Britain takes the lantern and goes out to see if anyone is there. Clemency remains by the fireplace, frightened by the noise. Suddenly she feels Marion's hand on her shoulder and Marion asks her to go out with her into the garden."

"Oh, yes, now I remember. The scene between Marion and Clemency must be very strong dramatically; but, instead, you have it filled with light drawing-room dialogue. Everything that Clemency and Marion say in this scene is sincerely justified, but both actresses are unaware of the action for the scene, which is to do the wrong thing, to commit a sin. This is how they should think of this scene and of their own action in it. For Marion a secret rendezvous at night in the garden verges on immorality, while for Clemency with her naïve imagination, it is a scene of seduction in hell. Marion is falling into the arms of Rokambola. Your mise en scène prevents the actresses from using their temperament and so robs the scene of its intensity. Play this scene in the rhythm, tone, and movement of melodrama, as you understand this genre. But you must justify everything you do, and everything you feel. Both of you should rush around the room, and you should think of all kinds of adjustments: Clemency almost ties Marion up with a kitchen towel to stop her from going into the garden; Marion almost breaks the lock of the garden door. But tell yourself that the time is short. Clemency is afraid that Britain may return any minute, and Marion is aware of Warden's quick temper. He might be offended if she is late for their rendezvous and he might not wait. The rhythm of this scene must be impetuous and rapid, the voices hushed but passionate, the movements sharp and jerky, and the adjustments spontaneous. Now begin the scene."

The actors didn't move.

Stanislavsky spoke: "What's wrong? Why don't you begin the scene?"

Stepanova said: "Well, Konstantin Sergeyevich, we are

planning our movements and what we are going to do in the scene."

Stanislavsky replied, "Did Marion and Clemency talk over their action?"

"Of course not." Both actresses sounded embarrassed.

Stanislavsky said: "So what's wrong? Why do you allow yourself to break the spontaneous logic of events for the sake of the nonsensical and theatrical? Such old clichés! 'You will do that and I will do this, etc.' A cheap bargaining among actors, tricks and adjustments seen in a thousand plays! Don't fix anything before the scene. This is the surest way to deaden the scene and your parts. The true adjustment will come on the stage as a result of the correct state of the actor in the character, from his desire to fulfil the problems of the part in the given circumstances. For fifteen years I have spoken again and again about this fundamental law of the actor's creative power. It's the only law that provides organic life on the stage. Act, but don't plan your action among yourselves beforehand. Action plus counteraction will provide the rest. The moment the director says, 'Begin!, Curtain up!' begin your action on the stage immediately."

And Stanislavsky said loudly and impressively, "Begin!"

As soon as Britain had made his exit, Clemency rushed to the door leading to the garden and locked it. At that moment Marion came into the room. "What are you doing, Clemency?" she exclaimed. "Open that door at once and stand by while I talk to him."

But Clemency put the key in her pocket and began to use all her ingenuity to stop Marion from making this fatal move. Marion faced a very difficult situation. She couldn't take the key from Clemency by force. She rushed about the room and her face and all her movements clearly expressed her panic to find a way out. But Clemency followed her, persisting in her arguments. This mise en scène was most expressive. Suddenly Marion stopped, gazed at Clemency with a long intense look, and then fell on her knees before the maid: "Clemency dearest, sweetest Clemency, you don't understand. I have thought it all over, I have decided. I can't hesitate anymore. I must take this step. Clemency, please help me!" And Marion sobbed bitterly, hiding her face in Clemency's apron. This adjustment, as Stanislavsky had explained, was spontaneously created by the given situation. Marion had to win Clemency's heart. This was her problem. Clemency, confused and embarrassed, also kneeled near Marion, and unexpectedly a very colorful, naïvely touching mise en scène was created.

"Send me to him," Clemency suggested as her last argument. "I'll tell him everything you ask me to. Only, please, please don't you go."

Marion understood that Clemency was giving in. She got up and raised Clemency from her knees, taking Clemency's hands in hers and holding them tightly. "Clemency, shall I go alone or will you go with me?"

After a short pause Clemency answered sadly but firmly, "I'm going with you."

Resolutely she opened the door, and, when Marion stepped to the threshold and Warden's dark figure appeared in front of them, she gasped and stepped decisively between the lovers, pushing Warden as far away as she could with her outstretched hand.

Stanislavsky interrupted: "Hold this mise en scène. This will be the final point of the second act. Gorchakov, please make a drawing of this mise en scène: half-open door, Marion standing on the threshold with one hand resting on the door post, and the other pressing her handkerchief to her bosom."

Without taking his eyes from the stage, Stanislavsky moved a piece of paper in front of me and handed me his pen.

"Konstantin Sergeyevich," I said, "I can't draw."

"Draw as well as you can," he said. "Don't talk, just draw, and later we will discuss it. The director must know how to sketch the design of any mise en scène in his notebook during the rehearsals. Sketch Clemency in front of Marion with her hand outstretched, as if to say, 'Don't come any nearer!'; Warden standing in a kind of demon pose (I have in mind Vrobel's picture, *The Demon*); a moon, a strong blue projector directed toward Warden's back, lighting his figure in silhouette—dark and somber. Marion and Clemency lit by direct light seem much paler. There is scarcely any fire left in the fireplace. It would be good to contrast the silence of this pause with some sound, perhaps the cricket's chirp, and then have the curtain come down slowly. Have you made this sketch?"

I replied, "I have, Konstantin Sergeyevich. I even drew the cricket by the fireplace."

Stanislavsky said, laughingly: "Very good. Now let's test it. We've done enough work for today. Now I want your complete attention. We spent a great deal of time today talking about emotion. But it is most important; you will come up against this problem over and over again in your acting and directing work. It is absolutely necessary to learn the basic principles. First, everything has to be prepared so that the emotion will come: the actor's concentration and his correct state of being on stage at that particular moment, either in rehearsal or performance. For this the character's biography must be as familiar as his own, and he must constantly fill that biography with new facts, even after the play is running. Then the circumstances given him by the author and director must be understood and must be perfectly justified.

"Second, you must define the exact feeling for each beat without being afraid to stumble upon an ugly one (as **Marion** did today). In my acting experience I have made some very sad discoveries for myself. For instance, when a Philistine loves, the most important element in his feeling is possession; when he suffers, he is trying to draw sympathy from those around him, etc.

"Third, after having defined what feeling the actor must have, we must analyze the nature of this feeling. For example, egotism is first of all pity for oneself.

"Fourth, after defining the nature of the feeling, the actor must search for actions which will arouse the feeling. This is the bait which the feeling will rise to.

"Fifth, having caught the feeling, he must learn how to control it. Remember that it is the actor who controls the feeling, not the feeling which controls the actor.

"Will all the actors in the scene we have just analyzed please prepare all their beats for tomorrow's rehearsal in exactly the same manner as we did that beat today. Until tomorrow then."

The Background of the Play and the Main Episodes

The next day we ran through the Lawyers Scene twice. Stanislavsky praised the actors for remembering all his remarks. Then we ran through the scene at the fireplace and the rest of the act.

Before the beginning of the third act, which commences with the party at Dr. Jeddler's to celebrate Alfred's return, Stanislavsky addressed all the actors in this scene.

"I want to warn you. Don't give yourself general problems such as being sad or gay at the party. It doesn't happen like that in life. Among the guests at any party or ball there are all kinds of people and each has a different problem. The host, regardless of his personal feeling, must be the host, making his guests feel at home, greeting them cordially, urging them to enjoy themselves—and by so doing, giving them the general problem of enjoyment. But we know how very little these words mean, because each guest has a personal reason for coming. Usually the least honest are those who say, 'Oh, I just came to have a good time.' They are the ones who have usually come for a very specific purpose—perhaps to meet a superior and have an opportunity to approach him about some important personal business. Another has come to find out the consequences of his scandalous behavior last night at the club. A third is in love and has come to suffer. He observes from a distance the object of his passion. A fourth has come because he had nothing else to do. The fifth has come to prove himself the life of the party, and he proceeds to flirt with all the ladies.

"The sixth has come to have a good meal. The seventh suffers from insomnia. He can't sleep in his own bed. He hopes somehow to doze for an hour, for he can always sleep in a noisy place. (Some people go to bad opera to sleep.) Poor fellow, if it weren't for parties and balls he would have a nervous breakdown from insomnia. And so forth. People, music, movements, the action which each person is trying to accomplish, lights, general activity such as card games and dancing, or a special incident such as Marion's elopement—all together create the party scene or, as we say in theatre terms, a mass scene. I don't like the term mass scene or crowd scene. I don't like it when the director stands before a group of actors and tells them to be sad or gay or frightened or surprised, because this denies the actor any individual initiative. In life, no matter how large the crowd is, each member has his personal life.

"Our best Russian painters showed this realism brilliantly in their pictures. Remember, *Morning of the Archers' Execution*, by Surikov. Then *Dnieper Cossack* by Repin. Also *Appearance of Christ Before the People* by Ivanov.

"How should one direct a crowd scene? How should an

actor behave in a crowd scene? Well, you've correctly planned this party scene: First, the guests arrive. Second, there are the individual episodes with the main characters. Third, a general beat for all the actors in the scene, with dancing, games, etc. Fourth, again an individual episode, with the actual dialogue of the play, and, fifth, the dramatic finale. This is practically a classic design for any crowd scene, but naturally it must be filled with real life, and for that purpose each actor in the scene must have his personal, individual problem. Besides, and this is strictly for the director, when you have an episode taking place down-stage, the action upstage must become almost silent but still continue actively in other small groups. The director should never stop the activity of the crowd when there is dialogue between the main characters.

"When I look out of my window in the morning, I always see clearly the background of the life in the street and then the highlighted episodes. Background: The superintendent of the house across the street and the woman superintendent from our house chat and exchange gossip. The children play by the iron railing of the house; passers-by walk purposefully or simply stroll. Episodes: Across the street a very fancy automobile approaches and blows its horn twice. Almost immediately a smartly dressed lady appears at the door. The superintendents stop gossiping, the children stop playing; the superintendents greet her most cordially, the children stare with great curiosity; the lady enters the car, the car drives off. The children wave and the lady waves back in friendly fashion. Only the passers-by are in the background at that moment. We use the same principle on stage. The scenic life should not stop at the entrance or exit of a character. It's very tasteless staging when everything stops on the stage for the purpose of emphasizing the entrance or exit of a main character. One must work for harmony of rhythm, sound, light, and action at each moment. Unfortunately, very often in our theatre, scenic harmony is interpreted as some stupid combination of music, plastic movement, and recitation. Please, let's begin the rehearsal—unless you have some questions."

After the rehearsal of the party scene, Stanislavsky asked the actors to come down into the auditorium. "I have just a few notes to give you," he said. "You played the scene well. I saw that each of you had an individual problem, but those who had dialogue were obviously worried for fear the audience might take them for part of the crowd. Because of that they made a lot of unnecessary movements. I have in mind the two lawyers' wives, whom we meet in the party scene for the first time."

The actress playing Mrs. Snitchey said, "But this is the character of our problem: to find out what our husbands are hiding from us."

Stanislavsky replied, "Then your behavior must be even more deft and subtle so that the guests cannot guess that you don't know what your husbands are up to. For the benefit of the guests you must be the personification of self-assurance. We know all the gossip. And you must show the audience only that you are beside yourselves because you don't know their important business."

"Konstantin Sergeyevich, we are surrounded by the guests; it is very difficult. How can we show our excitement to the audience without revealing it to the guests on the stage?"

"It's difficult but possible. And your text helps you."

"We are criticizing our husbands' attitude toward their work, but we have very few lines for this."

"Tell me the words," Stanislavsky said.

Mrs. Snitchey spoke her lines, "That nasty office!"

Mrs. Craggs said, "I wish it would burn down!"

Mrs. Snitchey said, "I wish it would collapse."

Stanislavsky laughed: "Well, that's quite enough for the audience to understand your state of mind. Speak those lines with strong indignation. You are doing it so that I can see your inner revolt, but this indignation overwhelms you. You're not controlling it. Your temperament is controlling you. Your hands, your shoulders, and your heads are moving violently. I want you to have the same inner indignation and to speak your lines with the same temperament without even moving a finger. And do not once raise your voice. Now do your scene following the text of the play. Use these three outbursts as often as you want between the questions and answers of your partners, but keep a poker face. Never accompany those outbursts with movement. In this way you will make your audience believe that the crowd doesn't hear you. Treat it as you would an inner monologue. Now, in order not to lose any time, go over your scene here in the auditorium."

They began the scene.

Dr. Jeddler greeted Mrs. Snitchey and Mrs. Craggs, "Well, the legislative power has arrived, but where is Mr. Snitchey?"

Mrs. Snitchey, following Stanislavsky's instructions, spoke very pleasantly, "Only Mr. Craggs knows that."

Mrs. Craggs answered with the same tone, "We are told nothing."

Mr. Craggs stammered, "He's—he's . . . well, there's a little . . . matter of business that k-keeps my partner rather late."

Mrs. Snitchey said, "That nasty office!"

Mrs. Craggs said, "I wish it would burn down!"

Mrs. Snitchey spoke, "I wish it would collapse!"

"That is not exactly what I meant," Stanislavsky remarked. "I wanted you to fill your lines with as much feeling as before. Keep the poker face but speak your words with tremendous intensity. Let's do the scene again."

Dr. Jeddler, Mrs. Snitchey, and Mrs. Craggs began, and we saw that Stanislavsky included himself in the scene. He greeted the ladies cordially, looked for Mr. Snitchey (whereas Dr. Jeddler had not), and laughed, reacting to the ladies (where Dr. Jeddler only listened). He paid especial attention to Mr. Craggs' explanation of Snitchey's absence.

Then (at my prompting) he took over the ladies' dialogue, first, smiled most charmingly at Dr. Jeddler, then his face literally hardened into stone when he turned to Mrs. Craggs and said through his teeth with the greatest intensity, "That nasty office!" And he did exactly the same thing when he said, "I wish it would burn down." His change from extreme cordiality toward his host to the bitter wrath with which the two wives denounced their husbands' work made Stanislavsky achieve a remarkably comic effect by means of the brilliantly stressed asides.

Stanislavsky asked the actors to repeat the scene once more. And then he said to Mr. Craggs: "I've heard you in the scene three times now and I can't understand why you don't trust yourself as an actor. You have a fine, subtle sense of humor, an expressive appearance, clear diction, plastic movement, right temperament but you speak your lines as though you were an extra who at last had been given a few words to say. You are trying to make an important monologue out of one sentence."

Mr. Craggs asked, "Konstantin Sergeyevich, are you trying to say that I'm over-acting?"

Stanislavsky answered: "The director has a right to tell an actor that he is over-acting only when he knows and understands this actor very well—when the director knows precisely in what aspect of his work he is over-acting, whether in temperament or in emotion or the characteristics of the role. First, I don't know you very well. Second, I don't think you are really over-acting. I think you are trying to be overly conscientious. You don't trust yourself as an actor, nor do you trust your importance to the scene. You are afraid that the audience has forgotten your previous scene."

Mr. Craggs unexpectedly interrupted: "Yes, yes, you're absolutely right. I was worrying for fear the audience would wonder who I was. Shouldn't I worry about that?"

Stanislavsky smiled: "You are excellent in the office scene. I am sure the audience will remember it. You see what a comedian you are? You make me laugh even now when I'm not in the mood."

"It's accidental."

"I know you comedians. You do nothing accidentally."

Mr. Craggs remarked under his breath, "I'm not a comedian, I'm a dramatic actor. I want to do serious drama."

Stanislavsky answered. He certainly heard what he had just said. "It is a very worthy ambition for a comedian. Be sure to test yourself in a serious dramatic role. No matter what the result, work in a different *genre* will widen your range. Now go over your scene again, lawyers!"

The scene went well. Craggs played extremely well. He was relaxed. He had a subtle humor and also showed a very serious anxiety concerning Marion.

"You see now how much an actor can do when he trusts himself, the author and the director," Stanislavsky said, addressing us and pointing to Mr. Craggs. "I am tempted to prophesy a great future for you, Mr. Craggs, if you continue to work as seriously as you do now. But I'm going to bewitch you with my evil eye."

Luzhsky interrupted: "I wish you would bewitch me with the evil eye. You have never been that generous with us old actors. You are very kind to the young ones, I must say."

Luzhsky had the special talent of relieving the tense moments in rehearsals with Stanislavsky by a joke or a witty remark. Also, he let us know in a subtle way that our work in the Moscow Art Theatre would not always be as easy and joyous as in these first months of our acquaintance with the theatre and with Stanislavsky.

Stanislavsky continued, "The young actor, like a puppy, must be treated very kindly for three months or until he is domesticated and then . . .

Luzhsky broke in, "Then for the next thirty-three years he will be whipped. We learned this 'method.' "

We all had a good laugh.

Stanislavsky said: "Well, now that we have rested a few minutes, let's go to work. Do the party scene on the stage."

Everything went well. The comic beats were gay and full of excitement, and the dramatic beats were serious and touching.

Finally, Stanislavsky concluded: "We can leave this act until the dress rehearsal. The next time we meet I want to give you my notes on the fourth act. Then we will begin our run-through. So long."

Actions and Problems

The fourth act takes place six years later. It consists of two scenes. The first is in the tavern owned by Clemency and Britain who are now married.

Stanislavsky began: "According to the author's construction of the Tavern Scene, all the characters in the play except Mr. Snitchey are sure Marion is dead. For some reason you are playing it as though you were unaware of this. Why do you interpret the scene this way?"

"As actors in the play we know that Marion is not dead," someone answered. "And the audience is certain that the leading character can't be dead so early in the play . . ."

"There!" Stanislavsky interrupted, with that special air of triumph he used when he caught the fault by the tail, as he called it—that is, when the director or the actor broke one of the basic laws of stage action. "This is exactly what ruins the spontaneous reaction of the audience. It's a grave mistake for an actor and director to make. You actors and your director know the plot, and you will be embarrassed when, in the next fifteen minutes, the secret of the play is revealed and you have not hinted it to the audience. Isn't that it? But who gave you permission to know the plot in advance?"

"But, Konstantin Sergeyevich, we must know it in advance in order to rehearse the play," I said.

Stanislavsky answered: "In order to rehearse—yes. But after you finish the rehearsals and the actors are playing, they must not only be unaware of what happens in the third and fourth acts, but also of what happens in the first act from the moment the curtain goes up. Are you sure what I will do in the next few minutes—even though we have a definite plan to rehearse the fourth act?"

"No, of course not."

Stanislavsky continued: "You see, you don't know. That's the logic of life. Although we plan a day ahead or even a year ahead, no one can be certain of his plan being fulfilled. The audience that watches a play has its own ideas of how the plot will develop, but it cannot be sure until the end. Even when watching such a well-known play as *Hamlet*, the audience still doesn't know how this play will be performed, but if the audience isn't familiar with the play, what right have you directors and actors to brag that you know? This only reveals the fact that you are not real characters, for they could not possibly know what will follow, and also you are not very smart or learned in your profession, like people who are afraid to be taken for fools. Now, play the scene as it is written without anticipating the next scene. Tell me, according to the text, who is certain that Marion is dead?"

"I am, Konstantin Sergeyevich," Clemency said.

"So am I," answered Britain.

"I learn of her death during the scene," Michael Warden remarked.

"What prevents your believing it?" Stanislavsky asked.

"Nothing."

"Then act as if you believed the sad news and use whatever reaction this calls forth."

Snitchey declared, "I know that Marion is alive, but now I realize that the fact that I told Michael Warden about Mr. Craggs' death . . ."

Stanislavsky asked, "Is your information true?"

"Yes."

Stanislavsky said, "Then telling Michael about the real death of one of the main characters at that point will only strengthen the impression that Marion is dead."

"I just realized that now."

"Play this scene in such a way to make the audience believe in Marion's death and you will see how grateful they will be for your deceit when they discover that Marion is not only alive but that she has been irreproachable in her conduct all these years. Begin the scene, please."

Because we emphasized the death theme instead of the lyric color that our nostalgia had given it, the scene in the tavern began to ring with dramatic force and conviction. Clemency and Britain talked seriously about the past years, since they now believed that Marion was dead. The sentimental flavor of their conversation disappeared and was replaced by short pauses, as they thought of what had happened. Michael Warden's arrival in the tavern in a somber mood confirmed the tragic news. Clemency's sorrow was real and deep. Without the lyric quality the whole scene was more compact, concrete, and forceful.

At the end Stanislavsky spoke: "Fine! I think you were afraid that the death theme in this scene would contradict

Dickens' sentimental genre. But this is one instance in which the actors and director, aware of the modern audience, have the right to disagree with the author's estimation of the situation. In Dickens' time sentimentality was in style. Such a death theme was usually underplayed and veiled with mere sadness. Today we have the right to talk of death as a serious fact, because to us the physical fact of death is not important but the reason why. In this way we must evaluate Marion's imaginary death. She performed an act of self-sacrifice for the happiness of another human being. She subjected herself to great suffering and died. Everyone talks about her with great respect in this scene. And our contemporaries, the Soviet spectators will be grateful to you for this kind of relationship to death, and will leave the easily aroused tears for the novel readers of Dickens' epoch. Our times are different and stern. Our attitude to events, even in the classic plays and novels, must be different, sterner, and more manly."

Luzhsky said, "If everyone believes Marion is dead in this scene, how should they react in the next scene when they meet her?"

Stanislavsky replied: "Just as one does in life in a similar situation. Suppose you receive news from the front that someone near and dear to you has been killed. Your sorrow is infinite. First, you can't believe it. You try to deny it. Then you are convinced that it has really happened. You evaluate the fact (of course, not being aware of this process) in relation to the past, usually thinking, 'Oh, how wonderful he was! How close we were!' Then, in relation to the future, 'He was planning to do this or that. We were dreaming of going here and there when he returned.' Now, in relation to the present, 'What am I going to do now without him? How shall I tell my daughter?' These thoughts call forth an outburst of despair and tears.

"Then time goes by; your sorrow is in the past but it

occupies a very big place in your heart. More time passes, and sorrow gives way to respect for one who has sacrificed his life for a fine ideal. Then suddenly the one you thought lost returns. He stands in front of you. Can you imagine how many steps one has to retrace in order to believe that he is alive—in order to accept the idea? Before you act it out for me, let's analyze the structure of the scene in which Marion returns. Let's establish for each one of you your relation to her return.

"The first beat: Alfred prepares Grace for the fact that Marion is alive. Second beat: Marion and Grace's meeting, and Marion's explanation of her past and present action. Third beat: the meeting between Marion and Dr. Jeddler, who knew she was alive all the time. Fourth beat: the meeting between Marion, Clemency, and Britain, who were sure she was dead. Fifth beat: the happy ending, which leaves the audience with the idea that Marion will be rewarded for her sacrifice by marrying Michael Warden, who is, of course, completely reformed. In this structure I see clearly two different types of meetings with Marion and her partners in the play. The first between Marion and Grace is deeply dramatic in its essence, especially dramatic for Grace, who must be thinking: 'It isn't only that Marion is alive but also that she has been hiding all these years because of me. How can I accept such a sacrifice? How could I, her older sister, fail to recognize ten years ago the thoughts and feelings of my beloved young sister? How wrong I was in thinking her capricious and light minded! And Alfred—whom does he love? And Marion—does she still love Alfred? She must—her love for him was so deep. What am I to do? What can I say?' "

"Konstantin Sergeyevich, please forgive me for interrupting," Grace said, terribly excited, "but I don't have all those wonderful words of that beautiful monologue in my text. All I have is a few broken phrases, 'Is it you, Marion?

Don't talk . . . don't talk . . . what are you saying, Marion? I can't . . . I don't want to hear it.' And then two remarks by the author, 'Grace is silent and hypnotized as she looks at Marion. Grace's eyes are full of tears as she embraces Marion.' "

Stanislavsky smiled, understanding her excitement. "The thoughts that I was trying to compose now, are they implicit in your words or are they something else? Does she or does she not have such thoughts as she listens to Marion's confession?"

"The thoughts are certainly the same," Grace answered sadly, understanding the meaning of his question.

Stanislavsky continued: "Don't feel so bad because the monologue in the scene is Marion's. You have just as powerful an inner monologue. Trust me. If you will say those words inwardly and if you will live them, then the audience won't take its eyes from your face as it reads your thoughts. Remember our scene on the swing in the first act when you had the monologue aloud and Marion had the inner one. The scene came out strongly and both of you as actresses were happy about it. Remember that to know how to listen to your partner means to know how to conduct the inner dialogue with him instead of waiting for your cues. Do you understand what I mean?"

"Yes," Grace replied.

"Have I convinced you?" Stanislavsky asked.

Grace said: "I'll try to do what you just said. I'll carry on a desperate inner monologue with Marion. Please tell me afterwards what was right and what was wrong."

Very happy, Stanislavsky answered: "This is wonderful. We've come to an understanding about the meeting of Marion and Grace."

He continued, "The second meeting is the one with Clemency and Britain. This is obviously a comedy scene. But it should be played very seriously. I will ask you,

Clemency, to fulfill the following problems when you see Marion for the first time: A) I don't believe that this is Marion standing in front of me. I am looking at the other people around me as though I am telling them, 'See what one can imagine!' B) Look at Marion. She stands on the same spot and doesn't disappear. She is surely a ghost. C) (Look at her a third time.) Suppose she is alive? How? I don't know anything. But suppose she's alive? Suppose it isn't a ghost? I must find out. D) I will. (This you will have to do the way you feel it.) 'My Marion!' I kiss her, embrace her, clutch her in my arms. E) No, I must be dreaming. I don't know how to hide my stupid behavior from anybody.

"During the pauses that you have, do you think you can do all that?"

"I will try, Konstantin Sergeyevich," Clemency said. "But please don't be angry with me if it doesn't come out the way you want it."

Stanislavsky said: "I will not be angry, because I gave you a very difficult task. And I ask all the actors on the stage to react spontaneously to everything Clemency may do in fulfilling her problems."

Britain asked: "What relation do I have to the resurrected Marion? My character is so different from Clemency's."

Stanislavsky replied: "In evaluating what is happening, you go through the same inner process as Clemency, but, as a phlegmatic person, you react outwardly quite differently. During the Marion-Clemency scene you stand like a pillar of salt and you suddenly come out with a most unexpected reaction only after everybody thinks the scene is resolved. But you have to find what it is for yourself. This reaction can take a different form at every performance. It can be a strong curse or stupid tears, things no one would expect from Britain. Is this design agreeable to you?"

Britain sighed deeply, well aware of the difficulty of his task. "Yes, it's agreeable to me, Konstantin Sergeyevich."

Stanislavsky continued: "Well, splendid then. Now you are to play all the interval beats between those two climactic scenes as you did in your original production. On stage, please."

The sisters played their meeting scene with a great deal of fire. Grace's eyes were filled with inner doubt and torment, while Marion's eyes pleaded with her to understand that she had sacrificed herself not only for Grace's happiness but because she had loved Alfred less.

Grace must have carried out her inner monologue fully, for her face did not have that mere listening expression which, I must admit, our actresses often had at rehearsals when Stanislavsky wasn't present. Her face, her eyes, her gestures, the turn of her head, sudden movements of her hands, all came as a result of her true inner monologue. And the short sentences of her text came as explosions of feeling that she could not hold back. The scene was now intensely dramatic and most colorful. Because of this, all the interval beats were deeper and more exciting. Clemency fulfilled her problems most interestingly. In dealing with her first problem—"I don't believe that it is really Marion standing in front of me"—Clemency threw two or three glances at Marion and at the others around her and then suddenly began to laugh. But, seeing that nobody joined her, she stopped just as suddenly. Accepting the idea that Marion was a ghost, Clemency instantly disappeared behind Britain's wide shoulders and carefully peeked out to see if the ghost had disappeared. When Marion said, "Clemency, it's I, your Marion!" Clemency started to move very slowly toward Marion, ever closer and closer. She touched Marion's hand and immediately ran back to Britain. She stopped, then came back and touched Marion's dress two or three times, twisting the buttons on the dress.

Then she cried wildly, "Marion!" and fell on her neck. At that point she quite unexpectedly began to embrace and kiss the rest of the actors, and followed this by kissing Britain, and then kissing Marion again and again. Her actions were a brilliant, unexpected realization of the simple Clemency's joy at the miraculous return of her deeply loved mistress. Following the abrupt end of her kissing scene, she sat on the bench in the corner by the table crying softly. She didn't dare to look at Marion anymore for fear that she might turn out to be a ghost after all. The actors, almost in tears themselves, began to console Clemency.

At that point, Britain, who had stood like a pillar of salt until now, put the bowl of his pipe in his mouth (he had taken it out of his mouth at Marion's first appearance). He reacted as if he were being choked by the tobacco—coughing and spitting. The scene was so funny that everybody on stage burst out laughing. It made a fine ending to the scene.

Stanislavsky was most satisfied and said: "Tomorrow we will have a run-through without stops. Three days before schedule." (This was said for Luzhsky's benefit.)

The Actor's State of Being

The next day we were just as nervous as we were on the first day we showed Stanislavsky our *Battle of Life*. Everything would be tested today. The result of his work with us during the last three weeks, and of our own work without him in solidifying (as he expressed it) the design of the scenes and the relationships between the characters.

As usual, Stanislavsky came ten minutes early for this last run-through.

"Is everything in order?" he asked.

"Yes, Konstantin Sergeyevich," I replied.

"Did you check the costumes, lights and props?"

"I did."

"What mood are the actors in?"

"They're very nervous."

"Where is Luzhsky?"

Luzhsky called from the back of the auditorium. "I'm here. I want to make sure that the actors can be heard from the back."

Stanislavsky said, "Fine. Let's begin."

The curtain went up. Stanislavsky didn't make many notes during intermission. His face remained serious and tense. He was very anxious about the outcome of this run-through. But when the curtain came down upon the last act he said, "Congratulations! You played correctly, seriously, and energetically, and you carried out the design precisely as we discovered it together. But I am warning you: don't get swelled heads. This is only the beginning, only the first run-through. This design will either die or bloom in new colors during the first ten or fifteen performances. Until then, we cannot be certain if it is good or bad. Pay attention to and concentrate on the play's inner action, its problems, and the precise inner and outer rhythm. Act, but don't emote!

"Now the schedule for the opening is as follows: Tomorrow everyone rests. The day after there will be a complete dress rehearsal in make-up, but without audience. Then, again, rest all day and in the evening another complete dress rehearsal with audience. A week from today will be the opening. Rest tomorrow but don't let go of your inner concentration. Think of the inner life of your character. Don't think of how you will do this or that moment in your part. Good-by—until the day after tomorrow."

Stanislavsky left without giving us his notes. When we

asked Luzhsky his impression of this dress rehearsal, he said: "Now you need audience, audience, audience. At this stage, without an audience, I really don't know what to say. Test yourselves the day after tomorrow. And then, with God's blessing, you will play before the audience."

The day after tomorrow arrived. Stanislavsky was at his director's table with Luzhsky by his side. We rehearsed the play for all it was worth. We tried our best. The actor's *state of being* was wonderful. I was aware of it during the intermission backstage, but Stanislavsky sat with a stony face during all four acts, not smiling once. I couldn't understand it, and I couldn't answer the actor's questions about his response.

After the run-through we all gathered around the director's table in a good and happy mood.

"How did you feel today on the stage?" Stanislavsky asked, tapping his pencil on the table.

"Fine! Wonderful!" the answers came from the actors.

"Even wonderful," Stanislavsky answered, with a shade of irony in his tone which gave us the feeling that all was not well. "I think you played very badly today. You were empty. You kept only the form of the design without the real inner content of the beats. For the sake of a brisk tempo, you slid over problems; you were satisfied with imitation, with reflection of feeling. You never aroused the true emotion in yourselves. It was easy and gay for you to act, but it was difficult and sad for me to watch you. Three weeks' work were wasted. We must begin all over again."

I doubt if I will ever forget the pause that then followed Stanislavsky's words.

"I don't know what to do now," Stanislavsky addressed Luzhsky. "The play is announced. Is it possible to hold it up for a time?"

"It's possible," Luzhsky answered, "but is it necessary?"

"I can't let the performance go on in such an empty cliché state," Stanislavsky said.

"It won't be like that," Luzhsky answered. "The youngsters just got carried away. You have been praising them too much lately. They felt too sure of themselves. They played for 'all hundred,' as the saying goes. But they have no right to play for 'all hundred' yet. The result was bad."

Stanislavsky asked, "What are we to do?"

Luzhsky said, "Explain to them that such an exhilarated state on the stage is deceptive. Sometimes an actor feels delightfully easy and gay during a performance, but then the next morning he meets a friend who says to him: 'Weren't you feeling well last night? Your performance wasn't as good as usual. Are you ill?' "

"Very well put, Luzhsky," Stanislavsky said.

Then, addressing the company, Stanislavsky continued: "You were all ill on the stage today. What was your illness? Self-assurance, smugness, imagining yourselves great actors. But I am worse than all of you. Once more I led myself to believe that it is possible with talented young people to change the performance, inject new life into it, and launch it on a long life in ten rehearsals. Of course it's all my fault."

Luzhsky said: "Don't accuse either yourself or the youngsters too severely. You will continue to get excited over new young actors, and the young actors will always get drunk on quick success."

Stanislavsky asked: "What is there to do now? There's not much time left."

Luzhsky replied: "There is no time left. My suggestion is to follow your original plan. The day after tomorrow test the performance with an audience. I think today will have been a very good lesson for them. Now the first run-through was fine. Perhaps, after some hard thinking, they will return to their proper working state and will renew their desire to fulfill the modest but difficult problems you established for them, instead of imagining themselves great actors."

Another long and heavy silence followed. Finally a question came from Stanislavsky, "Perhaps the actors or the director have some constructive suggestions to make?"

"We will never forget the lesson that you gave us today," I answered. "Perhaps we are not experienced enough actors to let our inspiration guide us on the stage, and it may be that we must work modestly and persistently for a long time to come. Permit us to repeat the play right now."

"Do you all agree with Gorchakov?" Stanislavsky asked. "Do you all see your mistakes as Gorchakov defined them? Your mistake was that you lived on stage in a general mood, not in the mood of your characters. You did not act. You weren't solving the problems which we discovered, established, and agreed upon for each character."

The actors answered that they understood their mistake and asked for a chance to prove it. They were ready to repeat the performance that very minute. They were excited and upset by their failure. Stanislavsky gave them a long and intent look and we could see how difficult it was for him to come to a decision. Then he looked at Luzhsky, searching for advice from him, but Luzhsky was silent. Stanislavsky looked at me once more, but I had nothing to add to what the actors and I had already said. Finally Stanislavsky said: "It's too late to repeat the play now. But I am ready to trust you once more. I will come to see your run-through before the audience the day after tomorrow. I will be most strict and demanding. Are you ready to undertake this important responsibility? Decide. It's up to you."

The actors looked at each other, debating inwardly, and then the bravest, Stepanova, said, after looking around at all the other actors, as if gaging their reaction, "I think,

Konstantin Sergeyevich, that I am expressing the wish of the whole company when I ask you to see our performance once more the day after tomorrow with the audience."

The rest of the company supported her.

"Fine!" Stanislavsky answered. "I think this is what we should do. Until then." And he left the auditorium.

Luzhsky followed him. We all remained in the auditorium for quite some time. We didn't reproach each other. We didn't complain or philosophize. We didn't promise each other to play better the day after tomorrow. We were deep in thought; for the most part we were silent. But for some reason we couldn't disperse.

"I thought I'd still find you here," Luzhsky said, as he reentered the auditoroum. "I had a good talk with Konstantin Sergeyevich as I walked with him to the big stage. And I think I have succeeded in convincing him to witness your performance the day after tomorrow with a kind heart. He likes to put on severe airs, but he is as worried as you and I."

His words breathed kindness and a keen awareness of our psychology. Just the fact that he had returned meant so much to us. The feeling that we were at the mercy of this final run-through left us. We realized that Luzhsky's concern represented the Moscow Art Theatre's. We tried to show him our appreciation but he kept repeating, "No need to talk about that. Go home now. All will be well."

The run-through with the audience was going well. Sitting next to Stanislavsky, I saw that he watched attentively and quietly. The audience applauded, and we had many curtain calls. Stanislavsky also applauded. But we were very anxious about his verdict.

"Good children, bravo!" Stanislavsky said, as soon as we had gathered around his table. "I believe you now. And I can work with you again. Remember that my task is to teach you the difficult work of the actor and director, not how to pass your time gaily and pleasantly on the stage. There are other theatres for that, other teachers and other systems. The actor's and director's work, as we understand it, is a poignant process, not an abstract creative joy about which ignoramuses make empty declarations. As we approach our work, it gives us joy—the joy of realizing that we are capable and have the right and are given permission to work at what we love. And the work itself gives us joy when we see that in fulfilling our task of putting on a play or playing a part we have brought something useful and have communicated to the audience something important and necessary for its life, development, and growth. I want to repeat the words of our great Gogol and Shchepkin: *The basis of creativeness in an actor or director lies in work, not in mood or inspiration or whatever word was in vogue during periods of decadence!*

"The process of work, including the performance, is a process that demands a great inner concentration and often great physical perseverance. The joy of creation certainly comes to the real artist when he has accomplished his goal by tremendous work.

"In your previous run-through you were flirting with the audience. You weren't concerned with either the idea or the theme of the play—actor-courtesans! Never do that! Never! Leave this kind of acting to the decadents, futurists, and cubists.

"Great Russian artists, actors, and writers never flirt with life. They have always worked to reveal the ugly and the beautiful and also to teach. Don't be afraid of the verb 'to teach' in art. I have spent many hours and many words in these three weeks trying to teach you. I have talked to you about so many general problems of our theatre art because I want you to know not only how to play your parts well but also how to develop the real artist in yourself. I have accomplished this through enormous work and many years lost in mistakes and digressions from the main, important line in art. I am transferring all my knowledge and all my experience to you in order to spare you the mistakes I made. You will have so much more time to advance our art if you will understand me and follow the road I have paved for you. You are the new youth who have come to the theatre since the revolution. I want you to understand the Stanislavsky method through work. There is no actual *method* yet; there are only a number of basic principles and exercises that I suggest an actor practice in order to train himself to become a master artist.

"Now what are those basic principles of my method? First, my method gives no recipes for becoming a great actor or for playing a part. My method is the way to the actor's correct state of being on the stage. The correct state is the normal state of a human being in life. But it's very difficult for an actor to create this state on the stage. He must be physically free, must control his muscles, and must have limitless attention. He must be able to hear and see on the stage the same as he does in life. He must be able to communicate with his partner and to accept the given circumstances of the play completely.

"I suggest a series of exercises to develop these qualities. You must do these exercises every day, just as a singer or pianist does his scales and arpeggios.

"My second principle concerns the correct state of being on stage. This calls for the correct actions in the progressive unfolding of the play: inner psychological actions and outer physical actions. I separate the actions in this manner intentionally. It makes it easier for us to understand each other during rehearsal. As a matter of fact, every physical action has an inner psychological action which gives rise to it. And in every psychological inner action there is always a physical action which expresses its psychic nature: the unity between these two is organic action on the stage. It is defined by the theme of the play, its idea, its characters, and the given circumstances. In order to make it easier for himself, an actor must put *himself* into the given circumstances. You must say to yourself, 'What would I do *if* all that happens to this character, happened to me?' I believe this *if* (I call it jokingly, the magic *if*) helps an actor to begin to *do* on the stage. After you have learned to act from yourself, define the differences between your behavior and that of the character. Find all the reasons and justifications for the character's actions, and then go on from there without thinking where your personal action ends and the character's begins. His actions and yours will fuse automatically if you have done the preceding work as I have suggested.

"The third principle of the method—the correct organic action (inner plus outer)—will necessarily give rise to the correct feeling, especially if an actor finds a good bait for it. The sum of these three principles—correct state of being, actions, and feelings—will give to your character an organic life on the stage. This is the road which will bring you closest to what we call metamorphosis. Of course this takes for granted that you have understood the play correctly—its idea and its theme—and that you have analyzed the character accurately. And beyond all this, the actor must have a good appearance, clear and energetic diction, plastic movement, a sense of rhythm, temperament, taste, and the infectious quality we often call charm."

"Then how is it that great actors like Mochalov, Orlenev or Dalsky played without these classic qualities and knew nothing of your method?" Luzhsky asked.

"You're talking of exceptional talents," Stanislavsky replied. "I offer my method to capable actors, and they are the great majority.

I asked, "What principles must the director know, Konstantin Sergeyevich?"

Stanislavsky answered: "All those I mentioned for the actor, plus three more, are essential for the director: First, he must know how to work on the play with the author, or without him, if the author is dead; and he must know how to make a complete and profound analysis of the play. Second, he must know how to work with the actor. This includes everything we have spoken of during the three weeks of rehearsal and will discuss and act upon in future productions. Third, he must know how to work with the scenic designer, the composer, the costumer, and all the rest of the production crew. The director must work on himself as much as an actor does, and he must do ten times more. He must be ten times as thorough and ten times as disciplined, because he must teach not only himself but the actors. Well, I think you have enough for today and the near future. I wish you all success on your opening night. I will be there."

The next day, October 7th, was our opening. The play went very well. But Stanislavsky could not see it. He was ill, kept in bed for a few days at the doctor's order because of overwork and anxiety. Luzhsky watched the play and telephoned reports to Stanislavsky at each intermission. We asked Luzhsky if it would be all right to bring flowers to Stanislavsky. He said, "I will telephone Lilina (Stanislavsky's wife) and tell her you are all coming. I know it will please the old man."

In twenty minutes the whole company was at Konstantin Sergeyevich's house. Lilina received us kindly and graciously and promised to give Stanislavsky the flowers, and our best wishes for his quick recovery and our gratitude.

The moment I arrived home my telephone rang. "Stanislavsky speaking. I want to talk to Gorchakov."

"I am listening, Konstantin Sergeyevich."

"I want to congratulate you once more on a good performance. And you're a fine fellow to have accepted the changes I made. The whole is always much more important than special details. How's the actors' mood?"

"Wonderful, Konstantin Sergeyevich. Thanks loads—for everything!"

"Thank you for the flowers. You and the whole company can sleep in peace tonight. Give them all my regards tomorrow."

"I will, without fail."

"All the best."

This was Stanislavsky's first telephone call to me. I put it down immediately on the last page of my director's copy of *The Battle of Life*.

A RUSSIAN CLASSIC IN VERSE

CHAPTER TWO

MUCH WOE FROM WISDOM

BY Alexander Griboyedov

The satire is laid in the town house of Famusov, a rich land-owner and government official in the Moscow of the first part of the last century. The author, Griboyedov, was the first writer

SYNOPSIS
OF THE
PLAY

who dared to raise the veil which covered the faults of his contemporaries. He struck with a firm and resolute hand at the base of the stupendous edifice of prejudices which centuries of ignorance had reared. The play created a sensation, not only in the literary circles of Moscow where it first made its appearance but in all classes of Russian society. A great number of its verses remain as proverbs to the present day. There is in Griboyedov more of Juvenal than Molière. His style is strong and concise, and it bears, from its very want of poetic expression, the aspect of severe satire rather than witty comedy. He smiles at the igno-rance and frivolity of his contemporaries, but, as a true patriot, he becomes bitter when thundering against the servile imitation of foreigners that distinguished his epoch. He is a caricaturist: a few words, a single sentence is enough to present a clear idea of every character in the play. The principals are the selfish, pompous, servile Famusov, who gives royal receptions to all Moscow and scolds his servant for being out at the elbows! Skalozub, the worthy old soldier whose head contains nothing but parades and rank, who always speaks, even to a lady, as if he were issuing orders to his regiment; Molchalin, Famusov's

123

secretary, who thinks it a part of his duty to assume the character of a romantic lover with his superior's daughter; Platon Mikhailovich, who tries to look contented under the yoke of matrimony but who has completely subjected his spirit and will to his pretty, determined wife; Sophie, Famusov's daughter, the true pattern of all the young ladies of her day, whose education was based on French novels and songs; the princess, with her six daughters, all smiles, fashions, and scandal-mongering; Zagoretsky, well-known for his cheating, whom everyone calls a liar and yet who is well received everywhere because of his dexterity in all worldly matters; and finally the hero, Chatsky, a young man of high talent, refinement, and sensitivity, who struggles vainly with the powerful spirit of prejudice. The majority is opposed to him, and Chatsky is vanquished in the combat. He is unfortunate because he is more clear-sighted than his contemporaries. He attempts to exhibit their faults and they call him a Jacobin; and when he speaks as a man of feeling would on seeing himself surrounded by treacherous friends, they immediately say he is mad.

As the play opens, Molchalin is having a rendezvous with Sophie. Famusov intrudes unexpectedly and expresses his displeasure in no uncertain terms. Sophie succeeds in mollifying him with some difficulty. Shortly after, Chatsky calls, having just returned from a long sojourn abroad. He is in love with Sophie, but neither she nor Famusov approve of him because of his frank tongue. Chatsky indulges in the passionate, ironic criticism of a person who sees his world through clear eyes.

He observes Sophie's interest in Molchalin and is eager to learn whether she really prefers him to Skalozub, the stupid army officer who is Famusov's choice for her. He cannot get any answer from her, as she is afraid of his cleverness and insight. Moreover, she resents his criticism of her suitors, particularly his criticism of Molchalin—which she attributes to jealousy.

At a ball which her father gives Sophie spreads the rumor that Chatsky has gone mad. The rumor is quickly believed by the guests, who resent his ironic comments. Chatsky is about to leave, as he has become aware that his audience has deserted him and he is disappointed that his homecoming has not proved more successful, when he is stopped by Repetilov, a garrulous and frivolous bore. Chatsky seizes the first opportunity to slip away unseen into a porter's lodge, where he overhears the departing guests as they discuss his supposed madness.

Chatsky is completely taken aback, and he is alarmed that Sophie may hear this rumor. He has not the slightest suspicion that she began it. Suddenly she appears and calls Molchalin. Chatsky hides behind a pillar just as the yawning Molchalin comes in from his room.

Molchalin proceeds to make love to Sophie's maid, Lisa, who tells him that her mistress is waiting. But both Sophie and Chatsky overhear this episode. Astounded at Molchalin's behavior, Sophie enters and rejects him, although he grovels at her feet. Her satisfaction that at least no one else has witnessed his treachery is short-lived, for Chatsky soon makes his presence known. Molchalin runs away. Chatsky bitterly taunts Sophie, who bursts into tears.

At this moment Famusov enters with his servants, and berates all concerned. He threatens to use all his social and political influence against Chatsky, but the latter announces—with cutting sarcasm for both father and daughter, as well as Russian society in general—that he has decided to leave Moscow forever. As the play closes, Famusov's chief concern is for what people will say.

IN THE FALL OF THE YEAR 1924, Stanislavsky and Nemirovich-Danchenko decided to do a new production of Griboyedov's *Much Woe From Wisdom*, using the young actors in the leading parts and most of the old actors from the previous productions in the minor parts. We young actors from the Moscow Art Theatre were very happy to learn of this decision. In the middle of October, Sudakov and I were informed that the two of us had been chosen as Stanislavsky's assistants, and we were asked to become acquainted with the play in detail. A week later, we were summoned by Stanislavsky for a discussion of the play. Luzhsky was present as usual.

The discussion took place in the evening in Stanislavsky's study. Stanislavsky had two large black notebooks on the table in front of him—one of which he used for his first outlines of discussions and rehearsals of the production at hand and the other for the rough draft of his future books. (These were published in English as *An Actor Prepares* and *Building a Character*.)

Stanislavsky addressed us: "You two young directors were chosen because our purpose was not only to revive *Much Woe From Wisdom* but to pass on to you, the young directors and actors, the ideas that were the basis for our work on the play in 1906 when it was first produced in the Moscow Art Theatre. Since you knew that you were to participate in this production, I expect you have read the book written by Nemirovich-Danchenko on the production.

126

But I would like to add certain things to it. You did read the book?"

"Yes," we answered, "we read Nemirovich-Danchenko, and also other material on Griboyedov."

"Very good," Stanislavsky said. "You should know the history of his society, the ideology of the period, its mode of life, and its morality. These things are the foundation of every realistic work of art. Many mistakes in the old productions of *Much Woe From Wisdom* came from the wrong approach of directors and actors to this play written in verse. It was an accepted opinion in the Russian theatre that a play in verse is an especially 'theatrical' work of art, and even a fine actor, when entrusted with a role written in verse, allowed himself to be stilted and to declaim in an elevated style thoughts he did not completely understand. He would cover his lack of feeling and understanding by accentuating the effective rhythm and putting the stress at the end of each line. We will fight all these clichés.

"But now I want to tell you about the most significant aspect of Griboyedov's remarkable comedy.

Patriotism

"*Much Woe From Wisdom* is considered a comedy. A number of scenes in it completely justify that style. But in this great play there is much of the author's bitter grief for his country and his people, the grief which stamps Gogol's *Inspector-General* and *Dead Souls*, and many of the comedies by Ostrovsky, and satirical plays by Sukhov-Kobylin . . . The great Russian classic dramatists showed their deep love for their people and their country by bringing out the tears which are hidden in laughter—a characteristic expressive of many Russian works of art.

"In 1906 we left Moscow with a heavy feeling to tour

Europe, our social and political dreams unfulfilled. And that is why, when we returned to Moscow, Nemirovich-Danchenko suggested *Much Woe From Wisdom* as our first production. It was accepted unanimously, with tremendous enthusiasm. We felt that the immortal text of Griboyedov's comedy expressed our thoughts and emotions at the time.

"I consider patriotism—the author's deep love for his people and his country—the most important aspect of Griboyedov's comedy. And when we performed it, we saw the opportunity to express with him our own love for our people and our condemnation of all that which, because of censorship, could not be expressed in other plays. In *Much Woe From Wisdom* we could openly say:

> A new star will be born
> A star of great joy!
> Russia will throw off the evil dream.

"Chatsky's monologues are the *fortochka* [a pane in a window which can be opened in winter when the rest of the window is sealed] through which the fresh and invigorating air of Griboyedov's thought rushes into the auditorium to stimulate hope for Russia's better future. In reviving *Much Woe From Wisdom* now, we know that both the young and old actors of our theatre, who devotedly love their country, want to make her an example for all the world's people who strive for genuine freedom. Our actors can express all their feelings through this comedy.

"The Russian actor is and always has been a patriot, no matter how much, in a fit of temper, he condemns all the defects of everyday living—and we still have many (oh, how many!). This comedy reveals them in a very colorful, satirical, and sharp manner. The actors must fill themselves with hatred for these defects which are still present in our way of life and in our characters—our ugly thoughts, actions, and intentions. But this just criticism of oneself and one's way of life is inseparable from one's love for everything that is dear and close. One shouldn't act this play in one key or in a state of indifference or callousness. Such a cold, destructive style is ruinous for any artist. It is foreign and strange to the spirit and character of the Russian people. In the western countries artists have a special ability to be virtuoso in their professions. They can remain restrained and not give all of themselves. Russian writers, painters, actors, and musicians cannot work that way. They burn themselves up in their work. They torture themselves, like Chatsky, with 'a thousand torments.' Like Chatsky too, they attempt to move mountains, so often beyond their strength. But if they do reach their goal, the greatest work of Russian genius is born.

"The young artist must be educated on the work of these artists, because patriotism is the true, real, indestructible power, the clear and vivifying source for the artist's creativeness."

"But how about one's profession?" Luzhsky said. "You have always taught us, Konstantin Sergeyevich, to put our profession above everything else in our lives. You always told us to love our theatrical profession and our acting work more than anything else."

"But why must we love it?" Stanislavsky said. "Is it for the sake of the profession itself, or for the profit or glory it brings an artist? No, only for the sake of serving society, the people, and our country. You know this well, Luzhsky, and your question is not one which is asked by a founder of the Moscow Art Theatre but by a certain group of contemporary young people. Yes, I know that now professionalism is often substituted for the important goal of art.

That is why Nemirovich-Danchenko and I have chosen this patriotic play with its patriotic theme for our theatre at this particular time.

"Professionalism in art is necessary. But it should never take the place of the goal which art serves. Remember Gogol's words, 'The theatre is a pulpit from which it is one's duty to educate the audience.' "

Stanislavsky glanced for a minute at his notebook and, with a characteristic gesture, crossed out the line at the top of the page. He continued: "We decided, upon our return from Europe this time to come back to *Much Woe From Wisdom*—as we did in 1906—not only because it is a sharp political satire on our past and on the aristocracy—its way of life, customs, and morality; not only because Chatsky's monologues will make our audience evaluate the question of freedom more deeply; not only because of all this but also because the significance of *Much Woe From Wisdom* lies in its expression of the Russian people's spirit. They are always ready to admit their defects openly, yet with a sense of dignity. In *Much Woe From Wisdom* one does not find petty joking and scoffing at the people. This comedy presents the question of reforming society bravely and confidently. The author knows that his contemporary society will not remain forever as he describes it and this makes the play a progressive and inspiring comedy. No other country has such comedies. Sheridan in England, Molière in France, and Heine in Germany criticize the society and the morals of their times, but they lack that citizen-consciousness and the feeling of responsibility for the theme undertaken which distinguishes the Griboyedov satire.

"The comedy was written by a citizen of his country with temperament and responsibility. *Much Woe From Wisdom* educates the audience, and, I would add, the actors, directors, and theatres. It educates them in three directions: patriotic, national, and artistic.

"When I speak of an artistic influence in *Much Woe From Wisdom* on audience and actors I have in mind not only the actors who are performing this comedy but all actors of the theatre.

"Griboyedov's language, his singularly forceful words, impress themselves upon the listener's memory for a long, long time. During the rehearsals the entire company and all the workers in the theatre begin to use quotations from the play in their everyday life and conversation.

"Griboyedov's language is so alive, so vital, and so expressive that one involuntarily uses his words to express one's thoughts. His vocabulary is immensely rich and diverse. For one basic word like love, he brilliantly adds power, ardor, and passion in a few lines. Do you remember?

> But do you find in him such passionate ardor, flushes
> That all the great wide world can hold?
> Except for you is dust and ashes;
> That every heart beat takes its measure
> And comes more quick for love of you,
> That nothing he can think and nothing he can do
> But has one mainspring—you, your pleasure.

"We will speak again later about Griboyedov's language in detail. Now I want to come back to the question of the importance of this play for our theatre."

Realism of Theme and Characters

"We are turning to this comedy now because a large number of young actors from the second and third studios have come into the Moscow Art Theatre company," Stanislavsky continued. "They will learn 'on their own skin,' as Shchepkin used to say, what realism in the Russian classic is, through their work on this comedy in verse, written a hundred years ago and seemingly rhetorical and exhortative. First of all, the theme is realistic. The themes of all Russian classics beginning with Fonvizin are, in my estimation, thoroughly realistic.

"I see none of the theatrical contrivances so many of our contemporary directors claim to see in the plays of Ostrovsky, Surhov-Kobylin, or Griboyedov. All this special theatrical treatment of these plays occurred in the days of decadence and symbolism, with actors and directors who did not want to dig into the truth of life, which is the essence of the Russian classics; or, again, by fashionable, half-baked contemporary directors who, for the sake of the theatrically effective trick—for the sake of self-advertisement, as our saying goes—would sell their own father —never mind Ostrovsky, Gogol, or Griboyedov. Give me one theatrical contrivance in *Much Woe From Wisdom* which I could not justify by the organic laws of nature and the mode of life of the period and I will believe you. (Laughingly.) No, I am lying, I will never believe you! In *Much Woe From Wisdom* there is nothing but the honest and true expression of life."

"Isn't it a theatrical trick when the servant fails to inform Famusov of Chatsky's arrival in the first act?" Luzhsky asked.

"What makes you think that the servant did not tell Famusov of Chatsky's arrival?" Stanislavsky asked in turn.

"Famusov enters Sophie's room saying, 'Oh, here is another . . .' And every actor who plays Famusov always interprets this phrase as though Chatsky's presence in Sophie's room at this moment was a great surprise to Famusov."

"Well—do I give that impression when I play Famusov?"

Luzhsky laughed. "It seems to me you too, Konstantin Sergeyevich . . ."

"Then, for the sake of theatrical effect and in order to

make the audience laugh, I play incorrectly. I should not be surprised by Chatsky's presence in Sophie's room. I should be upset to find that she has not one admirer, not one lover but two! Famusov was certainly told of Chatsky's arrival, but he was shocked to find Sophie and Chatsky in such an intimate pose when he opened the door. And the last words of Chatsky's speech, which are interrupted by Famusov's entrance, prove that Chatsky is very close to Sophie, perhaps holding her hand:

Why so far away? And now, 'tis well you've served me!
The jingling bells ring out, harmonious
And rushing headlong over this waste of snow.
By day, by night to her I go.
And she receives me, how? So stern and ceremonious
A full half hour I suffer from your coldness,—
The face of Virgin sunk in prayer, . . .

"Notice the dots after Chatsky's speech. They indicate that he didn't finish his thought: 'And yet I love you to despair.'

"This is what he wants to say to Sophie. And Griboyedov even stresses it by a stage direction: *A moment of silence.*"

And, as he read the stage direction to us, Stanislavsky seemed to become Chatsky. With deep tenderness and concealed sadness he looked at the imaginary Sophie.

He continued: "Surely Chatsky takes Sophie's hand and tries to embrace her while he is speaking to her. And at this very moment Famusov enters. 'The same picture again,' he says to himself. 'First, one holds my daughter's hand and now here is another.' " And as Stanislavsky found the new justification for Famusov's famous line, he spoke it with such distress that we all burst out laughing.

Luzhsky said, pointing to the young directors: "The audience reaction was the same!"

Stanislavsky laughed as he answered: "Absolutely right! It only confirms my original statement that the realism of *Much Woe From Wisdom* is so authentic, true, and typical of the time that it always gets a correct satirical reaction from the audience. You have caught me, Luzhsky. I, too, interpreted Chatsky's presence in Sophie's room as unexpected for the sake of the comedy reaction. And when I made myself analyze this moment more deeply in front of you, you yourself confirmed the fact that the audience reaction did not change, but that only the meaning and the content changed. From simply a purely comical moment it developed into a humorous appreciation of Famusov, the father who can't keep an eye on his only daughter. This interpretation is much more in keeping with Griboyedov's text. Now I know that I am going to say quite differently:

> Oh what a heavy charge, Creator,
> To be a grown-up girl's papa!

"The realism of the theme lies not in the love-intrigue: Chatsky's love for Sophie or Sophie's love for Molchalin, who in turn prefers a light affair with Lisa. This is not a comedy about Sophie's three suitors Chatsky, Skalozub, and Molchalin. The love intrigue is only a solid canvas on which the skilful hand of a brilliant dramatist wove the design of the play—the 'thousand torments' of a progressive, freedom-loving, free-thinking man when he came up against the stagnation and the retrogression of our society in the twenties of the last century. This drama—I would even say tragedy—of Chatsky (and all those like him) is the realism of Russian life which that genius, Griboyedov, described so truly. I don't mean because of the play's canvas that the personal relationships between Chatsky and Sophie, Famusov and Chatsky, and Sophie and Lisa should be neglected. On the contrary, only after establishing the solid canvas of their way of life will you be able to distribute the more colorful, complicated, philosophical, and ideological design of Chatsky the citizen.

"To limit yourself in *Much Woe From Wisdom* to showing only the mode of life of old Russia without stressing the progressive fight of Chatsky's political ideas against the society that surrounds him would mean to skip the most valuable element of Griboyedov's comedy—its social-revolutionary significance in Russian classical drama. You see the realism of the comedy's theme even in Famusov's entrance at the end of the first act. It is truly justified not only by the intrigue and the situation in which the dramatist places his leading characters but also by their specific characteristics. I want you young directors to reread the play and mark all the places which seem to you unjustified by the realistic, specific, and concrete routine of living— or, as I call it, 'the flow of the day.' We will discuss all your doubts during the rehearsals. The more doubts the better; it will be most helpful for all the participants in the production.

"Our work on the realism of the play should grow in sturdiness and should convince the actors of their need to act concretely. I say death to all the theatrical contrivances which those people use who cannot see in the Russian classics the expression of the real life of the epoch with all its passions, conflicts, thoughts, emotions, and ideas!

"Now let us analyze the realism of the characters. From time to time one hears voices saying that *Much Woe From Wisdom* is an outdated play. I don't agree. There are no Famusovs today, but there is—and I am afraid will be for a long time—Famusov's sense of values, his conservatism, his opposition to the new, his servility, his worship of everything that used to be ('In the days of Catherine the Great . . .'), his snobbishness, his bureaucratic arrogance, his belief that the position makes the person and not the person the position. Is all this only in the past? And how about Molchalin? Oh, it will take a long time until those despicable, subservient secretaries will no longer be around!

"You might say that Sophie doesn't represent the contemporary young girl. I will gladly agree with you, but, first, let me ask the Chatskys of our time, do you always fall in love with the finest and deserving girl?"

The question was put to us in such a serious tone that we answered it seriously.

Sudakov said, "It seems to us we love those who deserve to be loved, Konstantin Sergeyevich."

Stanislavsky continued: "In that little word 'seems' lies the drama of Chatsky and of many of you. Of course one never includes present company." And he looked gaily at us and also at Luzhsky. And Stanislavsky laughed at our gay but polite protests. "Now here is the very party scene from the play. But let's return to Sophie," he said in a serious tone. "If it is only human for contemporary Chatskys to err in their personal infatuations, and if it only *seems* to all of you that the girl you choose is perfection itself, then it is only natural to suppose, according to logic, that also among contemporary beauties, especially at seventeen, there could be some Sophies. Dreaminess, sentimentality, and the deep conviction that 'the one I love is different,' are characteristic of youth. Sophie's lack of appreciation for Chatsky's fine qualities does not necessarily mean that she is not clever or intelligent. Her reaction to him is influenced to such a great extent by her environment, her upbringing, and, most of all, the changeability of a young girl who is between the ages of fifteen and seventeen.

"I am stirring up these thoughts intentionally to prevent you from taking the path of the satirical-grotesque that deliberately, without inner justification, exaggerates certain traits of the characters. I don't believe that by some external means like ugly make-up, a red wig, or a fantastic collar, Molchalin can be made more ridiculous than Griboyedov makes him, by giving him his revealing speeches in the famous dialogue between Chatsky and Molchalin at the beginning of the third act. Before you directors begin to work with your actors—especially with the young ones—you must understand how, and from what historical circumstances Griboyedov created characters like Sophie, Chatsky, Molchalin, and the rest. You must also know what traits of character constitute their individual personalities and define their behavior in the family and in society. And also you must know why we want to present them to the contemporary audience. If you keep remembering these three problems in connection with the 'red thread' of the play, you will never digress from the realistic interpretation of your characters and you will express the play's idea fully and brilliantly through the characters and their behavior.

"It is very important to remember these problems in working with your actors so that the characters in this great comedy will come alive on the stage and so that the actors will forget that they're called types—those tags used for living creatures. What nonsense it is to call Famusov 'the noble father,' or Sophie 'the heroine,' or Lisa 'the soubrette,' or Chatsky 'the *raisonneur*'! What is so noble in Famusov the father? In what scene does Sophie reveal any heroism? And to call such a wonderful type of Russian servant a soubrette! And how can one call him a *raisonneur*—Chatsky, with his understanding of the world, his love of his country, and his pure and fiery passion for Sophie? These tags were the roots of cliché, the means of turning a great comedy full of social significance into a theatrical and artificial vehicle."

And again Stanislavsky took his pencil and crossed out

another line in his notebook. It was obvious that he was following a very precise, carefully thought out plan in his discussion with us today.

Stage Atmosphere

"The realism of *Much Woe From Wisdom*," Stanislavsky continued, "must be felt in the interpretation of the play's idea, in its content, in the actors' creation of living characters, and of course in every detail of the stage production—the 'stage atmosphere.'

"How is stage atmosphere created? First of all, by just as thorough work on minor roles as on the important ones. Petroushka, with the holes in his elbows, Mr. H., Mr. D., servants and footmen of the Famusov household, guests at his party with or without lines who represent the mode of life, all of them serve as a background to the leading and secondary roles. All these people have enormous significance in the creation of a true and realistic stage atmosphere. Is it possible to separate the role of Chatsky from the role of the servant who tells Sophie of his arrival? Suppose that a bit player appears on the stage, carefully costumed but unhappy in such an insignificant part, and indifferently announces, 'It's Mr. Chatsky come to call, Miss,' and, after showing Chatsky in, just as indifferently leaves the stage. Would such behavior help the stage atmosphere at the moment of Chatsky's arrival? Of course not. Such an appearance on the part of the servant would break the atmosphere created by Lisa, Sophie, Famusov, and Molchalin in the previous scene. Here, I'll give you another version of the same entrance: the young servant rushes into Sophie's room, upsetting the usual dignity of Famusov's household. He is out of breath from running upstairs and so he has to stop before blurting out enthusiastically, 'It's Mr. Chatsky come to call, Miss!' He speaks enthusiastically because, three years earlier when Chatsky left for Europe, this servant had been only a boy in Famusov's service who used to watch and admire Chatsky and Sophie in their adolescent games. His admiration for Chatsky was just as strong as Lisa's.

"And now Chatsky is back. While Chatsky is taking off his coat downstairs, the boy thinks, 'I'll run quickly to Sophie so I can be the first to break the news to her.' The rhythm of Chatsky's arrival can be brilliantly prepared by the rhythm of the servant's appearance: he lingers at the door of Sophie's room as long as he dares so he can see this first meeting between Sophie and Chatsky, but finally he leaves, throwing an admiring look at Chatsky.

"Lisa's relation to Chatsky has the same character as that of the other servants. Nor does the biography of the first servant necessarily have to be invented. During his three years in this household, he has graduated from a boy-servant to a young valet, as Lisa had graduated from general errand girl to Sophie's confidante. In this case the servant's appearance will not only be in harmony with the daily routine of the household but will contribute to the creation of the stage atmosphere. Petroushka, footmen, servants, all are very important figures, introducing the character of Famusov's household to the audience: as the proverb has it, 'Like master, like servant.' But in Famusov's household Sophie is the mistress and because of this Lisa's speeches are full of independence and freedom. The servants could actually be divided into two camps: those who are on Famusov's side and those on Sophie's.

"Look for what is typical of Khlestova in her servants, and for what is typical of Tugoukhovsky in his servants. Now what kind of officers would Skalozub have? There is important work for the directors with the whole group of guests in the third and fourth acts. One can bring in the guests again and again and thus create stage atmosphere.

It is such a large part of the directors' work in this play that we will devote a separate discussion to it. Of course the sets will have a tremendous part in creating the stage atmosphere. We are going to use the same sets that we used in 1906 and also in 1914. At that time we thoroughly studied the architecture of the 1820's and 1840's. Griboyedov places his first, second, and third acts in the drawing-room. We felt it would be better to play the second act in the salon. From the drawing-room set a small ballroom can be seen through the upstage doors. This gives the audience a complete illusion of the authenticity and reality of everything it sees. It also gives the actors a good stage atmosphere, and helps them to fill the life of the characters and to carry out their physical actions. Of course it will be more difficult for you new young actors who are taking over important parts in this version of the play to feel at home in these sets created before your time.

"Directors don't always bring their actors into direct contact with the designers but they usually have some awareness of the preparation of the production. Some directors even consult their actors as to the sets or at least some details of the sets. Our designers attend rehearsals, so those actors who are interested can talk to them, visit the studios where the sets are built, and learn the various designs. Sometimes an actor will ask, 'Is this the *fortochka* for our set?' And then when he says in rehearsal, 'I will slip the shutter and let out the heat,' he really knows what it looks like. In this way actors in the process of forming a new production take part in creating the stage scene.

"In your case you are given everything ready made—furniture, props, and costumes. And it is the director's responsibility to find the way to help their actors in that difficult process of making themselves at home in surroundings they did not help to create. I would even advise you to fool your actors. Tell them that you are planning new sets, new costumes, new furniture, and new props. That will arouse their creative imagination, and then you can imperceptibly sneak in all that has been done before. The nature of the actor's creative process makes him as trustful as a baby who believes that Robinson Crusoe's cave is under the table and dangerous Indians lurk behind the door. His childish belief in the events of the play are an integral part of his creative talent. By 'fooling' an actor you must arouse his creative vision. I'm talking about delicate, artistic fooling. I hope you young directors understand what I'm trying to say.

"Spend some time with your new actors in imagining what Sophie's room looks like and what kind of a house Famusov lived in. Even take them for a walk through the Arbat and point out the house in which you think Famusov might have lived. And then in a day or two, during the following rehearsals, tell them, 'The stage crew has placed some of the old set on the stage. They are going to remake some of it for the new production. What a pity! There is such charm and beauty in this set designed by Dobujinsky and Simov. Would you like to take a look at it? There is no one in the auditorium now. Let's go and sit there for a few minutes.' "

Luzhsky interrupted: "Oh, what a sly one you are, Stanislavsky! I see what you are driving at. In the auditorium you will let loose your magic *if*."

"That's right," Stanislavsky replied. "Sitting in the auditorium in front of the old sets, the director must say to his actors, 'If you happened to live in this room, how would you behave in it?' And the actors begin to imagine, 'Well, I would sit in that armchair when I say this or that. In such a moment I would move to that corner. I would look out the window at that point in the scene and so forth.' "

Luzhsky said: "And the next day at the rehearsal the actors would say to the director, 'Perhaps we should keep the old sets; they seem so comfortable. Why bother building new?' "

Stanislavsky continued: "Because the older actors, and we the directors and designers of the first production of *Much Woe From Wisdom* as far back as 1906, have used these sets for so many performances, they feel lived in; they seem like Famusov's home. You (and he addressed Sudakov and me) must enter the Famusov house on the stage without being prejudiced against the old production, without searching for the new for the sake of the new. And you must stimulate your imagination and that of the actors in relation to the old. I grant you it is a difficult but certainly not impossible problem. You must learn how to handle this kind of problem, because in your future work in our theatre you will often have to bring new actors into the old productions."

Sudakov said: "But we don't have to necessarily use the old mise en scène because the sets are old? One could find various mise en scènes in the same room to express the essence of a certain scene."

"Undoubtedly," Stanislavsky replied, "although I am inclined to think that in the final analysis, as you follow the inner action of the scene (of course with some minor changes), you will come to use the most truly expressed of the old. But, in any case, I want you to know that I will not restrain your creative search as long as it is guided by the desire to express the inner, the ideological, and logical nature of the event rather than the desire to enhance the moment on the stage for the sake of effect. In any case, be sure to let me know when the old-new sets are placed on the stage for the first time. Don't call your actors for rehearsal on that day. We directors will have our rehearsal with the sets."

"But of course the actors will be somewhere not far away that day—by chance," Luzhsky broke in.

Stanislavsky laughed. "Now you are the sly one, Luzhsky!"

Stanislavsky and Luzhsky laughed, and we understood that both of them knew something about the tradition of rehearsals in the Moscow Art Theatre that we young directors as newcomers did not know and did not even suspect but would learn the first day the set was placed on stage. Again, Stanislavsky crossed out a line in his black notebook, closed it, and addressed us:

"I should have talked to you in the same detailed fashion on the significance of lights, props, and sound effects in group scenes (don't forget that we'll devote a special day to the mass scenes), because all these elements are important for the creation of stage atmosphere, but it is getting late and we will discuss these things another time."

Stanislavsky looked at his watch, and, after a short pause, he continued, in an obvious attempt to sum up this first session on *Much Woe From Wisdom.*

"We often have been and are still accused of falling into a naturalistic expression of detail in our pursuit of the realism of life and truth in our stage actions. Wherever we have done this we were wrong. It is definitely bad and inartistic; it misrepresents our desired attempt to create a realistic performance. Realism in art is the method which helps to select only the typical from life. If at times we are naturalistic in our stage work, it only shows that we don't yet know enough to be able to penetrate into the historical and social essence of events and characters. We do not know how to separate the main from the secondary, and thus we bury the idea with details of the mode of life. That is my understanding of naturalism. But to discover the typical in life and to know how to express it on the stage is not easy. We don't have an exact recipe for this process yet. And that's why we often have to rely on the personal intuition of the artist and his experience.

"I am attempting to introduce a method for the self-education and development of the actor, but a definite system should also be found to determine a sense of values and a concept of life for every artist who is searching creatively for the truth and wants to be useful to society through his work. It seems to me that in the theatre we can achieve this only by following the realistic tradition of our great writers, painters, artists, and actors. That is why I find it so important for us, actors of different ages and directors, and for our new audience, to have this great realistic creation of Griboyedov in the theatre's repertory.

"Now begin to work on the play. Find the flow of the day in Famusov's house and the characteristics of the characters. Work out with Luzhsky's help the plan for the group scene in the third act. Penetrate deeply into the particular meaning of Griboyedov's language. Thoroughly examine his artistic conception. When in doubt, no matter how small the question, don't hesitate to come to me or Luzhsky for an answer. The best of luck to all of you."

The Group Scene

The next rehearsals of *Much Woe From Wisdom* did not exactly follow Stanislavsky's plan. We chose two casts of principals for Chatsky, Sophie, Molchalin, and Lisa among the new actors. Sudakov was to work with the first group and I with the second. Also, Livanov was entrusted with the part of Chatsky as a third lead, but Stanislavsky was to work with him. Stanislavsky sent a message to Sudakov and me through Luzhsky to begin our work with the actors immediately on the text, on the biographies of the characters, and on Griboyedov's verse. Luzhsky also told me that I was entrusted with the direction of the ball scene in the third act and the scene of the guests' departure in the fourth. Luzhsky suggested that I work out a scheme for the arrival and departure of the guests in the third and fourth acts, using Griboyedov's text and the old director's book from the 1906 production. During the next few days I worked out the following scheme: the successive entrances of the guests, their exits to the ballroom, their return to gossip, and their participation in the action of the third and fourth acts. Together with Luzhsky, we tested it carefully, made some necessary changes, and then selected mainly the youngest members of the company for the group scenes. And still, I was very surprised when a few days later I saw the following on the rehearsal schedule, "Tomorrow rehearsal of third act of *Much Woe From Wisdom* on stage with Gorchakov as director." Veteran actors of the theatre were called for that rehearsal, along with the large group of young actors. I was practically certain that the rehearsal would be conducted by Stanislavsky and that my name on the list was just a formality. I also understood that the purpose of this particular rehearsal was to break in the youngsters taking the small parts of the guests, but just the same I worried. Why didn't that notice say "Rehearsal with Stanislavsky?" Stanislavsky's name was among the actors to be called. Did this mean that I would sit alone at the director's table? How could I direct the leading players of the Moscow Art Theatre, who not only have been playing in *Much Woe From Wisdom* for years but who are also the best and the oldest actors in the theatre?

Merely the thought of it made me break into a perspiration of fear. Panic-stricken, I called Luzhsky. But, to my astonishment, Luzhsky was vague and noncommital. "Well, Nicolachki, what is there to do? You just have to begin to direct to the best of your ability. The order is from Stanislavsky. Don't worry, it will come out all right. I'll see you tomorrow after the rehearsal."

After! The most important thing was to know how to

begin the rehearsal. Afterward, I thought to myself, will be too late. Either I will be ruined in the first few minutes or I will manage somehow. And why did Luzhsky emphasize the order from Stanislavsky? What was he trying to say by that? Should I call Stanislavsky? Should I ask him directly what he expected from me and how he wanted me to conduct the rehearsal? But on the other hand, wouldn't that belittle my authority? What would Stanislavsky think of me if I confessed how petrified I was of tomorrow's rehearsal? And, again, this is not an original production entrusted to me but a revival. I have the right to know how the leading figures of the Moscow Art Theatre are accustomed to working. Besides, I came to the Moscow Art Theatre to learn, not to assert my prestige. At eight o'clock that evening I called up Stanislavsky.

"Konstantin Sergeyevich, this is Gorchakov who's disturbing you, but I just have to talk to you about tomorrow's rehearsal."

"Well, naturally, I have been waiting for your call for over an hour."

"You have been waiting for me?"

"Of course I have. I decided that if you are a serious, conscientious worker in the theatre, you certainly will want to talk to me before your rehearsal tomorrow. But if you are more concerned with your prestige as a director than with the essential work, then I will let you alone tomorrow. Come over immediately. You have already lost an hour. On your way here, gather all the questions that are seething in your head."

In twenty minutes I was in Stanislavsky's study.

"Where do I begin the rehearsal, Konstantin Sergeyevich? Must I give an introductory speech?"

"What do *you* think?"

"I would prefer not to give a speech. What do I have to say to the masters of the Moscow Art Theatre about *Much*

Woe From Wisdom that they don't already know? And, as far as the youngsters are concerned, I have had a number of discussions with them."

"All right, no speeches. Gather the whole cast on the stage. Skip the first part of the third act. There is no sense in doing this part when you have called forty actors for a definite time. Do you have the order of the guests' entrances in your director's book?"

"Yes."

"Show it to me. And explain the entrance of each actor and where and why."

The following fifty minutes were spent with Stanislavsky examining in detail the order of entrances I had worked out. These were the questions he asked me: "Why does that particular group arrive first?"

I answered, "These are the old people. Most of them are poor relatives. They have started from home very early because they have no carriages."

"Do the actors playing these parts know this justification?" he asked.

"Yes, they do, Konstantin Sergeyevich."

"Fine. That is right from an artistic point of view and it is also true to life. Do they come alone? Isn't there some poor young relative, perhaps a niece or nephew, who accompanies them?"

"I didn't think of that."

"Add some young girl to the group. She will hire a cab for them, see that they are neatly dressed, and see that the footmen take their coats properly. The old could not cope with all these things alone."

"All right, I will add Vronska to the group."

"Fine. Now, do your old relatives know their behavior all through the act? At what exact moment do they come in? Whom do they greet first? Whom do they know among the guests? Whom don't they dare to greet? Where are they during the dance? What part do they take in the gossip scene and how are they grouped?"

"I have prepared a list of their movements on stage from place to place," I told him, "and I'll give them this list tomorrow before the rehearsal. I was planning to set the final movement of each group during the rehearsal tomorrow on stage."

"Fine. Although the director should have a definite plan of movement for each group, he corrects his groupings for the most expressive forms."

I gave Stanislavsky my lists, in which I had set their entrances and movements and exits according to their relation to the other characters, events, and main beats of the act.

"Fine. Tomorrow we will see how it works out on the stage. Do all your guests know their biographies?"

"I talked to each one about his life and character in detail."

"Here," Stanislavsky said, "take this list. It's a questionnaire I prepared for your guests. See that they know all the answers to it before they come to the ball."

And Stanislavsky gave me a sheet of paper with the following questions on it:

"Who are you? Name, members of your family, their position in society. In what section of Moscow do they live? What street? What does their house look like? How many rooms do they have? What is the plan of the rooms? How are they furnished?

"What was the 'flow' of your day like today? What were the good and bad incidents of the day? What work did you do? Whom did you see?

"What is your relationship to Famusov? Are you his friend or his relative? How did you know of the ball? Are you acquainted with Chatsky? Khlestova? Gorichev?

"What is your outlook on the world? (Naturally, from

the point of view of Griboyedov's epoch.) What do you think of Chatsky's ideas? Of Famusov's ideas?

"What and to whom would you tell your impression of this ball?"

I promised Stanislavsky to go over their biographies and the flow of their day with the actors once more according to this questionnaire.

"It is possible that this detailed questionnaire may seem unnecessary and primitive to some of your young actors," he continued. "Griboyedov did not give a description of any of his guests. You must explain the necessity of this work to those who are doubtful. This is the only path to organic life on the stage. I have frequently been reproached for adopting the technique of the Meiningen Theatre in the handling of group scenes. This is not true. The Meiningen Theatre was strong in external organization of mass scenes, strong and formal. They used to order their writers to write small parts with at least two pages of text—for example, for every soldier in *Wallenstein's Camp*—and they ordered the actors to memorize it and repeat it mechanically during the mob scenes. In this way they created a false similarity to life. By loud and soft intonations and by a definite rhythm to the movement of the crowd, they solved the general stage problem only in its external aspects.

"My purpose is completely different. I want each actor, no matter how small his part, to create his life on the stage on the basis of a complete knowledge of the life of the period and his own personal observation of his contemporary life. I appeal to his conscious independent creativity. While observing the young actor in the group scene we can learn about his talent, his relation to theatre art, his ability to understand the play, his imagination, and his skill in combining all the elements of the method into the organic life and action of the stage. Please explain this to all the guests. I will watch the scene myself. It is very important to me that this scene be staged well and also that in the process of work the youngsters should understand their work and the significance of the crowd scenes in our performance. The ensemble is the first consideration of our theatre.

"It is important for me to develop in them artistic taste and a sense of the period. Now Gorchakov, what are the specific characteristics of the period that you as director find in the text?"

The Concrete Expression of the Epoch

"*Much Woe From Wisdom* was written by Griboyedov, Konstantin Sergeyevich, as he says in his letter to Katenin, to show the progressive man of the Russian people, Chatsky, in contrast to his society. *Much Woe From Wisdom* is a satirical comedy castigating . . ."

"Excuse me for interrupting you," Stanislavsky stopped me, "I have no doubt that you are capable of making an excellent literary and historical analysis of *Much Woe From Wisdom*. I don't think you understood my question. I am asking you what the distinctive characteristics of the epoch are that you as a director selected from the text and events of the play?"

"From the text and events of the play?" I struggled to remember the first pages of the play:

> 'Tis all Kuznetsky Bridge and those infernal Frenchmen
> Who send their authors, bards and fashions to their henchmen.
> They wreck our brains, they wreck our purses.

I read the first lines to Stanislavsky.

"Pardon me," Stanislavsky answered in astonishment,

"if I'm not mistaken those lines are from the fourth scene of the first act. How about the first scene? Isn't there anything there that's different from contemporary life?"

"No, it doesn't seem so to me." And I went through the first three scenes in my mind again.

"Well then, you are only acquainted with the epoch theoretically—only as a critic but not as a stage director. Let's read the play together."

I began the first line of the first scene:

It's dawning. Ah! How fast the hours go skipping!

Stanislavsky stopped me immediately. "Does the play begin with those words?"

I suddenly recollected, "There is an author's direction which I skipped."

"The play does not begin with the author's direction. Take the text."

I looked at the first page of the play. "The cast of characters?" I asked.

"That's right. Read the cast of characters out loud. Don't you see here some indication of the period?"

"Pavel Afanaseyevich Famusov, Manager in the Fiscal Office," I read and then stopped.

"What does manager in the Fiscal Office mean?" Stanislavsky asked me.

"He manages the affairs of some government office."

"Which one exactly?"

"I don't know, Konstantin Sergeyevich. I haven't thought about it."

"And why on this particular day didn't Famusov go to the office? According to the text, Famusov spent the whole day at home. Why?"

"To tell you the truth, Konstantin Sergeyevich, I haven't thought about this either."

"You were approaching the period from the wrong end,

from the conventional standpoint. Of course you should also know that. But, after having learned the general concept of the period, you must apply that knowledge directly to the text of the play. For our next meeting prepare the names of all government offices in Moscow that Famusov could have worked in and find out why that particular day he did not go to his office. Before your rehearsal with your four leading players you must be able to answer every question concerning the period in connection with the text of the play. Now let's continue reading the list of characters."

"Sophia Pavlovna, Famusov's daughter; Lisanka, servant," I continued.

Konstantin Sergeyevich stopped me again. "Now wait. Didn't you notice that Griboyedov calls the servant Lisanka in his cast of characters and then all through the play calls her Lisa, with the exception of the first scene of the first act? How do you explain that?"

"I don't know," I answered, "it didn't even attract my attention."

"Now think. Use your imagination. This also belongs to your work on the period in relation to the text."

"Alexei Stepanovich Molchalin," I continued, "secretary to Famusov, living in his house. Alexander Andreyevich Chatsky; Colonel Skalozub; Sergey Sergeyevich; Natalia Dmitrievna, a young married lady; Platon Mikhailovich, her husband; Gorichev"—I was reading quite slowly, pondering over those names and expecting to be stopped by Stanislavsky—"Prince Tugoukhovsky and the Princess his wife, and their six daughters; the Countess-grandmother; the Countess's granddaughter Hryumine; Anton Antonovich Zagoretsky; Khlestova, an old lady; Svoyachnitza . . ."

"What does the word *svoyachnitza* mean, do you know?" Stanislavsky interrupted me again.

"Yes, it means sister-in-law."

"Do we use that word for sister-in-law now?"

"Very seldom."

"Then this word is also typical of the period. Read further."

"Mr. H.; Mr. D.; Repetilov; Petroushka; and a few other servants who have speaking lines; a great number of guests of varied status; their footmen in the departure scene; Famusov's waiters. The action takes place in Moscow in Famusov's home."

"I noticed that about the middle of the list you began to read more slowly, much more slowly, obviously pondering over the names," Stanislavsky remarked. "How do you explain that?"

"I became aware of the fact that Griboyedov named his characters after their predominant characteristic. I read about this when I was becoming acquainted with material on the play but I didn't attribute any special significance to it. Now I see that the description of the status, kinship, or profession of the characters is listed in quite an unusual manner. To some of them he gives only their first name, their father's name, and the family name. In front of other names he puts the mark of their distinction first, like Colonel Skalozub, Countess-grandmother; Repetilov is given neither his first name nor his father's name, just Repetilov. Mr. H. and Mr. D. are known only by initials. Also, I began to see such descriptions as 'guests of varied status.' All these new observations made me read more slowly."

"I am sure that as you were pondering over the names of the characters a vision of the period flashed across your mind. This is an approximate process which the director must go through when seeking the elements of the period in the text. Skalozub's predominant characteristic springs from his being a Colonel. When Skalozub is drunk he may forget his own name and his father's but he will never forget that he is a Colonel. The important thing about Repetilov is that, no matter what his or his father's name, he constantly rattles, like a set alarm clock. By the way, the French word *répéter* means not only to repeat but also to wind. Mr. H. and Mr. D. are just general designations of people, but not any definite persons who have either a name or an important position in life. You see how much you skipped before when you began examining the period from the fourth scene of the first act? Now which events in the first three scenes do you consider typical of the period?"

Pondering over the cast of characters led me in the right direction. "The first event: Lisa, asleep in the armchair, is supposed to be keeping watch for Sophie and Molchalin; the second scene, the rendezvous between Sophie and Molchalin, one playing the piano, the other the flute; third, Famusov as head of the house is making his morning rounds and flirting with his servant Lisa. It seems to me that these events would be out of place now."

"Correct," Stanislavsky encouraged me. "Now you are on the right road. Tell me, what words in the first three scenes are typical of the epoch?"

I began to read the text of the first three scenes again to myself, but said aloud those words and phrases which, in my opinion, were characteristic of the period when Griboyedov wrote.

"Excellent," Stanislavsky interrupted me. "Enough! I'm not interested in a list of words which we do or do not use now. All I'm interested in is to make you aware of the characteristics of the language of the period. In any case, you are convinced now that, in those three scenes that you skipped over before, there are many words, expressions, nuances of thought, events, and characteristics of the text itself which give us a clear picture of the period and trans-

fer our attention from a general concept to the particular
example which is necessary for us—the concrete, distinctive expression of the period in this drama. So never limit
yourself to general knowledge. Certainly it is necessary,
but for the actor and director its concrete manifestations
are all important—its reflection in the minute changes of
the text, in the detail of events, in the nuances of the
author's thought, and sometimes even in punctuation.
Griboyedov has most interesting punctuation, which often
helps to understand his thought in relation to his characters. But we will talk about this when we work with your
four leading players. Now tell me in a few words something about these four young principals."

I was about to say that Sophie is a product of the time,
when I remembered my poor description of the epoch. My
mouth opened involuntarily but in a few seconds I deliberately closed it. It must have looked funny because Stanislavsky laughingly broke the pause.

"I guess you don't want to give me a general description
of Sophie as you attempted to do of the epoch. I'll help
you. Here is what I need to hear from you concerning
Sophie. Stepanova will rehearse this part with you. You
know her well from your work with her at the Vakhtangov
Studio. You know Zavadsky, Bendina, and Koslovsky
equally well. So whatever I shall tell you about your directing task in relation to Sophie will apply as well to Chatsky,
Molchalin, and Lisa. As a competent stage director you
have certainly read and know all that has been written
about Sophie's character. If you are not lazy you possibly
selected those phrases from the text that pertain to Sophie
and to those actions of hers which reveal her character.
You probably analyzed her relation to her father, to Molchalin, to Lisa, to Chatsky, and to her other acquaintances.
This is necessary preliminary work for every director.

"Now you were assigned to work on the part of Sophie

with Stepanova. By the way, do you have any objection to the actors we selected for you?"

"No, I agree wholeheartedly."

"Now tell me," he continued, "if you had to work with both casts, would you treat them in the same way?"

I wasn't quite sure that I understood Stanislavsky's question. Frankly, I would work with both in the same way. But I remained silent, because from his inflection I felt that some other answer was expected from me.

"Silence doesn't always mean consent," Stanislavsky broke the pause. "Your silence obviously does not express consent but doubt."

"You are right. I know that you don't expect a conventional analysis of Sophie, but I cannot think of any other and I don't know where to begin."

"Begin with the living person who is given to you to reflect Sophie. Begin with Stepanova. Tell me what you think is right in her as a person and an actress for Sophie and what you think she lacks."

That question made everything clear to me. In a few minutes I told him all my observations of the creative individualities of the four actors in relation to the roles they would rehearse.

"Compare each role with the qualities of the actor who will portray it. Your demands on an actor must be guided exclusively by the material in the role. Develop the inner qualities of the actor necessary for the character and fight all his personal characteristics that are contrary to it.

"Stepanova, you were telling me, is taciturn and reticent. To a certain extent this is correct for Sophie, who has been brought up without a mother and with no other companions but Lisa. But Stepanova is restrained in her feelings and somewhat too intellectual. This is bad for Sophie. Sophie is sensitive, sentimental, capricious, and wilful. Let Stepanova find out for herself what she needs to do to stimulate sentimentality in herself. I suppose caprice and wilfulness are easy to arouse in any woman. An actor must have at his command all the inner qualities which you are trying to develop in him for this or any role. The moment he needs to cry, he must cry. If he needs to remain cold or indifferent or severe, he must do so. There lies in the nature of every gifted actor the seed of every human feeling and sensation. One only needs to find the right bait to arouse him. He must have the willpower to control these feelings, to stop their action when it is necessary, or to change them. An actor must control his technique as the pianist-virtuoso does his instrument.

"Feelings and sensations are the keyboard of his piano. An actor must know the tone and overtone of every human feeling. He must know how to increase or diminish the pedal (the moderator) at will. He has the full score of the composition (the play) in front of him. Before the pianist touches the keys of the piano he hears the notes with his inner ear. The images which the composer had in creating the symphony rush through his mind. Thus an actor, before pronouncing the first words of his text, always hears the character speak, sees in his imagination some of the scenes, and begins to get the feeling of the play. Then the process of transforming the text takes place —transforming it into actions and into the characters, their thoughts, words, and behavior, and into the conflicts, passions, and ideas given by the author. But the instrument of the pianist, the piano, must always be in perfect condition. Observe with what love and attention musicians take care of their instruments. Have you ever observed how the great violinist uses his chamois, how particular he is in ordering the right case for his precious violin, how touchingly he handles it? Could you ever conceive of an artist-musician using an instrument that is out of tune?

"The nature of the artist in the theatre, with all his inner and outer qualities, is as precious an instrument as the violin of Stradivarius. I always ask myself why we treat ourselves so neglectfully. Why do we play so often on the stage on a broken, out-of-tune clavichord? Do I make myself clear?"

"Very clear, Konstantin Sergeyevich."

"When you work with your young actors, see that they study the human psyche as the finest instrument of the dramatic art in which they work. See that they study the laws of physical life, the physical actions which involuntarily affect the human psyche and arouse sensations and emotions. First of all, see that your young actors are in complete command of the senses of hearing, seeing, and touching. An actor, especially a Moscow Art Theatre actor, knows that he must see and hear on the stage, but that there is still a gap between his knowing it and doing it. In life it is different. If a person has to open a door or close a window or read a book or listen to what is going on in the next room, he just does it. On the stage he does the most familiar everyday action approximately as he does it in life, indicating the action but not performing it fully. But he must perform it not only precisely as he does it in life but in a more heightened, colorful, and emphatic fashion. He performs the actions of seeing and hearing on stage under special conditions with the emotional response of an audience of a thousand people—some directly in front of him, some to the right, some to the left, and some high above him.

"All the actor's actions and behavior form one unbroken chain of the role's action. I suggest," Stanislavsky continued, "that the actor learn his character's behavior not only from the moment of his appearance on the stage, but, at the very least, from the morning of the day in which his actions in the scene and in the act take place. This will help him to understand and assimilate the character so much better. I also suggest that the actor examine the flow of the day thoroughly and in detail before he appears on the stage."

"Konstantin Sergeyevich," I said, "in *Much Woe From Wisdom* all the roles begin their action in the morning."

"Not all; far from it. Perhaps only Famusov's," Stanislavsky replied, thinking a minute. "Sophie's day began, if one can put it that way, yesterday. From the moment she sent Lisa to Molchalin with an invitation to a night rendezvous, her night became her day. And that 'day' must have exhausted her: playing music all night with Molchalin, then Chatsky's arrival, then a visit from Skalozub, then preparing for the ball. She has not slept for two days. This is a very important circumstance for the actress' physical state of being. Lisa also has been watching all night and can scarcely say when yesterday ended and today began. The same applies to Molchalin. And Chatsky surely did not sleep during the night, as he came toward Moscow anticipating his meeting with Sophie after so many years. What do you think Skalozub has been doing that morning before he visited Famusov? And how about the rest of the characters?

"Now begin your work with the young actors by a thorough examination of the flow of their day! A day so tied up with yesterday (as happens so often in life) that one is not sure when yesterday ended and today began!

"Now let me talk about the actual rehearsal tomorrow on stage. As you see, it has begun today for you as director."

Stanislavsky laughed at this accidental demonstration of what he meant by the flow of the day.

The Director-Organizer

"Let us now sum up our discussion of tomorrow's rehearsal. So—you'll give no speeches. I, as the supervisor of the production, will say a few words to the company before you begin the rehearsal.

"First of all, the director must create the correct conditions for the actor not only on stage but in the wings. In the first years of the Moscow Art Theatre, Nemirovich-Danchenko and I used to work out the planning and placing of the sets in such a way that there was a vacant space between the flats of the sets not in use and those of the current scenes. When an actor comes on stage and sees the reverse side of the sets, the vacant space between them, he gets a feeling of lightness and an actual physical illusion of entering the house and rooms of Chekhov, Ostrovsky, Griboyedov, etc. He has a chance to prepare himself for that entrance. He collects his thoughts and feelings for his role.

"For this purpose the director must arrange the whole area of the stage in such a way that it corresponds to the atmosphere of the play. The stage must be immaculately clean. The sets for the current production must be neatly arranged. The sets for other productions should be suspended from the flies. The prompter and all the stage crew must be neatly dressed in working clothes. Fresh air should circulate throughout the stage area at each intermission. The assistant stage manager must be confident, relaxed, like our Alexandrov, an artist wholly enthusiastic about his work. Now all this together creates a festive and exultant atmosphere for the actor's entrance. This atmosphere tells the actor so much better than any words that he is the most important person on the stage and that he is expected to have a most serious and profound relation to what he is about to do on stage in the following minutes. Everyone working in the theatre considers his appearance before the audience to be the most important thing. In the theatre everything and everybody exists to give the right conditions for the actor's creative state of being.

"Use the beginning of tomorrow's rehearsal to insist upon these conditions and then to check them. The sets should be on stage promptly at the time designated for rehearsal. Props must be ready and so must those personal additions to the characters' costumes, such as canes, lorgnettes, glasses, and handkerchiefs—things that an actor might want to use during this rehearsal. I would like to stress the importance of using the shoes of the period at rehearsal. Shoes define the walk of a character and the plasticity of his movements and these, in turn, define in many instances the rhythm of the character. Lorgnettes, canes, glasses, reticules, boutonnières, and dance programs will keep the actors' hands occupied and at the same time keep their attention on period details. These objects are very important to the actor's physical behavior on stage, for many large and small gestures of his role. Also these objects can even influence his inner action.

"Let me repeat, everything must be prepared for each actor, beginning with Chatsky and going through the last servant of Famusov's household. If you will take care of this, or see that your assistant has taken care of it, you will make a great impression on actors and stage crew. 'Aha!' they will say to themselves, 'this looks like a very well-organized rehearsal. See what pains the director takes with minute details.'

"Then you show your concern for the actors. The third act is the group scene. Many actors are involved in it: the leading characters, guests, and servants. Prepare places in the wings where all of them can wait so that each is near his proper entrance. To have to stand and wait is tiresome, even for the youngest actor. Their attention begins to wander and, before you know it, they are talking and joking, which is most undesirable. Place a number of comfortable armchairs for the older people who have played many years in the theatre, and chairs and benches for the rest of the actors. You don't have to tell each actor which belongs to him. In a well-brought-up family of actors bureaucratic servility has no place. The feeling of comradeship and mutual respect prompts the members of the theatre collective to decide to whom the first place belongs —according to his talent and his ethical qualities as a human being and as a citizen. In our day we place the ethics of comradeship particularly high and I want very much to develop these qualities in our youngsters. Prepare the stage for rehearsal with great care. Remember that the director-organizer must be extremely attentive to his guests and to the audience, and that he must be just as concerned about those who carry on their shoulders all the artistic and ideological responsibility of the performance. I am talking once more of the actors.

"The next rule for rehearsals concerns the economy of working time for actors, stage crew, and technical staff. Actors work twice as well when they are aware that their time is being used productively. When an actor sees that the director spends the previous rehearsal time in showing off or philosophizing too much, thus abusing his power as a director (the director is master of the rehearsal and an actor will submit to his orders), the slightest mistake on the part of this type of director will shake the actor's respect very quickly. That is why we know of so many instances in which actors much prefer to work with so-called 'working directors' than with the exceptionally talented, brilliant artist-director who does not know how to organize either his work or that of his actors. The 'organizer' in the director is one of his most valuable qualities. Now how should you organize the time and work of your actors during tomorrow's rehearsal?

"First, distribute among the actors playing the guests the various beats of the text at which they enter. Don't be stingy with them. Better to give them more of the text so that they have plenty of time before their entrance. Nothing hurts the creative impulse of a young beginner as much as being given only a few words for his entrance cue. Besides, tell your youngsters to answer that questionnaire I gave you. Tell them that I will see the answers myself and will choose the best three or four biographies for my book *The Work of an Actor on His Role*. Also, please tell them that in the very near future they will be given lessons in dancing, plastic movement, and the special motions of the period.

"Choose a day in which you will take the youngsters to the Tretiakov Gallery and also to the Museum of Forty Years and the Bachrouchin Museum. All this will prepare them better for their parts.

"Give the list of entrances to Alexandrov and his assistant. Also, talk over with him how you will stop the rehearsals; whether by ringing the bell or by sending on stage someone specially assigned for this purpose. Mark down exactly which scenes you will run through before the first break, which before the second, and so forth. Are you planning to finish the first act today or will you need tomorrow also? Fix the program of tomorrow's rehearsal for yourself and inform your actors if you find it necessary. When you see that a certain part of a scene must be repeated a number of times, do so. Don't inconvenience yourself in any respect. But also don't abuse this right. Don't under any circumstances let anyone leave during the rehearsal. Don't allow any smoking. Use my name in announcing this before the rehearsal. Decide beforehand when and how long your break will last. Stick to the schedule of rehearsals and breaks. I would suggest ten minutes for smoking. Twenty minutes for breakfast and tea after an hour of rehearsal.

"Tomorrow everyone will 'examine' you for your organizing ability and they will also examine you on whether you are a director who knows his work. You must be able calmly to answer every question concerning the mode of life, the content, and the red thread of the play and its characters. During more intimate rehearsals you will analyze all questions of a psychological nature. You don't have to answer them tomorrow. As far as I can judge from our meeting tonight, you are well prepared for the part that Luzhsky and I entrusted you to play tomorrow and for the next few months, so you have nothing to be afraid of. I wish you success. I will watch and in case of any difficulties of course I will help you. But unless there is an absolute necessity, I will not interfere with your rehearsals. It might undermine your prestige. It is a most revolting spectacle in the theatre for an older director to butt into his young co-director's rehearsal and display his right to make this or that correction. This petty egotism and this desire to show off on the part of the senior director is easily interpreted by the actors as fear of parting with some of the laurels with which such a chief-director has crowned himself in his imagination long before the opening of the play. The actors soon understand that such a chief has no desire to have his younger colleague learn and develop.

"When you reach my position and have young assistants of your own who are students and co-directors, concentrate on building their self-confidence and encouraging them in their work; don't look only for their mistakes, especially when you are in the presence of others."

I returned home that evening in quite a different state of mind. I was most eager to carry out Stanislavsky's suggestions and instructions to the best of my ability. I stayed up late that night preparing all the material for the rehearsal, and I made a fresh copy of all the notes I had been given by my genius-teacher.

Rehearsal on Stage

The next day I came to the theatre an hour ahead of time. Alexandrov was already there and didn't seem to be surprised to see me there early in the auditorium. He joined me immediately and asked about the order of rehearsal. I turned over to him the plan of the guests' entrances and the lists of the cast which Stanislavsky had approved. He began immediately to study them, stopping only to ask me several questions, largely repeating those I had gone over with Stanislavsky. I was pleased to answer him, knowing that my plan for the guests' entrances had been accepted and confirmed by Stanislavsky. I, in turn, asked Alexandrov if the personal props of the guests were ready.

"Let's go on the stage and see if I have distributed them correctly," this excellent old worker in the Moscow Art Theatre answered me, the young director, without any sign of false pride.

Of course everything was on stage just as Stanislavsky had suggested. In a few minutes I noticed that the stage crew were watching me closely, perceiving that Alexandrov had given over the stage to the young director. This morning their serious attitude as they vigorously shook hands with me was especially encouraging on this, my first day as a director on the big stage of the Moscow Art Theatre.

Alexandrov and I covered the entire stage, checking the sets, the opening and closing of doors, and the backgrounds which were to be seen from the audience.

"Konstantin Sergeyevich is especially strict and critical about the position of furniture and props in relation to every door—that is to say, the staging of these backgrounds," he explained to me, with a special professional intimacy, as he straightened a picture on the wall behind one of the doors.

(The set by Dobujinsky for the third act consisted of three sections. The first, a large drawing-room with steps leading to the ballroom, which was placed below the drawing-room and could be seen through the open door. Behind the ballroom, on the same level as the drawing-room was the third section, consisting of two rooms, whose doors also led to the ballroom.)

"I can't stand it when he throws his criticism at me from the auditorium," Alexandrov said.

But the tone of his voice and the touching concern with which he was arranging the stage in the spirit of Stanislavsky's demands indicated just the opposite. I am sure that this fault-finding was what he loved and appreciated most in his work.

When Alexandrov and I came down into the auditorum, the cast had already assembled, and in a few minutes Stanislavsky appeared. He came to the director's table and asked if everything was ready and everyone was here. Alexandrov, after checking the lists, confirmed the fact that everyone was present.

"Please give me your attention for a moment," Stanislavsky began. "Today we are starting to rehearse the revival of *Much Woe From Wisdom*. Some of the work has already been done with the new actors in the principal roles.

"What will be left of the old and what added? All the best of the old production and all the best of the new. If it is possible, we will build even better sets and create an even better scenic atmosphere for the original members of the company. If it is possible, we will try even harder to give our young performers the thoughts and feelings which excited us in the days of the first production of *Much Woe From Wisdom*, which enabled us to create an exciting and patriotic production of this play in those difficult, dark days in Russia . . . In the revival the old and the young generations of the theatre will be united in one artistic ensemble. This fact is of the greatest value to me.

"We are starting our rehearsal with Famusov's ball. I find it advisable to hold this rehearsal on stage, because the actors in this scene will understand what is expected of them by the author and our theatre, after they have been given their physical actions in the third and fourth acts and have rehearsed in the sets. Gorchakov will conduct the rehearsal of the third and fourth acts, as I will be occupied with my part as Famusov. Luzhsky, Gorchakov, and I designed the plan for these acts, and, when we have worked it out, Nemirovich-Danchenko will put his final approval on it.

"Today we'll rehearse the third act from the entrance of the guests to the moment of Chatsky's appearance. The pause before Sophie's entrance, described in Nemirovich-Danchenko's book, *Much Woe From Wisdom in the Production of The Moscow Art Theatre*, is familiar to all of you. And we will elaborate on it in the auditorium rehearsals. We will work every day in the auditorium on the dancing, bowing, and ways of walking of the period. Next time I will ask all the guests to wear their shoes from the play. Now, please, everyone on stage. Gorchakov and Alexandrov will begin the rehearsal."

Stanislavsky started to climb the steps leading from the auditorium to the stage and he was followed by the actors playing the principal parts. The guests left the auditorium through the side doors in order to be at their places on stage in time. Without a word from me the curtain came down. With some anxiety I looked over the auditorium. Nobody was in it except me. This gave me a feeling of relief. Nobody would watch my behavior during rehearsal.

Before the day was over I learned quite by chance that Stanislavsky had given strict orders to let no one watch rehearsal; indeed, he even left instructions to lock the doors. A few days later I had an opportunity to ask him why he gave such orders.

Stanislavsky answered me. "Those who are idle and curious should not be allowed at rehearsal when neither we directors nor the actors are sure of the outcome of our work at that point in its development. The director must be left alone in an empty auditorium and must be assured of complete privacy. He should be able to concentrate on the rehearsal on stage. Actors who are rehearsing the play must stay in the wings, even when they are not in the scene. Under no circumstances should the actors be allowed to come into the auditorium to watch other actors rehearsing. This diverts their attention from thinking, between scenes, about the flow of their day. Of course in the case of an older, experienced director whose concern is to pass on his knowledge and experience to the young directors, it is another matter. He invites a group of people to the rehearsal for this specific purpose. Before the rehearsal he explains his purpose and he prepares himself beforehand as a teacher and director for it. The character of this rehearsal will be different."

How right Stanislavsky was! How nervous the director can become in listening to those actors who are not in the scene or to the visitors to the set, whispering in the auditorium! How his attention can be diverted from the stage by the presence of unoccupied people! How much time is usually wasted on answers to friendly advice on which way is better for an actor to do this or that on the stage! And how nervous it makes the actors on stage to hear the whispering and the hushed voices in the auditorium! I was most grateful to Stanislavsky for leaving me completely alone in the auditorium that day.

The curtain went up. Molchalin and Chatsky exchanged their last words in the scene. Lisa slipped out of Sophie's room, gave an inconspicuous sign to Molchalin to enter it, and then disappeared through the other door. Chatsky remained alone.

Next the bell was heard announcing the arrival of the first group of guests. The first beat of my ballroom scene began from that bell sounding in the vestibule of Famusov's house. The doors that led to the lower hall opened wide and a butler appeared in the drawing-room at the head of a large group of servants carrying the poles to light the chandeliers and candelabra. The butler said:

> Here, Philka, Phomka, look sharp! Don't talk!
> We want the card tables and candles, brushes, chalk.

I felt that without being seen I was in the Famusov house myself. I knew how much time the guests needed to take off their wraps downstairs, to climb the stairs to the ballroom, to pause a while there, to meet the other groups, and finally to enter the drawing-room. I think that my impression of Famusov's house was the most accurate and valuable sensation that I had as a director at that rehearsal.

We went through half the act. Each group of guests went over their entrances, crosses, and exits from the drawing-room to the ballroom several times. Stanislavsky remained on stage all the time as Famusov. When the first break came, I announced the schedule for the rest of the day: the length of the break and of the rehearsals. So began the big rehearsal of *Much Woe From Wisdom*. At the same time, work was continuing on the remodeling of the sets and the collecting of furniture and props.

The day came for the directors to rehearse with the sets. Stanislavsky was sitting in the auditorium examining very carefully the drawing-room set of the first act.

"Here is what we are going to do now," Stanislavsky

said, smiling. "Can you ask Stepanova, Bendina, Zavadsky, and the rest of the two casts of principals to come here— that is, unless some of them are busy rehearsing?"

Then he addressed the stage crew: "Light the stage area fully. Take the furniture out of the drawing-room and place it outside, so we can use the wings as a furniture store. Take the pictures down from the walls and hang them outside as in a shop. China, porcelain, bronzes, table-cloths, rugs, and carpets also must be spread out some-where on the stage outside the sets. Make it all look like a showcase or the window display of some antique shop. While you are doing that, I'll have breakfast." And with a gay and mysterious look on his face he left the auditorium.

Alexandrov and the supervisors of the different depart-ments were somewhat amazed, but no one would think of questioning Stanislavsky's order, so they began imme-diately to follow it. On one side of the stage area Alex-androv and Titov (the chief mechanic) arranged the fur-niture to look like a furniture store. From somewhere in the basement under the stage they dug out two additional suites of antique furniture, the upholstery of which was embroidered handsomely in flowers on black wool. So these pieces, together with the three suites that belonged to the play, made a real furniture store . . . There was even an improvised cash box and a sign over it, "Ware-house. Mr. F. Stupin & Sons." On the other side of the stage area they arranged a window display of the bronzes, porce-lain, china, and so forth. On screens they hung the pic-tures, prints, etchings, and lithographs. This latter gave the illusion of a picture gallery.

With what creative enthusiasm they discovered things and put them to use! No one interpreted Stanislavsky's order as a whim. Every one understood very well that Stanislavsky had conceived—and perhaps had found— some new opening to creativity in our complicated dramatic art and the stage crew were trying to help him with their ingenuity to realize his new idea.

Stanislavsky returned and looked over the arrangements. "Bravo! Bravo! What resourcefulness! What inventiveness! I didn't expect this much to be accomplished in half an hour. How many of the actors are free?"

"Stepanova, Bendina, Androfsky (the second Sophie), Koslovsky, and Zavadsky."

"Ask them to come on stage."

He addressed the actors, who joined him on the empty set: "You see in front of you an empty room. You are supposed to be very familiar with the character of that room. A week ago, Famusov, the master of the household took a fancy into his head to send the furniture of this room to his country estate. He had time to send away the old furniture but not time enough to buy new. He was ill or something. And tomorrow there is going to be a ball at his house. I, as Famusov, entrust you, Sophiushka, and you, my brother Molchalin, to choose, buy, and have delivered today everything that is necessary to furnish and decorate this drawing-room. Take Lisa with you. Chatsky and I will remain in this room. You can ask our advice as to where to place this or that object or picture. Chatsky can be most helpful, as he has known our house from childhood. Put two armchairs in the corner of the room for Chatsky and me."

"Where do we go to buy furniture?" Androvskaya asked, who, along with the rest of the actors, did not know of Stanislavsky's plan.

"Oh, excuse me, I forgot to tell you. Of course, on the Kuznetsky Bridge. It's just around the corner. As soon as you are out of this room you will see it. Now please stay in your characters. Be serious. Shop as Sophie, Lisa, and Molchalin would."

Outside the door the actors were truly amazed to see the

Kuznetsky Bridge. Alexandrov and Titov, together with other members of the stage crew, were in charge of the furniture store. Morosov was in charge of the antique shop and Gorunov of the art gallery. And during the following two and a half hours the actors were busy buying the furniture and the rest of the objects for the drawing-room with absolute seriousness and enormous enthusiasm. They brought furniture into the house, arranged it, put rugs on the floor, and hung pictures, often asking Stanislavsky's advice. They took back some things and exchanged them for others. Before the rehearsal ended, the room looked as though someone had lived in it a long time. Everything seemed complete to the last pillow on the sofa, and the actors had had a wonderful lesson in how to treat objects on the stage as their own possessions. It proved to be a most important improvisation for them in that it taught them how important stage atmosphere is. This realization of stage atmosphere is what Stanislavsky and Nemirovich-Danchenko considered absolutely essential to the performance.

Before leaving the auditorium Stanislavsky asked the actors how their rehearsals with Sudakov and me were progressing, and he promised to visit one of them soon.

Rough Sketches for a Role

Stanislavsky's rehearsal with the first four leads took place a few days later. The actors played the first act for him, improvising their movements, as I had not set the mise en scène. To our surprise, on Lisa's cue, "Oh, master . . ." Stanislavsky answered with Famusov's line, "Master, yes! It's you, naughty girl, you harum-scarum . . ."—and the rest of the speech. (During our previous rehearsals the stage manager had read Famusov.) And after his last famous phrase:

> Oh, what a heavy charge, Creator,
> To be a grown-up girl's papa!

Stanislavsky looked gaily at the actors. "Well, was it terrible to play a part in verse and on top of it to have to play with Stanislavsky?" he asked.

"Oh, terribly frightening! All my insides hurt," blurted out Bendina, who had played Lisa with her usual spontaneity.

"Remember that sensation. That's exactly how Lisa feels when Famusov finds her by the clock," Stanislavsky remarked, contented with Lisa's reply.

"Well, how did you feel?" he addressed Stepanova seriously. "After my scene with Lisa you could anticipate my playing the next with you."

Stepanova answered: "Though I expected you to play Famusov in my scene, I hoped with all my heart that something would interrupt the rehearsal and you wouldn't come on stage for my scene."

"Did Sophie wish Famusov to appear in her room when she was saying good night to Molchalin?"

"Not for the world! Of course not!"

"Then you also remember that my intrusion into the scene frightened you. Remember, you are afraid of your father. This is very good material for Sophie's feeling in her first few scenes. How did Molchalin feel about my appearance?"

Koslovsky said, "My heart went into my mouth. I could hardly answer you."

"That's correct. You must remember that sensation and use it. You must have had more time to adjust to my participation in the scene." Then he addressed Zavadsky: "But you were self-conscious in your scene with Sophie because you felt I was observing you not as Famusov but as a director."

"That's exactly how I felt," Zavadsky replied.

Stanislavsky said, "It was good that you gave your complete attention to Sophie rather than to your criticism and mockery of the members of the English Club."

Zavadsky said: "My problem in this scene is to look at Sophie and compare her with the girl I had known three years ago. I must find in her face the new and yet recognize the old characteristics. I must admire this Sophie who is new to me."

"Your problem is correct. But you must realize it with much more intensity and daring. Then your love and desire for her will be clearer. But why were all of you rushing your lines as though you could not finish them soon enough? I tried to slow down my scenes with you, but you threw me into your tempo. Did you notice my attempt to slow you down?"

"Yes, Konstantin Sergeyevich," Stepanova answered for all of us, "but no matter how much I tried to slow down my thoughts, my tongue would not obey me. We always want to speak verse faster than prose."

"You should fight that desire," Stanislavsky answered her. "Of course speech in verse is much more thoroughly saturated, compressed, and dynamic than speech in prose. And just because of that it demands greater skill in expression from an actor; a fast delivery does not always contribute to this. Sometimes a poet expresses one basic thought in seven or eight lines, as Pushkin does in *Boris Godunov*, in the impostor's speech to Marina:

> I swear to thee
> That thou alone wast able to extort
> My heart's confession, I swear to thee that never,
> Anywhere, not in the feast, not in the cup
> Of folly, not in friendly confidence,
> Not 'neath the knife, nor tortures of the rack,
> Shall my tongue give away these weighty secrets.

"It takes many lines—indeed, a whole stanza—to express this one impulse, promise, and oath. It is significant that there is only one period and eight commas. Say it with one breath if you can. But a speech in verse is not always constructed like that. Yet, the rhythm should always be felt—or, to be more correct, the constant change of rhythm, which depends both on what is being described and on the thoughts and feelings of the characters. The speech in verse is always filled with an inner rhythm, but not with the same one all the way through. In Griboyedov's verse, the change of rhythm in one scene or in one beat is very obvious. Here is an example: Lisa is awakening, one rhythm; she sees that it is late ('The house is all astir'), another rhythm; she's caught with the master, a third rhythm; she's trying to avoid his love-making, a fourth; he leaves, a fifth; and so on during each role all through the play. So far, all of you have been delivering your speeches in one rhythm, the so-called rhythm of poetry—as an actor does who appears on the 'smart' stage to read 'poetry' instead of prose. But one should not slow the reading mechanically or deliberately speak the role written in verse more slowly. How then must you find within yourself the organic rhythm that the events in a play in verse call for?

"First of all, as in a prose drama, one must establish the logic of events and the flow of the day for the play and for each character. I think you have already done this. I saw no lack of logic in your behavior, in your relationship to each other, or in your physical actions that were called for by the content of the first act."

"The big étude that we had in furnishing the drawing-room helped us tremendously," Zavadsky put in.

Stanislavsky continued: "I willingly believe that. Concrete physical action serves as a guide for an actor to belief in the reality of the play's content, in his existence in the given role, and in the relationships with which the author connects all the characters. But Griboyedov's thoughts, images, and words are in your way. They are not yours. The words are foreign to you; they are not created by your own imagination. How can an actor help himself in such a case? You realize very well how long it takes a writer to create the characters of his play—how many rough sketches Pushkin made for *Boris Godunov*, Gogol for *The Inspector-General*, and Griboyedov for his *Much Woe From Wisdom*, or other great writers before the final draft of their great work is completed.

"In order to make this text your own, each one of you must make for himself the rough sketches which Pushkin, Gogol, and Griboyedov had to make to reach the perfection of their thoughts, images, and language. Of course, they had their great talent and inspiration, but they equally needed labor, tremendous labor, to bring their conception to that degree of perfection that we are so enthusiastic about. Let us render what is due to them for their talent and inspiration, and let us labor so we can understand the road they have traveled and the words and images they so meticulously used to clothe their thoughts.

"Please, all of you, prepare right now two or three rough sketches of one of the important beats in your roles. You, Stepanova, think of a few rough copies of your dream. You, Zavadsky, the enumeration of Famusov's friends and acquaintances; Lisa, your description of Skalozub; Molchalin . . ."

Koslovsky interrupted: "Molchalin does not and must not have any fantasies. He cannot allow himself to think of anything but the accepted on any subject."

"Don't shirk a very important exercise," Stanislavsky replied. "Tell me, what other presents, besides those three little ones, are you going to make use of to buy Lisa's affection?"

"Konstantin Sergeyevich, must we give our rough sketches in verse?" Bendina asked.

A pause followed this question. The actors were very much afraid that this was exactly what they would have to do. But Stanislavsky was only amazed at her question.

"Our Bendina writes verse," Zavadsky said half jokingly, "and it's easy for her to speak in verse. We couldn't, no matter how we tried."

Everybody, including Stanislavsky, laughed. Bendina was very embarrassed.

Stanislavsky answered "Rough sketches in verse? No, I don't insist on it! But let's all try it in prose, please. Who is the bravest? I would like to hear all four of you in succession, in order to compare your sketches and make my remarks on them at the same time. Then I'll hear the new ones. We must compose three or four for each one of you, so let's begin immediately.

"Allow me, Konstantin Sergeyevich," Stepanova said.

Stanislavsky replied, "Please," and he took his pencil ready to go ahead with notes.

Stepanova started her sketch as Sophie: "Where do I begin, father? Imagine . . . first, in my dream I am swimming in the lake . . . there's such a silence around me as is possible only at dawn before the sun rises. I gather water lilies to make a wreath. You will ask me for whom? For the one who is in the boat with me and who guides it. It seems to me that I would go anywhere with him. I trust him, I know him. Perhaps he doesn't come from the nobility. He is not handsome nor rich. But with him. . . .

Stanislavsky interrupted her as Famusov:

Oh, daughter, spare the blow and say no more.
No match for you if once he's poor.

Stepanova continued: "Suddenly there is a horrible rumble. The lake is in an uproar. From the bottom of it monsters appear. There are mermaids, fish with animal heads, and with them as their leader are you, father—and you're green, wet, and slippery. All of them attacked our boat— you were pulling me under water; others attacked my dear one who was steering the boat. I want to stay with him, but you drag me with you. 'I wake and there is someone speaking.' Excuse me, Konstantin Sergeyevich," Stepanova interrupted her rough sketch, "but this line is from Griboy- edov's text."

Stanislavsky laughed: "It means that your rough sketch at this point coincided completely with Griboyedov's final text. Now work on another variation of the dream. Who is next?"

Bendina answered: "I have a rough sketch of Skalozub."

Stanislavsky asked, "In verse?" He laughed, then said, "Go ahead."

Bendina began as Lisa: "Your father would like to see you a distinguished lady, a countess or perhaps a duchess. But our nobility do not always jingle gold in their pockets. In order to live gaily and give large parties one needs a lot of money. So here is our Skalozub. He is not a count —oh, but how rich he is! Although he's not clever, he talks a lot. Though not brave, someday he surely will be an admiral. That's all."

Stanislavsky spoke: "In the first place you spoke prac- tically in verse. And secondly, why an admiral?"

"Well, I didn't want to stick to Griboyedov's text. And perhaps Skalozub might be transferred one day to com- mand a cruiser."

Stanislavsky replied, smiling but serious: "The purpose of our exercise is not to keep away from Griboyedov's text at any price. Changing the general into an admiral is ab- solutely out of the question. Your approach to the rough sketch is much too primitive. I am asking for much more in your improvisations. You must reach the root of Griboyedov's thought and discover what compelled him to write this particular beat of the text. Zavadsky, would you like to try to find that thought in your monologue about the members of the English Club and then dress it in picturesque form?"

"I will try." Zavadsky began his rough sketch about Famusov. He described him not only as a member of the English Club but also as a Free Mason, a frequent visitor to the group to which Repetilov mysteriously refers in the fourth act.

His satiric generalizations and his sharp characterizations of the uncles and aunts helped make Zavadsky's rough sketch a most interesting one. Stanislavsky was very pleased. In the next half hour the actors competed with each other in their different variations of their rough sketches. Evidently they were reaching perfection because they consistently met with Stanislavsky's approval.

Stanislavsky remarked: "Now you know how one must work on Griboyedov's text. You widened your conception of the thoughts and events in this part of the play which we chose to work on today. And this is the way you must compose rough sketches for all the important moments in your roles."

Harmful and Useful Over-Acting

Stanislavsky began a new subject: "Let's discuss some other important aspects of your roles. After you have made Griboyedov's text your own and have learned to speak it without declaiming, forcing, and straining, you must fill the text with Griboyedov's feelings. You must create those feelings in your heart; you must live them on the stage. Youth is usually outspoken in actual life. The young are not shy in expressing their feelings and relationships. Restraint comes to one as one gets older.

"On the stage, in our dramatic art, it is quite the opposite. The young actors are shy of their feelings in rehearsal and on stage; especially in our theatre the young actors are afraid to over-play. Let's stop for a few minutes to examine this word which is used so widely in our theatre language. The actor over-plays—that is, he exaggerates his actions and relationships on stage—for many reasons. Perhaps he has not analyzed the logic of his character's thoughts. Or he has skipped or overlooked the intermediate transitional thoughts that connect the main ones. In order to fill those gaps he strains himself in the transitory, light, and simple places in his role so that he can hide these flaws in his work, and he tries to express the main and the accessory thoughts with the same significance. In another instance the actor skips a very important fact in his evaluation of the events that influenced the composition of his role. He didn't think it over, or find the right relation to it, or connect it to other events in his role. Why does this happen? Quite often for trivial reasons: perhaps just at the time when he was about to work on this place in his part, friends interrupted his work. Next day during the rehearsal, when the director brings this gap in his role to his attention, the actor, hating to admit why he did not work on it, tries to justify himself. 'Well, after all I'm a talented actor. I don't have to work out every detail of my part. It will come somehow.' It does 'come somehow' sometimes, but very, very seldom.

"Our great actress Fedotova used to tell us young actors, 'Work! One must work, my dear. Work and not sit by the window and wait for inspiration, for a visit from Apollo. He has too much on his mind to remember you.'

"Ability to work and toil is also a great talent, an enormous talent. As a result of it, inspiration comes. Thus, let us go back to the question of over-playing. The actor also loves to put on a feeling he lacks and has not developed in

himself. He understands that to speak Chatsky's monologue: 'What's this? Can I believe my ears or do I blunder?'
coldly and without 'a thousand torments' is impossible.
So he postpones work on the monologue until later. He says
to himself, 'Perhaps if I work out the part up to the monologue, the monologue will come out by itself.' But this
monologue is long and full of changing thoughts and feelings. And this kind of a monologue will not come out by
itself, without being thoroughly worked out. The actor
neglects his work on it and the opening approaches. There
is no longer time to work on it seriously, so he decides,
'Well, after all I'm a professional actor. I have a good
voice, good diction, and excellent temperament; it will
come out all right.' But, as a result, he has to over-act. The
actor does not communicate to the audience the authentic
thoughts, the torments, and the depth of emotion which
Chatsky is filled with in this monologue. Usually he just
shouts and howls, increasing his tempo more and more as
he reaches the last phrase. And because it is his one sincere
desire to say this last 'My carriage! Here, my carriage!',
it does come out effectively, and the actor, satisfied with
himself, accepts the applause—for part of the audience
will always applaud him. It saw him working on the stage,
shouting, swinging his arms, and running about. It was
obvious that he was tormented by something. The question
is by what. He is tormented by not having his monologue
worked out, or thought through, or filled with genuine
emotion. He's tormented by that, yes, but not by the
thoughts and feelings that bring Chatsky at this point in
his monologue to a stage of rage and frenzy. The actor
over-acts as a professional in his trade, but Chatsky lives
as a real person, a person of great ideas, thoughts, and emotions. Now this is one aspect of the conception of 'over-
playing' in our theatre art.

"The myths about the intolerance of over-acting in our

theatre are greatly exaggerated. Also the myth about my intolerance for over-acting—based on my favorite cue to the actor, 'I don't believe you'—is exaggerated. You and I are just beginning our creative work together, so let's try to understand clearly and precisely what I call 'over-acting' and also the matter of my directorial despotism. I know too well how often I am called a despot. Possibly at times I am one—when as director, teacher, and educator I lose control of my temper. Please believe me that after such outbursts I feel ashamed. I ask you in advance to forgive me these bad traits. I have always fought them, I still am fighting them.

"Now about my frequent remark, 'I don't believe you.' First, I want you to understand that I do not use that expression in a personal way, or because I am over-demanding as a director, or because of some directorial caprice (I know I am accused of that, too). I only use it from the spectator's point of view, from the point of view of the ordinary spectator at the twentieth performance, the type of person who I always feel is by my side during every rehearsal, no matter when or where it takes place. It is only when I as an ordinary spectator at the twentieth or thirtieth performance (not as the opening night spectator and not as the 'mama and papa' audience at dress rehearsal) do not believe in what is going on, or in what the actor says in relation to this or that event, or in how he feels at this or that moment in his role, it is then and only then that from the vantage point of a neighbor-spectator I throw at you as a director, 'I don't believe you.'

"I am of the opinion that the director has the right to say to an actor, 'I don't believe you,' when he is absolutely sure that it is the audience in him saying it. But he doesn't have the right if he is speaking as the professional theatre man or, even worse, as the subjective esthete or snob. Therefore, don't ever be afraid to hear from me, 'I don't believe you.' Know that at that moment I detect in your thoughts, actions, and feelings, not some particularly subtle error in your actor's skill but the most elementary mistakes in the logic of your behavior on stage or in the logic of your inner sensations and relations to a certain event of the play. Accept my 'I don't believe you' calmly, seriously, and trustfully.

"Now let's go back again to over-playing. The types of over-playing that I mentioned before are harmful, but there are useful and even necessary ones."

Stanislavsky glanced merrily at our surprised faces. "Yes, yes, that's exactly what I said. It's useful and necessary. Let's make clear at first that I was describing types of over-acting by actors *during* the performance. But in the process of preparation and during the rehearsal period, over-playing sometimes is not only useful but necessary."

Stanislavsky laughed openly as he saw our shocked faces.

How could we help being shocked? His present statement contradicted sharply everything we had learned in following his method. It contradicted everything that we had ever been taught at the Moscow Art Theatre.

"I'm not joking," Stanislavsky continued, with a smile on his face, "and I most seriously repeat that to over-play during the rehearsals is sometimes necessary for an actor. And the director must not only allow it but suggest it. Of course you are interested to know when over-playing should be used and how to combine it with all those demands on your inner technique which you follow in using the accepted method of work in searching for the truth.

"Let us remind ourselves what started our discussion of 'over-playing': the concept that ideas, thoughts, and events of the play must not only be perfectly understood by the actor but also filled with emotional content of definite power. I have been telling you all along that every feeling is the result of the actor's thoughts and actions in the given circumstances. However, the strength of the feeling depends on the temperament and the creative imagination of the actor. How is the young actor to develop his imagination and his temperament? By intensifying, strengthening, and broadening the given circumstances to the highest degree. Stepanova, you must be terribly frightened when Famusov finds you with Molchalin in your room early in the morning. I cannot blame you, a young actress, for not preparing anything in yourself for that moment of action. You are excited when you answer Famusov's questions, but this is not what Sophie feels at that moment. Your head is not swimming when you say, 'My head goes round'; you don't feel giddy; you are breathing normally when Sophie cries from fright, 'My breath I have hardly found.'

"At the same time you understand perfectly the text of your role, your thoughts, and your relationship to the events of the play. You know the principles of the method very well. As an individual, you are perfect for Sophie. And, as I said before, all this has created in you a certain feeling of excitement, but your feeling at that particular moment is not of the same strength and intensity as Sophie's. Do you agree with me?"

"I agree with you," Stepanova replied, "but I was thinking that with each rehearsal my excitement will be stronger and deeper."

"How many rehearsals will you need for this?"

"I don't know."

"And I don't know either, because both of us don't know how strong the feeling must be to satisfy you as an actress and me as the director-audience."

"What am I to do?" Stepanova asked.

"Over-act," Stanislavsky replied, "immediately, right here and now. Over-act Sophie's excitement as much as you can. Imagine and thoroughly believe that when Famusov finds you and Molchalin together you have nothing on but a night gown."

"Oh, my God, but . . ."

Stanislavsky interrupted her, "Don't intellectualize, please. But answer me now as if at this very moment, during this rehearsal, you are half-undressed."

And Stanislavsky quite suddenly began improvising as Famusov:

"What is it? What happened? Why are you here? Why so early? For what purpose? And in such a state! Where are your clothes?"

Stanislavsky looked at all four actors with such great hostility that we realized that the two young girls and two young men were caught in the early morning in improper behavior.

"And why did God make you meet at such an unearthly hour . . ." he stared directly at Stepanova with a definite question. Stepanova blushed deeply under his stare, and for some reason began to straighten her dress. Suddenly she was almost screaming as though defending herself from Famusov's ugly suspicions:

He's only just come in this minute!

And almost in a whisper Molchalin said, "Straight from my walk."

Stanislavsky answered in a thunderous voice. And he continued to abuse Stepanova:

And you, miss, straight from bed and off you start your
  dancing
With some young man in tow. Respectable it looks!
All night you read absurd romances
And here is the fruit of all these books. . . .

Before he was through, Stepanova was choking, with tears. Stanislavsky suddenly started attacking Zavadsky with the same force.

His voice thundered through the theatre, as it always did when he spoke to someone who made him lose his temper.

But Zavadsky understood Stanislavsky's intention and did not let him finish Famusov's monologue from the fourth act.

In the same tone he answered with Chatsky's monologue. Zavadsky spoke the monologue with much bitterness and passion. Then on his last phrase he spontaneously jumped from his seat and left the auditorium.

"He's really off his head!" Stanislavsky addressed Lisa seriously.

Bendina, who was watching what had been happening, started to answer him, as excited as the rest. "Dare I, master . . ."

"Silence!" Stanislavsky severely interrupted her, and then continued:

> Off to your cottage, march! You will go and feed the
>   chickens.
> Aunt! Country! Wilderness! Saratov!

An intense pause followed this. In spite of Stanislavsky's humorous remarks which followed these lines, we did not laugh this time. Zavadsky quietly returned and sat down. Stanislavsky drank some tea, which was always there on the director's table for him. "Well," he said, "we all overacted to the hilt. In order to keep in line with you, I was forced to shout. But now we've learned how far our characters would go if they were not restrained by the conditions of time, by the surroundings, by the line within which the character grows, and by an artistic sense of proportion. At times all of you had sincere notes. You, Stepanova, when you were trying to talk and were fighting your tears; you, Zavadsky, beginning from the words, 'Thus my delirium is past! I have cast my dreams away. The veil is down at last.' The entire monologue sounded strong, sincere, and convincing. Try to remember what thoughts urged you to speak these lines and what your state of being was.

"But we all tried too hard. We pressed the pedal of emotion at the expense of thoughts and relationships. We were over-playing, but for what purpose? We learned what are the limits of our own feelings; for me how far I can go in a state of rage; for Sophie and Lisa, how far in a state of fright; how far you can go in bitterness and disillusion, Zavadsky. As far as the plot of the play and the characters are concerned, our feelings went in the right direction. But I can say for myself that my anger was not organized. I forced myself too much. I shouted much more than Famusov would have in the given circumstances. In other words, I too was over-acting. Now I know that such strong wrath is too much for Famusov. But I also learned that the energy I have been using in rehearsals and performances is not enough. My Famusov was too soft. Perhaps I minimized his ugly traits in order to make him more pleasant to the audience. What was wrong in 1906 and 1914 is obviously out of the question today, when we know so well and understand so much more about the scandalous role played by the majority of the nobles and gentry in recent times. Thus, I also must change my old design of Famusov and find a new one proper for his thoughts, actions, feelings, and relationships.

"If I were asked how many rehearsals I will need to make the change, I would answer like Stepanova, 'I don't know.' But there is a way to find out for myself the limit to which I can go in my feelings. That is to force myself to experience these feelings for a few minutes by straining all my will and imagination, even when I am fully aware that the character could not possibly have such will and imagination. An exaggerated feeling comes out as a result, one not justified by the author's given circumstances. For example, Sophie could not possibly be found in her night gown with Molchalin.

"But I consider this temporary over-acting admissible and even useful, although it is done only for a few minutes during the rehearsal. It's a trial shot of emotion directed at the necessary target. The bullet does not always hit the target at once. It also hits under or over the target—that is, until the gunner learns to shoot precisely. Of course I myself have never had an opportunity to shoot off a cannon, but I have read about it and that's how it's done.

"It's the same with an actor. First, he doesn't give enough feeling. The young actors are shy of *living* their roles on the stage"—Stanislavsky stressed the word *living* —"and in his mature years, the actor over-does and gives too much of his feelings. He over-acts because his experience tells him that it is his emotion that gets the spontaneous response of the audience.

"Where does the solution lie? How does one find the golden mean, that vital and artistic truth of feeling for which we are striving? Only by constant training and everyday exercises, not only in the primary principles of the method (attention, relaxation, etc.) but also in its more complicated aspects (fantasy, imagination, emotion-memory, etc.) can an actor be certain of filling his role's problem to the utmost—precisely, colorfully, and expressively.

"Most likely you have observed that in life the most insignificant person has a strength of emotion that is quite unexpected, when he comes up against difficult circumstances—or 'is caught by the throat,' as the saying goes. He plays a scene with an exceptional sincerity and emotional infectiousness seldom found in a play. It shows that a person can arouse in himself, if necessary, the most powerful feeling. Shame on you actors that you can't feel on stage what an ordinary human being can bring up

within himself when it's necessary! That's why I'm not
inclined to indulge the young talented actors and actresses
in their shyness as I would amateurs playing charades at
a party. That's why I won't indulge the experienced actors
in over-acting during the *performance*"—he stressed the
word performance.

"You should not only forgive young actors their over-
acting during rehearsals in the special instances when they
are trying to feel the extent and power of emotion in the
character, but you should encourage them. The experienced actor should never be allowed to over-act during the
performance or to exploit his feelings before the audience.

"Why do I talk about over-acting at almost the first rehearsal of *Much Woe From Wisdom*?" Stanislavsky continued, after a moment's silence. "Because this play is
considered cold and rational. But just from the short étude
we did today you feel how exciting and fiery it can be.
Just imagine how Sophie and Lisa can play their scene if
the scene preceding it between Famusov and Sophie is
played at full strength!

"Well, Lisa," he addressed Bendina, "begin your speech
immediately, and without thinking, having as a tuning
fork only my 'Silence.' "

And Konstantin Sergeyevich snapped the word "Silence!" at Lisa with such force that she exclaimed in
despair:

> Well, come, you are lucky, miss, what fun to think he is
>   gone!
> But no! We'll do the laughing later on;
> The prospect's black; I've not a tooth but chatters.
> It's not the doing wrong, it's what they say that matters.

The infectiousness of Stanislavsky's temperament was
so great that Bendina, always talented at improvisations,
filled these four phrases with an outburst of despair and

half-fainted as she pronounced her cynical truism. Responding on the same plane, Stepanova answered her as strongly:

> Let blame who likes. It's not from that I'm shrinking.
> It's what Papa will do that sets me thinking,
> Rough, ruthless, quick to take amiss,
> He always was, but after this . . .

With special expressiveness she spoke the last three words of the sentence: "you, yourself, can judge!"

The whole scene between the young mistress and her servant became extremely active and colorful. Both of them were very frightened, as they had disgraced themselves, and they were anxious to find a way out of the situation they had created and to avoid the humiliation of banishment to the village. When they brought up the names of Chatsky and Skalozub it was as if Sophie were searching for someone she could marry immediately. During this scene Stanislavsky kept urging Lisa, "Give it to her; give it to her! That mean woman—that's it!" Through her lines:

> Well, that's just it, miss, you despised my stupid warn-
>   ing,
> Thought my advice beneath you far,
> And there you are!

Then further on, he practically instigated Sophie and Lisa against each other. Then Sophie against Lisa, "She'll get such a thrashing from me one of these days, that Lisinka!" He prompted the direction of her thought when she was saying:

> Be careful! Don't forget I won't be put upon!
> Perhaps I have behaved with neither rhyme nor reason,
> I know. I please myself. But tell me, where is the
>   treason?

The scene gained new sharpness under such unusual prompting of the thoughts and relationships from which the text is spontaneously born. The actresses performed with fire. Because of this, Chatsky's arrival caught them unaware. Stanislavsky continued this unusual prompting during the meeting between Sophie and Chatsky. Often, in the most unexpected places in the text, he would whisper to Chatsky, "Oh, how beautiful she is! What a beauty!" He continued the exclamations a number of times during the rest of the scene. Zavadsky understood what Stanislavsky wanted, and, after the second or third prompting, he combined very expressively his chiding thoughts and words with admiration for Sophie—with tender looks and short pauses which stressed his fascination with her. Likewise this prompting of his inner line of feeling produced an immense gain in the whole scene: it attained reality and was cleared of the slightest rhetorical or narrative tone.

Stanislavsky used just one remark to prompt Sophie during the scene: "What ill wind brought you here?" But he changed his intonation each time he said it, giving subtle gradations to this idea. At one time his intonation implied, "This is the last straw!" another, "Go to the devil!" and another, "You will pay for this, just wait!"

At the end of the act Stanislavsky joined the young actors as Famusov. After all these exercises, the last scene of the first act rang emotionally deep, clear in its thought, and vivid in its character.

The Director's Work with an Actor

"Now you have the right to ask me how you can combine the work you have been doing under my direction with the work I demand of you in the method, when you are working by yourself," Stanislavsky said.

"The most important function of the director, as I understand the definition, is to open all the potentialities of the actor and to arouse his individual initiative. To compose rough sketches from the text fulfills this problem excellently. Of course in the final analysis the actor cannot use his own words for his part, but through his rough sketches he penetrates deeply into the train of thought and images of the author and shows his individual initiative in that direction. The knowledge and mastering of the elements of the system is not enough to draw out his feelings and make them alive. The director must constantly excite and kindle his actors' imagination. How can it be done? By relating the subject of the play and the separate moments of the play to real life as it unfolds today before our eyes. Learn to see and hear. Love life. Learn to bring it into art, fill your vision of the part with it. The director must keep each rehearsal in a creative atmosphere. In that way he helps an actor create a full-blooded vision of the role, and helps him think of the events of the play vividly and feel them strongly. To accomplish this, allow your actors to over-act during rehearsal, and then free them from over-acting by having them imaginatively adapt their acting to the concrete circumstances in which the characters in the play might find themselves.

"The logic of the inner and outer action—that physical action which comes as a result of the problems which the director gives the actor—will give him a sense of proportion which won't allow him to digress from artistic truth. Constantly check all the actions, thoughts, and feelings of your actors with their over-all problem—the idea of the play.

"Work creatively during the rehearsal. Fill it with your own initiative.

"Rehearsals are not lessons on a method in a dramatic school. They are the process of the embodiment of the author's thoughts and ideas into living, active human images. Work, and use all your acquired knowledge of the method but do not use it for the sake of demonstrating this knowledge for itself. The method is only the means for the realistic embodiment of the dramatist's ideas but it is not an end in itself! I cannot repeat this statement often enough, because I feel that our directors and teachers of acting sin precisely in this direction. I understand the cause of this. It is not difficult to learn to teach the method, or to teach the youngsters to be attentive and relaxed, and to have good relationships with each other, providing that the youngsters that come to our dramatic school have not been spoiled by dilettantism, amateurishness, or by schools where students are taught to represent the character rather than to live it. In a word, it isn't difficult to teach the separate elements of the method, but it is difficult to teach an actor how to link all the elements tightly together for his correct and creative state of being at rehearsal or in performance. It is difficult to channel the actor's knowledge of the method's principles—plus his own thoughts, experiences, and feelings—toward the creation of a role on the stage and, finally, to the over-all problem of the author's idea. For that, one must be not only a pedagogue but a director who thinks independently, a person and an artist in the full meaning of the word: one whose perception of the world is open and broad-minded and whose understanding of the problems and the goal of art is most profound.

"Not every teacher of the method possesses these qualities. I must add that the director must know how to embody all the actor's experiences in the living artistic image, using the play's material and the actor's professional qualities. Also, for a fine artist knowledge of the system is not enough. It is not enough to know how to live your role on the stage. You must have a strong, well-trained voice of pleasant—or, in any case—expressive timbre, perfect diction, plasticity of movement—without being a poseur—a face that is beautiful and mobile, a good figure, and expressive hands."

Stanislavsky glanced at the actors' faces. They were obviously measuring themselves against these requirements. "In addition," he smiled, "the actor must have vivid imagination, and he must be able to translate what he's observed into his characterization on stage. In addition, an actor needs to have an infectious stage charm. Now you must be very curious to know what this 'stage charm' is and how to bring it out and keep it during your creative life. I am sure this interests you no less than the Stanislavsky Method."

"Yes, yes—oh, very much!" came the chorus of actors' voices.

"We will talk about it some other time, separately, when we have clear heads." And, as usual, Stanislavsky wished us success in our work without him, and left the auditorium.

During the following six weeks, Stanislavsky rehearsed the two casts of principals in the first, second, the beginning of the third act, and the end of the fourth act of *Much Woe From Wisdom*. He met two or three times with other actors playing important parts. He also met with all those whose parts were new to them and with the participants of the group scenes. Then there followed the rehearsals on the stage in costume and make-up, and finally the opening night came.

The new and the old generations of the Moscow Art Theatre worked together in this play, and so the young people entered the theatre company. The guest scene in the third act and the departure in the fourth proved an excellent school for the young actors, as Stanislavsky expected they would. He remained in the wings all through the performance, constantly keeping his eye on the guests, the servants, and all the others in the group scenes. He saw to it that they did not lose their creative mood or their concentration on the problems, the relationships, and the correct rhythm—the totality of those elements in the actor that make him alive and active, no matter how small his role. An exciting factor of this first appearance of the young actors on the big stage of the Moscow Art Theatre was playing with Stanislavsky as Famusov.

Stanislavsky Plays Famusov

It is six o'clock in the evening. *Much Woe From Wisdom* is playing tonight on the big stage of the Moscow Art Theatre. A sleigh drives up to the stage door. The tall, heavily wrapped figure of Stanislavsky steps out. He enters the stage door. At that hour the dressing-rooms and wings are still empty. The actors who rehearsed during the day have left for their five o'clock dinner, and the actors appearing in tonight's performance will arrive at seven P.M., an hour before curtain time. Then, as now, the curtain went up in the Moscow theatres at eight o'clock.

Stanislavsky takes off his overcoat with the help of Maxim, who is invariably waiting for him at that hour, and goes to his dressing-room. Any one who meets Stanislavsky by chance in the wings greets him silently. No one calls him by name—this at his request. It is not a whim or an eccentricity, but the request of an artist preparing himself for his role. Because I know this, I ask Stanislavsky if I may come to watch him put on his make-up and costume for Famusov.

"If you keep silent or ask me only very simple questions,

I won't mind," he answers, "but if you want to discuss questions of some importance I would rather you came after the performance."

"When people greet you before the performance does it bother you?" I asked him.

"Yes, it does. I don't want to be talked to in the theatre before the performance. I begin to think of my role in the morning. I think of what my Famusov lacks. I try to enter into the world of Famusov's thoughts. I don't want to be disturbed by idle talk. But of course I'm not a lunatic, and I'm perfectly aware of what goes on around me."

Stanislavsky spends a great deal of time on the make-up for Famusov, although it isn't complicated. Before putting the slightest touch of make-up on his face, he leans back in his chair and examines intently his face reflected in the big, three-sided table mirror. At times his lips whisper something but I can't detect the words. His face constantly changes expression, as though he is talking to himself in the mirror. He seems to be asking himself questions and also to be talking to someone else. Sometimes he talks to me. "How do dramatists live now in Moscow? To whom are your friends married? How much do you spend for your dinner? What is the cure for such-and-such sickness?" and so forth. His questions are never related to theatre life.

After completing his make-up, he asks me to call his wardrobe man and dresses with infinite care, as Famusov would. He comes on the stage long before curtain time. Before his first entrance, he takes a few steps away from the door and then sneaks up on tiptoe to the last two or three steps. (This is the entrance when he catches Lisa unaware.) Before his second and third entrances in the same act, he stands far away from the door, and, after the signal is given him by the stage manager, he walks quickly to the entrance. Following the custom of the period, the doors are thrown open wide by Famusov's servants. Starting so far from the entrance gives him an impetuous rhythm. During rehearsals with us he paid great attention to this. He demanded brisk rhythm, energetic actions, and clear-cut delivery from himself and his partners all through the play.

Stanislavsky's Famusov was always sincere; all his actions were justified. He was the personification of a man who had reached the top in the Moscow of that time: a genuine lord and master, not too clever and not stupid. He had many interesting details of character. For example, when he listened to Chatsky's last monologue, he rolled a small wax ball from the candle which he carried into the scene, and during each of the latter's accusations he stuck each ball to the trunk of the candle as if to say, "Remember this!" This physical action which Stanislavsky used while listening to the long monologue was familiar to the audience. In this fashion such Famusovs used to listen in church to the reading of the twelve gospels on Thursday of Holy Week. The audience understood the adjustment instantly. He was completely engrossed as he listened to the monologue.

Stanislavsky sat by the round table, facing the audience, attention divided between Chatsky, who was pacing the floor on his right, and Skalozub, who sat on the sofa at his left smoking a *chibouk*. He frowned at Chatsky in warning fashion after each phrase, as though asking him to stop talking. Then he turned to Skalozub with his most ingratiating smile, as though feeling sorry for Chatsky. The severe looks and ingratiating smiles grew more intense, and he changed from one to the other more and more frequently, until at the last words of Chatsky's monologue he began to mix them up so that Skalozub was receiving the threats and Chatsky the smiles. This so petrified Famusov that he vanished into the next room, from which he called:

Oh, dear, I see the dangers growing,
Sergey Sergeyevich, I'll be going.

Stanislavsky's Famusov kept the play moving in a briskly energetic rhythm. The critic Afros in his review of the first production of *Much Woe From Wisdom* accused Stanislavsky of over-burdening his part with studied characteristics. In 1925 there was no trace of this; on the contrary, he played with the lightness of a virtuoso. His intonations were most expressive and varied from one performance to another under the influence of the special circumstances of the particular performance.

His Famusov was a brilliant satire on the swaggering, rankly ignorant, narrow-minded, self-opinionated Moscow official. But his satire was so subtle, sharp and alive that it had both an historical and a realistic authenticity. All the characters in this 1925 production were permeated with this subtle, sharp satire.

It is difficult to judge how much Stanislavsky succeeded in correcting the defects of the first two productions of *Much Woe From Wisdom* and how much he succeeded in inspiring the old and new actors with his remarkable ideas on Griboyedov's comedy. But unquestionably this production played an important role in building the new young company of the Moscow Art Theatre. And, most important, it affirmed the idea of the play and its realistic truth— these two steadfast fundamentals of the Soviet Theatre.

VAUDEVILLE

CHAPTER THREE

LEV GURYTCH SINITCHKIN
BY D. Lensky

The plot of Lensky's old vaudeville is very simple. A Russian provincial town in the first half of the nineteenth century has a local theatre managed by one Pustoslavtzev (the word means "empty fame" in Russian). Lev Gurytch Sinitchkin has just made his début with this theatre as a guest artist in an important dramatic role. Sinitchkin has a young daughter, Lisa, whom he is preparing for the theatre. Lisa has looks and talent. Prince Vetrinsky, a rich landowner and a back-stage habitué of the theatre, falls in love with Lisa. Vetrinsky wants to take her to his Kharkov village, but Lisa doesn't love him and does not want to elope with him. The theatre is her only passion. Sinitchkin asks Pustoslavtzev to give Lisa her début in his theatre. But the manager isn't interested: he has a very useful prima donna, Surmilova, who is admired by the local patron of the arts, Count Zephirov, and, before Lisa's appearance, by Prince Vetrinsky also.

SYNOPSIS OF THE PLAY

At the dress rehearsal of a new play with songs and dances by the local dramatist Borzikov, Surmilova refuses to rehearse. She is in a bad mood, having quarreled with Vetrinsky. Sinitchkin decides to use this to his advantage. He sends Surmilova a letter Vetrinsky has written Lisa. In this note, which has no salutation, Vetrinsky had written: "Come at dusk to the city gates. I will wait for you there in my carriage. We will drive to my place at Rasgulyevo for dinner."

Surmilova pays no attention to the fact that the note is without a salutation and interprets it as an attempt on Vetrinsky's part to mend the quarrel. She maneuvers an hysterical scene on stage; then, after complaining of a migraine headache, leaves the dress rehearsal. She refuses to play the performance that night. This is what Sinitchkin has been waiting for. He suggests that Pustoslavtzev let Lisa play Surmilova's role that night. Lisa knows the part by heart. The manager hesitates to do this unless Sinitchkin can get Borzikov's consent. Sinitchkin and Lisa go to see Borzikov, who is very upset to think his play may not be performed that night. He agrees to hear Lisa read. Lisa and Sinitchkin play the main scene for him and Vetrinsky who drops in on the dramatist unexpectedly. In spite of Vetrinsky's objections, Borzikov is warmed by Lisa's fresh talent and gives his consent to her début that night. But no question is decided in Pustoslavtzev's theatre without Count Zephirov. Lisa, Sinitchkin, and Borzikov go to see him. Vetrinsky rushes to Surmilova to persuade her to play the part that night; he doesn't want Lisa to have this opportunity. Everyone gathers at Count Zephirov's apartment. The Count takes an immediate liking to Lisa and gives his consent to her début. But now Surmilova enters with Vetrinsky. She announces she will play tonight. Sinitchkin naïvely asks Surmilova if she isn't going to have dinner with the Prince. A quarrel flares between Zephirov and Vetrinsky. Zephirov reproaches Surmilova for being unfaithful. Surmilova faints. Under pretext of looking for smelling salts, Sinitchkin takes her reticule and finds the letter from Vetrinsky, which he then gives to Count Zephirov. The latter, enraged by this final proof of Surmilova's betrayal, leaves for the theatre to tell Pustoslavtzev of his consent to Lisa's début.

That night both actresses are there to play the role. Both put on make-up and costume for the part, but the shrewd Sinitchkin arranges it so that Vetrinsky, back-stage, looking out for Surmilova's interests, falls into the trap under the stage and Lisa makes her entrance first. Lisa has a tremendous success. The victory is hers. The young actress' sincerity of emotion, talent and genuine youth triumph over the machinations and intrigues of the fading prima donna.

TWO MONTHS before the beginning of the 1925 season it was decided that the Moscow Art Theatre would leave for a long tour to Kiev, Odessa, and Tbilisi (Tiflis), and that the young group that had entered the theatre in the fall of 1924 would not be included in this tour. Thus, our summer intermission would be at least three or four months, much too long a time for young actors to be without work. As usual, when faced with a dilemma, we went to Luzhsky for advice.

Luzhsky said to us: "Go on a summer tour of your own. Make a not too elaborate production of *Lev Gurytch Sinitchkin*, which is practically ready. Dramatize some of Gorky's short stories and use them as an evening of one acts, and take your successful production of *The Battle of Life*. We will give you the sets and costumes for it."

We accepted this good advice with joy. Kedrov, then a beginning actor and also an amateur designer, made light and witty sets for *Sinitchkin*. We dramatized the Gorky short stories, *Malva*, *Chelkash*, and *Strasty-Mordasty*. Through Luzhsky's help, we received written permission from Gorky at Capri to use his stories. In this way our young group had three productions in our repertoire by May, 1925. The Board of Directors of the Moscow Art Theatre gave us money for our traveling expenses and sent Butiugin as our advance man. So we toured the cities of the Volga region as a "grown-up" theatre.

The standards of their own theatres were fairly high in all these cities, and they had great respect for the Moscow Art Theatre, which they knew well from newspapers,

201

magazines, and personal visits to Moscow. Suddenly they saw a poster, which announced the young artists from the Moscow Art Theatre, but they didn't see any familiar names on the poster. We had to overcome a perfectly understandable distrust in every city we toured. As a rule, we played our first performances to a half-empty theatre, but at the end we played to sold-out houses. The best reviews were received by members of our company who in later years became famous members of the Moscow Art Theatre, such as Kedrov, Stepanova, Bendina, Orlov, and Blinnikov. A fine comradely discipline united us. We did all the work ourselves. We put up the sets, kept our costumes in order, took care of the make-up, and ran the performance. Our wonderful teachers, Stanislavsky and Nemirovich-Danchenko, had taught us from the very beginning how to be independent and how to carry the responsibility for ourselves and for the reputation of the theatre.

What Is Vaudeville?

In the fall of 1925 the season of the Moscow Art Theatre had begun. After giving Stanislavsky a report of our tour, we asked permission to show him our production of *Sinitchkin*, which had been most successful in our repertoire. He allowed us to show it at a closed matinée, saying, "One cannot play vaudeville without an audience."

Stanislavsky used to tell us: "The audience creates half the performance. Their acceptance of the play is like water to a flower: the seemingly hopeless spots in the play suddenly begin to bloom and the most mediocre talents shine. When the audience does not accept the performance, then neither the praises of friends nor occasional articles in the press nor the hymns of praise of those within the theatre itself will save it. They may postpone its demise, but it will never survive more than twenty or thirty performances. Now don't rush the opening night, but also don't over-rehearse. Don't strive to perfect the play to the point where neither actors nor director have anything more to add. The performance always lacks two or three days of additional work, but, if the conception is right and it is on the right road, one performance before an audience is equal to five rehearsals. The play ripens before an audience and reaches its full strength only after fifteen or twenty performances.

"On the other hand, when the performance is wrapped too warmly in the cotton of superfluous rehearsals and is pampered too much, it begins to wither, as it lacks the new food which can only be supplied by the audience."

We played *Sinitchkin* on the afternoon of October 13, 1925, before a full house that included Stanislavsky, Luzhsky, and a great number of the important actors of the Moscow Art Theatre. We received a fairly good response, although we were very nervous and did not give as good a performance as we had during the summer. After the performance, Stanislavsky told us: "A good production, well-played. It has daring and talent. Good fellows! I am very glad to have seen it, because now I feel so much better acquainted with many of you."

He addressed Orlov, who played the role of Borzikov, the writer, "You have a great deal of humor and a very good feeling for the character of your role." And to Stepanova, who played a middle-aged actress, he said, "I did not expect such a sharp characterization and such control from you." To Komissarov, "Your Count Vetrinsky is correctly conceived and played with real vaudeville ease. You, Bendina, are charming and graceful as Lisa. The whole performance is light and elegant. It shows much humor and inventiveness on the part of the director. I congratulate you all."

Then after a short pause he added: "I have a suggestion to make. Play *Sinitchkin* three or four times a month at closed matinées without benefit of publicity. Meanwhile, let's have some rehearsals on it. These rehearsals will solidify your performance, and then we will not be afraid to show your production under the aegis of the Moscow Art Theatre. Agreed?"

We were very happy to work with Stanislavsky and to play before an audience at the same time. Stanislavsky had played in many vaudevilles in his youth and was considered quite a connoisseur of this *genre*. We told him that it was more than agreeable for us to learn from him the secrets of this complicated form and, then, with his blessing, to present it to Moscow audiences.

"I probably know some of the 'secrets,' " Stanislavsky said, "because I have played much vaudeville and operetta and have seen even more. And as long as fate brought us together on this play, I would like to give you all I have learned during many years of acting and directing in vaudeville.

"Now what must you learn? Your understanding of what you are playing in *Sinitchkin* is not completely clear. You don't yet know what world of feelings you must live in while performing this type of play. I intentionally use the word 'world,' because vaudeville is a world of its own, inhabited by creatures whom one does not meet in comedy, drama, or tragedy. There is an accepted notion that vaudeville is a very special kind of symbolic form, and that, as a result, you should not be guided by the laws of logic and psychology in directing vaudeville. The world of vaudeville is a perfectly realistic one but the most unusual incidents occur in it every step of the way. The life in vaudeville flows according to all laws of logic and psychology, but it is constantly interrupted by the unexpected. Characters in vaudeville are ordinary and realistic. One should not consider them strange creatures. On the contrary, they are most ordinary people. Their only strangeness is their absolute credulity about everything. For example, if I fall on my knees and declare my love for you at this moment, Lisa, you must believe my love without a second's hesitation, and, if you like me and your heart is free, you are compelled right here and now to answer my love with your love. And no counts or dukes can ever part us.

"A good vaudeville is always democratic, the aristocrats serving as evil creatures. They're not worth much, nor are they either very rich or very aristocratic. But to distinguish them from the good characters they are made counts or princes or dukes.

"Another characteristic of vaudeville is its musicality. Does this necessarily imply that the actors playing in vaudeville must have perfect musical talent? Good musical qualities, such as a good ear, voice, and sense of rhythm, are useful to any actor, but, along with these qualities, all the actors in vaudeville must know how to love to sing and dance and, what is most important, they must love to do it. The vaudeville character lives in that special world where you express your thoughts and feelings not only in words and actions but also in dance and song. And the vaudeville dance and song are special. They have nothing to do with the dance and song of opera or even of operetta. In operetta one must have a very good singing voice and excellent skill in movement—*cascade* as the French call it, brilliant as a waterfall or fireworks. In vaudeville everything is a thousand times more modest than in operetta. But charm in a song or a dance is very necessary. I remember two excellent vaudeville actors, Varlamov and Davydov. Varlamov could not move too fast because of his weight, while Davydov could move but did not find it necessary. Var- lamov danced so well with the movement of a foot, toe, heel, or even a hand that I would exchange a first-rate American tap dancer for a few seconds of him. I grant the superiority of the American tap dancer in external bril- liance, technique, and masterly skill. But no one can outdo Varlamov, Davydov, or our other great Russian vaudeville performers for the charm of the dance as an inner urge to move—a dance of joy, using whatever they want: fingers, handkerchiefs, shoulders, or even some special dancing walk.

"In vaudeville the actor must love dancing and singing even if his voice is worth only three kopecks—'only for himself,' as the saying goes—and even if he's pigeon-toed. But when that Russian pigeon-toed girl danced as a gypsy in the vaudeville *Daughter of a Russian Actor* or as a *kazachok* or as a hussar, people wondered where she got such energy, temperament, and 'soul.' This is the artistic charm of the Russian actor which makes up for his lack of technique and appearance.

"Vaudeville is a modest, unpretentious genre in its plot and characters, but—as Lensky, the author of your vaude- ville, has Sinitchkin say—'it is full of soul and warmth.' "

The Secrets of the Genre

We looked forward to this rehearsal with Stanislavsky with much anticipation. Rumors spread through the theatre that either Stanislavsky would play some old vaudevilles for us during this rehearsal or he would play the part of Sinitchkin. Everybody in the theatre was plan- ning to visit our rehearsal and had anticipated the pleasure of seeing Stanislavsky in vaudeville. Luzhsky received a great number of requests for permission to attend. Luzhsky asked Stanislavsky, who answered, "No one is to be allowed at the rehearsal except Luzhsky and the actors in the play. The rehearsal will be held in the lobby of the little theatre. A small orchestra—a quartet—all the props, furniture, and costumes must be ready for the rehearsal."

Of course, all those who had planned to come to our rehearsal were envious, and the mysterious air that surrounded it made us even more excited.

Stanislavsky obviously was getting ready for the event. He summoned me to his house and ordered me to prepare as many props as I could possibly find.

"You must have no less than fifteen canes," he said to me, "ten ladies' umbrellas—preferably parasols—the same number of lorgnettes, handkerchiefs, envelopes with letters, snuffboxes, kid gloves, small bottles of smelling salts, bunches of flowers, ladies' scarfs, ladies' hats and hand bags, men's cloaks and top hats. Believe me, without all this rubbish it is very difficult to play vaudeville. Please ask Luzhsky and Alexandrov about the effects that might have been used for the Borzikov play in *Sinitchkin*. Ask them to prepare for our rehearsal a moon, a sun, a sea, thunder, lightning, clouds, an earthquake—so it will be done exactly the way it was during the last half of the nineteenth century. You have two acts that take place in a theatre. You must create the atmosphere of a provincial theatre of those days. Perhaps something of this atmosphere can be used by your actors for the justification of their characters."

And I could easily guess from seeing Stanislavsky's smile that in his imagination he already saw some of the moments at rehearsal and the style of acting.

Vladimir Sergeyevich Alexeyev (Stanislavsky's brother), who was a music expert, not only in opera but also for operetta and vaudeville, was present during our conversation. The year before, he had given us lessons in rhythm under Stanislavsky's supervision. Now Alexeyev was sitting before the open piano. In front of him were some threadbare music sheets. I suspected that the two brothers had been going over old vaudeville music. My suspicion made me linger as I put my coat on in the vestibule of his apartment, after I had said good-by to the two brothers—and, sure enough, in a few seconds I heard the voice of Stanislavsky singing a vaudeville tune, accompanied by his brother. I confess that I stayed on eavesdropping in the vestibule. I had never heard Stanislavsky sing before—and, what is more, in vaudeville. I forgot my disgraceful behavior, as I stood there in my coat, hat, and galoshes, glued to the door. Stanislavsky crooned with ease and grace, phrasing Lensky's couplets.

Then Stanislavsky talked about something with his brother. Suddenly I heard a whisper right next to me: "They have been playing and singing together the past two evenings." Frightened at being caught in such unbecoming behavior, I turned, only to feel more embarrassed to find that Lilina, Stanislavsky's wife, was joining me in eavesdropping.

"Now Kostya will probably sing Laverge's couplets. He sings them magnificently," Lilina informed me in the tone of an accomplice. She accepted my presence there by the door quite naturally. Before I had time to answer her, there was a chord on the piano in the drawing-room and then the soft voice of Stanislavsky came through, stressing the end of each line slightly and crooning the last verse in recitative. But he sang the refrain in full voice, enunciating the absurd words with perfect clarity.

And suddenly I heard a soft woman's voice answering with the same musical phrasing. I was afraid to stir, afraid I might stop Lilina, who was answering Laverge from behind the door, so modestly and so touchingly, without being either heard or seen by him.

Stanislavsky sang two more couplets, and twice again I
heard the words answered by Lilina at my side. Then I
was aware of being left alone by the door of the drawing-
room. I told no one of this touching duet, but it made me
understand Stanislavsky's words about the special world
that characters in vaudeville live in, when I saw with what
naïve credulity and adoration Katherine (Lilina) listened
to her sweetheart Laverge. I felt that she had instantly
entered that small French village of the vaudeville, where
the heart of the peasant servant was broken by the arrival
of the splendid barber, Laverge, from the city. How many
memories of their young theatrical years must have passed
through the minds of Stanislavsky, his brother, and Lilina,
his wife and leading lady. Operettas and vaudevilles were
in the repertoire of the Alexeyev Circle and the Society of
Art and Literature. These were amateur dramatic groups
from which many of the first actors of the Moscow Art
Theatre were selected. The Moscow Art Theatre itself developed from this serious amateur work of Stanislavsky's
youth.

Luzhsky and Alexandrov carried out all Stanislavsky's
suggestions. The Moscow Art Theatre workshops were
ordered to make a sea, consisting of ten waves tied by loose
ropes to the edges of the framed benches. These waves,
swinging in varied rhythm, were very effective. A very
large canvas of an indeterminate sea color was spread in
front of the "waves." The walk-ons and some of the stage
crew lay under the canvas; some were on their knees and
were moving in different directions (the canvas rested on
their heads and shoulders); they made the breakers on the
sea downstage. A flat surface of a boat was made behind the
last line of waves, and the bottom of it was divided in half
so that one could carry it on his head and "swim" with it
either by raising or lowering it in relation to the horizon.

The sun rising from behind the sea was done in the same fashion.

As a reward for all his wonderful preparations, Alexandrov was allowed to be present and even to take part in the extraordinary rehearsal.

The Extraordinary Rehearsal

At last the long-awaited time came. We all gathered at eleven o'clock in the large foyer of the little theatre. The furniture of all five acts of *Sinitchkin*, music stands and a piano for the quartet, the screens covered with canvas to indicate the scenery, props laid out on the tables, costumes spread on the chairs, and lighting apparatus jammed the large foyer and made it look like a scenic warehouse. We couldn't imagine how Stanislavsky could rehearse in such chaos. He arrived at five minutes of eleven with his brother and Luzhsky.

Alexandrov had been in the theatre since nine that morning and had checked with me all the objects that had been gathered from the four corners of the theatre.

"Is everyone here?" Stanislavsky asked. "Can we begin?"

"Everyone is here, but don't you think it's rather crowded?" Luzhsky replied.

Stanislavsky carefully observed the room. "What is going on in the two adjoining rooms while we are rehearsing?"

He pointed to the two large rooms we could see from the open door of the foyer.

"Nothing, Konstantin Sergeyevich." Luzhsky answered. "They are usually locked to keep out the noise from the corridor."

"Wonderful! Close the doors leading to the corridor. We are going to rehearse in the foyer and in these two rooms simultaneously."

This was our first surprise. Rehearse in three rooms simultaneously? How? Stanislavsky didn't give us much time to speculate.

He said to us, "All five acts will go on at the same time in these three rooms." Out of his pocket he took out a large sheet of paper that was covered with circles, lines, and arrows and made some corrections on it, evidently because of this change in our rehearsal space. "I suggest the following," he continued, examining his design carefully. "The room on the left will be occupied by Count Zephirov, and our fourth act will be played there too. The room on the right by Borzikov. Arrange it as his study, where he is supposed to create his immortal plays. Do you know what play Lensky was making fun of in your vaudeville?"

"I think *Peryanka*, or *Maiden of the Sun*," I replied.

Stanislavsky continued: "That's correct. Now you, Borzikov, sit by your table and write a new Peryanka. Sinitchkin and his daughter will visit you here with Count Vetrinsky. Meanwhile, arrange the place with the help of your servant. We will use the foyer for the scenes that take place on the stage. They need more room because of the scenery and the number of people that appear in them.

"Sinitchkin and Lisa, arrange two small rooms, one on our right and one on the left downstage. Your living-room will be in front of our director's table. Put one more table here and three bentwood chairs. You'll need nothing more.

"Orchestra, please use the further corner of the foyer. You can shut yourselves away from us with a screen. Alexeyev will be in your section. He will tell you when and what you are to play. He and I talked it over. Please, everyone take your places and begin."

Utter confusion reigned. Only the musicians and Alexeyev took their places, and Alexandrov went with them to put up the screens. The rest of us stayed where we were.

"What's the matter?" Stanislavsky asked. "Is something not clear?"

Of course, nothing was clear, but not one of us had the courage to say so. Luzhsky came to our rescue, as always. "It isn't quite clear, Konstantin Sergeyevich," he said, "whether all the actors speak their lines at the same time or not. It would be quite difficult for you to understand them, and I am afraid they will try to shout one another down."

Stanislavsky replied: "No one must raise his voice. We must speak in the register natural to the given circumstances and the size of the room. I'll be moving from one group to another, and I shall take part in the action of each group as a person who logically could be there. I will visit Count Zephirov, probably as his old friend Prince Amoursky. I will come exactly at the hour when his *poulardes* are there, and perhaps some beauty will fall for me. To Borzikov I will appear as a fledgling dramatist. As a professional courtesy this great playwright will not refuse to read my first effort for the stage. To Pustoslavtzev I will come as an actor looking for a job. I can meet Sinitchkin and Lisa any place. As far as Surmilova is concerned, I will try to court her, appearing as a guest artist from some operetta company invited to come to the amateur performance of the governor's wife. I want you all to begin your lives in every corner of this foyer and the two adjoining rooms from the morning of that crazy day: get up, dress, have your coffee, and begin your day!

"Zephirov in his apartment, Surmilova and Borzikov each in his corner; Chakhotkin, prompter and tragedian, is just getting up from a drunken night spent on the sofas of the theatre . . ."

"Konstantin Sergeyevich, I don't have a tragedian in my company," Pustoslavtzev interrupted him.

"In those days it was inconceivable for an acting company to be without a tragedian," Stanislavsky answered. "Yours probably is drunk somewhere, and you may have to hire another temporarily."

Stanislavsky smiled slyly at this.

"Mitka and the assistant director will come this morning to the theatre to put up the sets. They will be followed by Pustoslavtzev. For some reason Vetrinsky comes very early to Sinitchkin's and Lisa's house. I would like to see the morning of the vaudeville in every spot of this foyer. I can very easily manage to observe all of you, and it seems to me that each one can relax so much better if he does not have the director's eye on him all the time."

Luzhsky broke in: "In other words, Konstantin Sergeyevich, you want them to play one big étude on the circumstances and situations of this play. Did I understand you correctly?"

"Perfectly," Stanislavsky replied. "This is an étude on a familiar plot with familiar characters. You can use the thoughts and lines of your parts if you feel the need and if they fit beats of the étude.

"But the morning begins for Lisa and Vetrinsky with the text of the play. The étude will be much easier for them. I would like to hear not only the author's lines but also the characters' thoughts spoken aloud."

"What do you want the musicians to do?" I asked.

"Let them be the musicians of Pustoslavtzev's theatre," Stanislavsky answered. "They have also come onto the stage for rehearsal. But the conductor hasn't arrived, so they are tuning their instruments. At one time the violinist scrapes something from the overture of Borzikov's play, but most of the time he is occupied in finishing off one bottle after another and alternating this with eating pickles."

"But, Konstantin Sergeyevich, our musicians are not actors. They may not know how to play the scene," Luzhsky said.

"Well, let them do the best they can. It is very important that everybody in this étude be a part of it. No onlookers please. I myself will be a part of the étude. I will ask you —Luzhsky, Alexandrov, and Gorchakov—to find places for yourselves and an occupation in our étude. Then we will all feel perfectly free. We will be completely immersed in the world of this vaudeville and its people. We will be filled with their interests, sorrows, and joys. This is the only possible way to find the scenic atmosphere of this genre, which is so foreign to most of you."

Luzhsky answered: "Is it all right for me to play the part of Knurov, a character from Ostrovsky's play, *The Dowerless Bride*? I will begin my part with a stroll through the streets of the town. Then I'll drop in to visit Surmilova; then I'll go to the theatre to watch the rehearsal for a few minutes. I think that this is how Knurov spends the first part of the day."

"Brilliant idea!" Stanislavsky said. "Go ahead. Gorchakov I would suggest that you play the part of a reporter on a small local newspaper."

I answered, "I will run from place to place, covering whatever is going on and will try . . ."

Stanislavsky interrupted, giving me a wink: "You will write down all you see. Do that without fail. Also, have an interview with each character; it will help the actors widen their conception of their parts."

I understood that Stanislavsky wanted to have a detailed record of this étude and had quickly thought of this way for me to record it without anyone in the étude knowing what I was doing.

Alexandrov spoke from the corner of the foyer where all the props were gathered: "And I've got myself a job as a prop man in Pustoslavtzev's theatre. I am already at work."

Alexandrov was sitting on a bench gluing together the parts of a prop sun. He gave us the sense of an old actor who had seen better days and now found himself reduced to the position of prop man. He achieved this effect by an imperceptible quality in his voice as he answered Stanislavsky and by the light movement with which he messed up his hair and pushed his glasses to the edge of his nose. He put all his love for the theatre even into this occupation though. His stage charm and his promptness and ease in responding to Stanislavsky's suggestion immediately influenced us to accept the reality and practicality of what Stanislavsky had asked us to do.

The actors went quickly to their places and put on their vaudeville costumes. So the rehearsal—if it could be called such—of this day of our life with Stanislavsky in the world of vaudeville began.

Count Zephirov arranged a very luxurious study-boudoir in the room to the right of the foyer with the help of his servant and attended to his morning toilette with the thoroughness of an eighteenth-century marquis.

Borzikov, the writer, laid out clean sheets of paper in various places in the room to the left of the foyer: on his writing table, on stools, on some kind of bureau. He even tacked up some of the sheets on the wall, and some were scattered on the floor. He moved from one place to another in his dilapidated house robe and slippers, unwashed and uncombed, with a goose quill in his hand. His servant, Simeon, followed him with the inkwell. Obviously Orlov, who played the part, had decided that Borzikov was incapable of writing his play in any order, but, like a chess player who demonstrates the game simultaneously on twelve boards, he was inspired by running from one sheet of paper to another, writing a word here, a sentence there.

now in a fit of dissatisfaction tearing up into shreds part of his great creation. The result was amusing, and it suddenly explained the fantastic illogical contrivances of Borzikov's plays.

The chorus girls, walk-ons, stage crew, and the assistant director, Nalimov, wrapped themselves in shawls and fur coats (a wonderful period touch because any stage in those days was very cold even in summer) while waiting for the rehearsal. They settled cozily among the sets and props and began a card game. Surmilova sat in front of her letter basket in morning negligée. Sighing, she read and reread her letters. She lit the candle and burned some of them with a tragic smile—a pastime worthy of a fading prima donna. Sinitchkin snored on an old sofa in his room, refusing to burden himself with any thought whatsoever. Lisa in a modest house robe sat in front of the mirror in her tiny room and zealously twisted her hair on curl papers. Count Vetrinsky was having a shave in the barber shop. Pustoslavtzev was strolling with Knurov (Luzhsky) and was trying to interest him in his theatre. All these episodes of the étude were going on simultaneously and had been going on for a few minutes when Stanislavsky got up and entered the scene.

With a very serious but somehow servile manner, he greeted Pustoslavtzev and Knurov. The two men answered his greeting casually and passed him. They continued their stroll, talking to each other. Stanislavsky remained on the spot waiting for them to pass him again. He had on a wide-brimmed felt hat and held a dark piece of cloth over his arm. Of course, all the actors started to watch him out of the corner of their eyes. Pustoslavtzev and Knurov realized that they were about to take part in a scene which Stanislavsky had planned. And, sure enough, he greeted them again in a more servile manner, bending low so that his hat touched the ground. Knurov and Pustoslavtzev stopped for a second, looked at the bending figure, and then looked at each other, puzzled, as though saying, "What does this fellow want of us?" But again they went on their way. At that moment, Stanislavsky made the ugliest possible grimace in their direction, then wrapped himself in the piece of cloth as though in a cloak, pushed his hat to a jaunty angle, crossed his arms on his breast, straightened himself proudly, and declaimed in a thunderous bass voice: "Even in rags, goodness is respected."

That voice naturally forced the two men to stop. "What are you up to, my good fellow?" one of them said.

" 'Those born to crawl, will never fly,' " Stanislavsky spoke a completely unexpected line from Gorky with the same thunderous voice.

"Nobody forces you to fly, my good fellow," Pustoslavtzev answered him, true to his character. "Why do you howl on the street?"

"I intend to enter your company, Master," his answer followed.

The theme of this meeting immediately became clear to the participants and to the rest of us, who, of course, from that moment on forgot about our individual episodes. The following scene developed:

Pustoslavtzev began, "Who do you think you are, trying to enter my company!"

Stanislavsky said mysteriously and ominously, "Haven't you learned to recognize the beast by his walk?"

Pustoslavtzev exchanged glances with Knurov. "Upon my soul, I don't recognize him, my good fellow."

Stanislavsky became even more gloomy and ominous, but spoke in a natural tone, "I am a tragedian."

Pustoslavtzev and Knurov said at the same time, "Oh, that's what you are."

Stanislavsky answered, "Does the name of Goremyslova-Gromoboeva mean nothing to you?" (This name is derived from two Russian words, meaning, respectively, "sorrowful thought" and "thunderous battle.")

Pustoslavtzev exchanged looks with Knurov, as though to say, "Oh that notorious drunkard." Then he continued: "It does mean something to us, but I'm not in need of a new tragedian. I have enough of my own."

Stanislavsky answered in a powerful bass voice: "Those in your company are not tragedians. They are squeakers. However, do you need any other actors?"

"We need a good comic, old man," Knurov replied. "We need a buffoon, so that people can laugh and relax in the theatre. Our ears are ringing from your tragic howlings. We are hungry for a good vaudeville, like those in Moscow. But we don't have a good vaudeville comic. That's how it is."

Pustoslavtzev said: "Upon my soul, it's true. I need a comic who can sing. I don't need you, old chap."

Before our eyes Stanislavsky changed from the tragedian to Laverge the barber, and, after giving Alexeyev a signal, he began to sing.

He repeated the verse twice to everyone's amazement. All the while he was making eyes at the chorus girls in a most comical manner. He stood on tiptoe and gesticulated with imaginary scissors. Then suddenly he stopped singing and addressed Pustoslavtzev: "May I depend upon an engagement?"

Pustoslavtzev answered in genuine amazement: "How do you do it, old man? One minute a tragedian and the next a singer of verses?"

Stanislavsky said: "A despicable comic can never rise above himself. But a genuine tragedian remains an artist even in vaudeville. If you please, my advance . . ."

Pustoslavtzev replied: "Well, it looks as if we can't help but engage him. You've caught me, old man. Take it."

He tossed him a three rouble note, which Stanislavsky took and scornfully twisted in his fingers to test its genuineness.

Knurov said, "Here's some from me, old man." He gave him a five rouble note. "And whenever you are free, drop in, old fellow. I'll treat you to a meal."

Stanislavsky bowed low: "Flattered, sir. Satisfied, sir. Now I'm on my way to the Temple Talin."

Stanislavsky made his way to the group of walk-ons— and the rest of us continued our études, but, of course, we still watched him stealthily.

Count Vetrinsky found it necessary to drop in at the theatre before his visit to Sinitchkin and his daughter in order to be closer to Stanislavsky, or rather to join the étude which Stanislavsky was about to begin.

Stanislavsky greeted the new company and somberly introduced himself. Then he stopped in front of a chess table, where the leading man, Chakhotkin, was playing with the director, Nalimov. The following scene developed:

Vetrinsky started, "Tell me, my lass, has last night's 'debutante' arrived yet?'

Various of the chorus girls spoke up: "Ah, Count Vetrinsky! Good morning, Count. Nobody has come to the theatre yet. Which 'debutante' are you looking for?"

"I must see Sinitchkin."

"Ah, Sinitchkin," the chorus girls said. "What attracts you about him? Is it Lisa by any chance?"

Stanislavsky approached Vetrinsky, "Are you looking for trouble, sir?"

"What's that?" Vetrinsky exclaimed.

Stanislavsky continued: "I would not advise your honor to cast your eye on a *jeune fille*. Our theatre charmers are simpler and with their talent outdo any virgin. Come on, my lasses, let us show the count that we are as good as any stars from the city, or even European stars. Sit here, Count. In a minute we will transport you with us to the birthplace of Cervantes in tropical Spain."

With these words Stanislavsky ended his role as a tragedian.

The Language of Objects

"Will you please take hats and cloaks," he addressed the actors, "canes, and ladies' fans, especially those of you who are in Borzikov's play *Alonzo in Peru*?

"In vaudeville and operetta, actors come across characters from all over the world. A discharged Russian soldier, a savage from the island of Turlipatan and a pirate named Surkuf and a Prince Moraskin, every kind of dancing girl and official—all these types should be equally interesting and important to an actor. He must believe in their existence with the naïveté of a child and treat them as living human beings. The whole world of vaudeville must become an actual reality.

"Now objects in vaudeville have their own language. An actor should be able to say as much with an object as with words. For example, take the light walking stick of the hero-lover in vaudeville. In the hands of a good vaudeville actor, it will reveal everything about its owner. Now he is gay and sure of himself, hurrying to a rendezvous. His walking stick skips along next to him."

Stanislavsky takes the first walking stick he sees and with extraordinary grace walks across the foyer. He hums and purrs some melody to himself, then whistles, and the walking stick literally lives, telling the thoughts and the state of being of its owner. Now it runs, hurries, and skips along with Stanislavsky. Suddenly it stops by itself, seeming to check the movement of his body. He stands still. And the walking stick in his hand tells us its owner is puzzled.

Which is his sweetheart's window? The walking stick strolls from one imaginary window to another and hesitates. Should it knock at one of them? It seems afraid of something. (Probably papa or mama.) It meditates and finally makes up its mind and quickly knocks at one of the windows. Instantly it hides behind Stanislavsky's back, and he pretends he is just passing by and has stopped to read a poster on the lamppost. Now the walking stick carefully peeks out from behind his back, "There she is!" His beloved appears at the window. The walking stick joins its master in greeting the lady. The conversation continues. The walking stick asks, "Is anybody else at home?" The answer is positive, "Nobody!" And the walking stick joyfully dances in his hand. It twists about in his fingers and starts ahead toward his beloved. But on the threshold of the house its master suddenly stops short and looks carefully up the street. "Oh, the devil take it!" The walking stick worries: "Something must be wrong! Could it be papa returning early? Most likely that is it."

Suddenly, in a fit of despair, the strong fingers of Stanislavsky break the stick in two. For a second, the broken parts are still living and quivering in his hands.

We anticipate that, following the clichés of the stage, he will angrily throw them away. But Stanislavsky surprised us again. He shoves the broken pieces in the pockets of his coat and proudly walks by the imaginary father with the symbol of his broken heart in his pocket. The parts of the broken cane stick out pathetically, but the steps of its owner are firm and energetic. And after he takes a few steps he is whistling and humming to himself again. A vaudeville hero never gives up. There will be a new cane, a new rendezvous, and a new beauty to captivate his heart. Meanwhile, forward! always forward! life is so wonderful!

Completely forgetting all about our étude, we surrounded Stanislavsky and asked him if we understood his pantomime correctly. Each one gave him a different version, but each used the same plot. Stanislavsky confirmed our interpretation and suggested that we do similar improvisations while we were still hot on the scent.

"Let the men use their canes and the ladies their parasols and fans."

Then he showed us how one should talk with a fan. The fan quivered in his hand like the wings of a wounded bird, revealing his excitement. Stanislavsky's figure, face, and half-closed eyes were seemingly calm. Only the movement of his hand and a slight trembling of the closed fan showed his inner excitement. Then the fan opened with a sharp impulsive movement, flying up and hiding his face for an instant, and just as suddenly it lowered and closed. We understood that in this brief moment the face hidden by the fan had time to give vent to feeling and time for a deep sigh or a short laugh. And it was possible that the hand lightly brushed away a tear with the aid of the fan. Then the fan, with a scarcely noticeable movement, ordered someone supposedly nearby to come closer and sit next to him. The fan stopped trembling. It opened calmly and began to sway softly in his hand as though listening attentively to the person sitting next to him. Then the fan smiled and even laughed. (We swore to him later that that's exactly what we heard.) The fan clossed again for a second and lightly struck the hand of the person next to him, as though saying, "Oh, you are mean!"—and then suddenly covered the blushing face. Now his eyes entered the conversation. First, they sparkled from under the lace-edged fan; then they looked over the fan and half hid behind it.

Only those who have seen Stanislavsky's eyes—full of an extraordinary brilliance, now laughing, now sad, capable of expressing the heart's subtlest emotion—can visualize this marvelous étude-improvisation. For the next two hours he made us all do a number of études with many other vaudeville objects. Stanislavsky used his brilliant illustrations of the language of objects not only to stimulate our desire to do these improvisations, but also to reveal the naïveté of approach to objects and relationships which is necessary for actors in vaudeville.

Stanislavsky later continued: "A letter in vaudeville can be just as much of a character as the rest of the cast. It is not simply a piece of paper given to the actor by the prop man according to the author's direction. In your direction of this vaudeville Sinitchkin takes a piece of paper from Lisa's room as though it were a letter from Vetrinsky to Lisa. The author's stage direction treats this differently.

"A famous master of vaudeville techniques such as Lensky certainly knows better than you the law of an object's life in vaudeville. He makes Sinitchkin bring from Lisa's room a copy book in which Vetrinsky had written a few words to Lisa with no salutation. That is why Vetrinsky's message which has no salutation is not a letter but merely a few lines written in the copy book. And Sinitchkin's first impulse is to destroy them. He tears the sheet out. If it were a letter, he wouldn't be able to realize this typical reaction of an indignant father. If he had torn and crumpled a letter of Vetrinsky's, he wouldn't have been able to send it to Surmilova. Now see what happens. By tearing the sheet from the copy book, Sinitchkin gives vent to his emotion and, then, holding it for a few seconds in his hand, he suddenly sees it not as a sheet of paper but as a letter. You have an accidental move here, but one perfectly natural within the father's relationship to his daughter, a move that always will serve to bring the mainspring of the play alive before the audience—a fake letter from Vetrinsky to Surmilova is concocted. It is not by chance that we see Sinitchkin first with a large object, a copy book, then with a sheet of paper with Vetrinsky's handwriting on it, and finally with a second sheet torn from the same copy book, from which Sinitchkin makes an envelope. Sinitchkin writes on the envelope, because he is afraid to forge Vetrinsky's handwriting on the letter itself. He takes for granted that Surmilova will not pay too much attention to the handwriting on the envelope. The author has worked out all this for a definite purpose—to attract the audience's attention to the letter. Now the audience will look for this letter in each act.

"You treated this letter negligently, not attributing to it its function as a mainspring of the play's action. Think how this letter 'lives' later—what a furor it creates in the second act in the theatre during the rehearsal, and how it passes from hand to hand in the fourth act, in the Count's apartment when Surmilova faints. This is an interesting scene in which the life of an object calls forth a chain of new actions and relationships between the characters.

"In vaudeville one can always find an object which plays a leading role. Sometimes the title of the vaudeville is taken from it. Remember *The Bewitched Omelet*? During thirty minutes of the action, everyone wants to eat this omelet but cannot. Something stops each one. If it were not for the omelet, there would be no vaudeville. The naïveté of the vaudeville consists in just this: all the adjustments, relationships, and emotions—love, friendship, hatred—center around the desire to eat the ill-fated omelet, and no one can eat it until the complications are resolved. One must believe most sincerely in the contrived complications, for only then will he have the naïveté and credulity which is absolutely necessary for vaudeville.

"Not only the main object must live. In this play, *Lev Gurytch Sinitchkin*, the copy of Borzikov's play is another object of great importance. Sinitchkin tries to get hold of it just as passionately as Vetrinsky seeks to kidnap Lisa and bring her to his estate, just as passionately as Pustoslavtzev craves for big box-office receipts or Borzikov for glory."

Life in the Image

The time was flying fast. Around two o'clock that afternoon Luzhsky mentioned the intermission.

"We cannot lose time," Stanislavsky said. "Let's try to include lunch in the flow of the characters' day. Pustoslavtzev has a buffet in his theatre, so let's have a small buffet in this corner where his company has settled down. They will have their lunch there. I will come to Count Zephirov's for lunch, and I am sure that, as one of the city's élite, Knurov is cordially invited to join us. Sinitchkin and Lisa will have yesterday's borscht for lunch, or they may send out to the tavern for it, providing that Vetrinsky offers to pay. Of course, Vetrinsky will lunch with them. Surmilova may invite Borzikov for lunch. This would be typical of such a prima donna. She lacks a few effective, showy lines for her part, so she decides to bribe Borzikov over lunch to write these added lines for her."

Luzhsky interrupted: "Konstantin Sergeyevich, the orchestra is not a part of the vaudeville. Can they go to a real buffet for their lunch or must they too eat here?"

Stanislavsky answered seriously: "The orchestra belongs to Pustoslavtzev's theatre today, and they must eat at his buffet. Prepare bologna, pickles, and dark bread. There will be enough for everyone."

Alas, our real buffet did not have the food that Stanislavsky described so appetizingly and which was in keeping with the period of the vaudeville! Of course, we didn't tell him this. He was completely in the artistic fantasy he had created. At that moment, he was a remarkable example of how an actor must believe in the given circumstances. In this way Stanislavsky turned the simplest moment of life into an interesting exercise. It was very amusing to see the waitresses of the Moscow Art Theatre buffet pulled into our game-rehearsal.

"Quench my thirst, my beauty!" Chakhotkin, the hero-lover, addressed one of the girls pompously, holding up his glass for her to fill with tea. In the beginning the waitresses laughed with embarrassment, but later, seeing everyone around them serious, they involuntarily began to fall in with the rest. I remember a very appropriate answer the head waitress gave Chakhotkin when he asked for cold tea. Understanding perfectly what he meant by cold tea (it is an expression used in Ostrovsky's plays), she answered: "Go to the bar for cold tea. For your information, you are not in a saloon but a theatre."

Stanislavsky did not demand elaborate dialogue from us, but he was strict to observe our true evaluation of the atmosphere and our relationships to each other. Stanislavsky again began his lunch at Zephirov's table as the tragedian. He immediately pointed out to Mordvinov (who played Zephirov) that the latter treated him with too much respect during the luncheon. "You forget that you are a Count, while I am only a poor actor you are treating to lunch."

Zephirov replied in character: "Enough, enough, my good fellow. Your stomach is filled. Go with God's blessing."

The contented Stanislavsky bowed exaggeratedly to the Count and began to go from one étude to another with his plate and fork under his arm. By now, the actors understood this étude and had adjusted themselves accordingly.

Surmilova and Borzikov met him kindly but did not invite him to their table. They put a mug of beer for him on a little stand by the window.

"Have you a good voice, master-tragedian?" Borzikov

asked him. "Or do you only know how to shake your head so as to frighten the audience?"

"I wish you were dead, miserable creature!" Stanislavsky bellowed in a thunderous bass.

"Are you by any chance a deacon?" Surmilova asked him.

"I am a bell ringer from Nizhni-Novgorod," he answered perfectly seriously, and the conversation continued in the same vein for a few minutes more.

Stanislavsky finished his luncheon tour at Sinitchkin's house. "Gorich, my oldest friend, good afternoon to you!"

He entered Sinitchkin's room with his arms wide open.

Sinitchkin responded: "Gromoboev, my bosom friend, where have you come from? My brother!"

The two fell into each other's arms and began to kiss according to the custom of the time.

"Who is that? Diana? Thalia? Venus?" Stanislavsky exclaimed, staring at Lisa.

"You don't recognize the child you played with in her cradle?" Sinitchkin pompously declaimed.

"It is she! She! Come to my arms, beautiful child!" Stanislavsky kept up with him.

"Embrace him, Lisa, on his bosom. You will find asylum from storms and misery," Sinitchkin said. "He is my true, my oldest friend," he improvised.

Lisa shyly greeted Stanislavsky, who was looking her up and down admiringly. Suddenly he addressed her with lines from the play:

Oh you tender daughter of a criminal father,
Weak support for an unhappy . . .

Vetrinsky finished the verse, "fool!"

Stanislavsky picked up the challenge immediately. "And who is that?" he asked, pointing to Vetrinsky and scowling.

Sinitchkin replied: "He claims to be an actor from Kharkov. He wants to engage Lisa."

Stanislavsky said: "Engage . . . ? Kharkov . . . ? Never! Our daughter will see her first footlights in Moscow. Only Moscow is worthy to contemplate this diamond."

Sinitchkin said doubtfully: "But, my friend, they have their own diamonds there . . ."

Stanislavsky interrupted him: "Paste! Artificial chips!"

Vetrinsky entered the argument: "You are mistaken, old man. This young lady will not be given a chance in Moscow. If she is to build her career, she should start in small theatres. Some of our landowners in Kharkov have fine theatres. I can take Lisa to a friend of mine, Count Vetrinsky, who has an excellent *corps de ballet*."

Lisa replied indignantly, "I in the *corps de ballet*?"

Stanislavsky said, "This virgin in a *corps de ballet*?"

He signaled to the orchestra and there commenced that charming musical accompaniment which is so much an integral part of Russian vaudeville.

The Art of the Couplet

After two measures of the musical introduction, during which he assumed the pose of Lisa's firm guardian, Stanislavsky spoke his last line of prose to the music.

"Are you aware, gentlemen, of what talent is here?"

And, with musical precision, he began the first words of the couplet:

> She is above Malatkovsky.
> To her, if I am allowed to say,
> Not the Kharkov theatre, but Moscow,
> Fate promises to adorn her way.

Stanislavsky pronounced these lines with perfect rhythm, a naïve belief, and a serious, proud paternal feeling for

Lisa. He sang the ending of the first three lines softly, and then sang the fourth line of the verse in a brilliant full voice.

We were so impressed that we burst into applause, completely forgetting our characters and études. But the applause did not stop Stanislavsky, nor did it cause him to come out of character. With imperturbable seriousness and even more power and feeling, he still followed the rhythm and melody of the simple tune as he pronounced the following verse:

> She just has to learn!
> I will answer for it myself.
> On the stage she will shine
> No less than Repina herself.

And he expressed in four short lines the image of an old man, a failure on the stage and in life, who adored this young girl, believed unquestionably in her talent, and foresaw her fate. Then he signaled to Lisa and Sinitchkin, "Now let's sing together." He gave the orchestra a sign, "Next number!"

This was a duet between Lisa and her father. Carried away by Stanislavsky's example, Lisa (Bendina) sang the first lines with a touching grace:

> The theatre is my father.
> The theatre is my mother.
> The theatre is my destination.

Sinitchkin joined her more timidly:

> Oh, if I'm allowed to say
> My child, my creation!

Stanislavsky corrected him immediately by using the repetition of the verse, singing with enthusiasm and feeling:

Oh, if I'm allowed to say
My child, my creation!

His voice trembled with tears, and on the next line Sinitchkin, inspired by him, sang with true pathos:

Sacred fire in your heart . . .

Then Vetrinsky began to sing:

Oh, old clown! How funny you are!

Stanislavsky interrupted him: "This cue is an aside, and, although it is set to music, you should not sing it. You must give the line in the rhythm of the melody but say and speak it as in drama, revealing your relationship to the words without emotion. Use the technique of the aside."

Stanislavsky asked Sinitchkin to repeat his line, "Sacred fire in your heart," and he did exactly that—threw aside Vetrinsky's line with a striking lightness and an amusing expression on his face. (Oh, old clown, how funny you are!) Then he sang with Sinitchkin.

At this moment, when all of us were expecting the final line to be sung with full voice, Stanislavsky abruptly stopped singing and said to Lisa in a prosaic tone, "Give me a handkerchief." Then, suddenly without losing a measure of the melody he sang *fortissimo*, "From the chest of drawers." This is how Lensky had indicated it should be done in his script. The effect was stunning. During one short musical number Stanislavsky had used several ways of delivering the vaudeville verse: recitative; a melodic, light singing of the line; then, singing only the last words of the line; then, a simple realistic speech arranged to music; and, finally, singing with a full voice.

Right there and then he made all of us talk and sing our vaudeville numbers. With his inexhaustible inventiveness, he divided us into three groups, appointing Luzhsky as head of the first, Alexeyev of the second, and himself of

the third. Each group was given half an hour to prepare
their couplets, duets, and chorus numbers for a competi-
tion. Before the contest began, Stanislavsky said: "The art
of true vaudeville singing is very difficult. The vaudeville
tune has no independent musical value. It must be easily
understood and instantly remembered by the audience.
Therefore, its musical phrasing must be graceful, rhyth-
mic, and uncomplicated. As soon as the audience catches
the music, it immediately transfers its attention to the
words. The actor must have irreproachable diction; his inflections must be rich and precise, and must express his
relation clearly to the content. A real singing voice is not
absolutely necessary, but a musical sense of the rhythm and
the measure, a true ear, and elasticity of voice are necessary.
His ear must be sensitive to all the nuances of sound, from
piano to *fortissimo*. He must feel the meaning and the
phonetics of every word in the verses.

"One can learn all this only by constant practice in singing softly and crooning the verses, and of course always
coordinating them with the laws of the logic of inner action that give rise to true feeling in the actor. The couplet
should never be without 'soul.' Couplets almost always
serve as the culminating point of the scene. That is why
they usually contain the strongest acting problems and
must be filled with emphasis and sincere feeling. Those
who think that vaudeville couplets are an entertaining
diversion from the main action are mistaken. A couplet is
usually combined with a dance. But the dance in vaudeville is a light, charming movement supplementing and
stressing the rhythm and music. Sometimes the dance
gives an actor the opportunity to stress some characteristic.
Dance in vaudeville has nothing of the 'can-can' quality
that it has in Offenbach's operettas. Dance in vaudeville is
as naïve, restrained, and chaste as vaudeville itself."

Stanislavsky said to me: "I strongly advise you never to

separate the singing and dancing from the inner action.
The plot of the vaudeville must subtly merge in the couplet and the couplet in the dance. Because of this, an actor
must make his prose flow into the verse and the realistic
movement into the plastic: music, dance, words, acting,
and feeling in vaudeville must merge in one. This is the
beauty of the *genre* and at the same time its difficulty. I
think working on a vaudeville is very important for the
actor's development. In vaudeville he trains all his most
important skills: belief in the plot no matter how naïve
it may be, building a character (most of the characters in
vaudeville are strongly defined with very definite characteristics), continuous inner action, sincerity, and basic feeling. The great Russian actors Shchepkin, Martynov,
Davydov, and Varlamov were brought up on vaudeville.
Vaudeville taught them clarity of diction, versatility of
inflection, rhythm and elasticity of speech, sincerity, simplicity, and naïveté of feeling."

The Soul of Vaudeville

Stanislavsky stopped and looked at us. Then he said, as
though summing up today's extraordinary rehearsal: "The
true old-fashioned vaudeville always gives off a warm human feeling, because it tells you in its own language about
the suffering and joy of ordinary people. Vaudeville is
always realistic in spite of its music, song, and dance. The
latter is its poetry, but not its 'specialty,' as stage stylists
of theatre art used to insist not so long ago. They were
concerned in preserving only the form, and they deliberately forgot that vaudeville has a 'soul,' an inner essence.
The 'soul' of vaudeville is its truthfulness to life. Let us
agree that vaudeville reflects life minutely like a drop of
water—but life, not theatrical mannerisms of acting and
directing. Let the captious French critic-academicians re-

gard the charming songs of Béranger as less than the pompous Corneille and Racine. For me there is more life and truth in one simple song of Béranger than in a complete volume of a pompous French classic. The seed of any role in vaudeville lies very close to the thought and feeling with which Béranger composed. Vaudeville was born among ordinary people at fairs and markets. The people's interests are dear and close to it as they are to the songs of Béranger. The slight element of satire in many vaudevilles, including your *Sinitchkin*, springs from this. The satiric element is not strong, of course, but it spices vaudeville and gives it at times a contemporary aspect.

"You see what a difficult *genre* it is? Truthfulness to life, sincerity of emotions, a realistic approach with at times a touch of satire, grace and poetry, rhythm and a sense of music—all these elements must be in your performance. Let us now put into practice all that I have been talking about. Search for these qualities, and work to develop them. Vaudeville is a magnificent school for the young actor."

Evening was approaching, but Stanislavsky worked tirelessly with us on the dances, songs, and individual scenes of the vaudeville. His imagination was inexhaustible in discovering devices, means of expression. The bargaining scene between Sinitchkin and Pustoslavtzev, as they established the conditions under which Lisa should work in the latter's theatre, is laid backstage. Stanislavsky suggested that both actors play it squatting behind the last line of waves of the pasteboard sea. Both must do duty as prop men as well as actors. He suggested putting the prop sun on Sinitchkin's head (he will raise it as the cue comes for this in the middle of their bargaining) and the boat that sails on the horizon directly over Pustoslavtzev's head.

Some of the comic effects took a most unexpected turn. Excited by the bargaining, the "sun" and the "boat" forgot their function, to the horror of the rest of the cast. At one moment the two rose to their full height, revealing themselves among the waves and using the most inappropriate movements for the sun and the boat (especially when they brought out a bottle to celebrate the signing of the contract).

Stanislavsky told the *corps de ballet* to return after their entrances and manipulate the waves. They had little time between entrances and exits, so several comic incidents occurred when they rushed to push the waves. All this gave an authentic picture of backstage life at Pustoslavtzev's theatre.

Besides these backstage activities, there was also the natural effect of Vetrinsky falling down the trap. Stanislavsky brought into action all the theatrical mechanisms usually hidden from the audience. The scene between Lisa and Sinitchkin, in which she leaves the stage for a few minutes to change into her costume, was unusually effective. He told Lisa to put the costume on right there on stage and told Sinitchkin to help her. A charming scene was evolved: Sinitchkin bustling about his daughter like an old loving nanny—adjusting her wig and false braids, correcting her make-up, adorning her head with a diadem of paste jewelry, and all the while trying to give her courage to face the audience.

As we worked on these scenes, we came to understand the importance of a correct and talented expressiveness which had the power of an interesting physical action organically tied to an inner action and the actor's problem and which was not artificially invented by either actor or director.

Stanislavsky did not remain at the director's table but participated constantly as an actor, now in one scene and then in another, very often playing different parts to show how they must be approached and treated. For me as a director this rehearsal served as an object lesson in the stimulation and influence upon the young actor of a director's personal participation in the rehearsal.

Stanislavsky gave us two more rehearsals on *Sinitchkin*, but he could not finish the production, as he was needed for the play at the Bolshoi Theatre. We played *Lev Gurytch Sinitchkin* a few more times at special matinées and then postponed the opening until the following summer, when we played it on our second tour for the Moscow Art Theatre.

A MODERN FRENCH SATIRE

CHAPTER FOUR

MERCHANTS OF GLORY

BY Marcel Pagnol WITH Paul Nivoix

The scene is set during World War I, in a provincial small town in France. The play is about the family of M. Bashelet, a petty employee in the municipal office. M. Bashelet's son, Henri, is at the front. The mother and father, Henri's young wife, Germaine, and Bashelet's goddaughter, Yvonne, are constantly worried about him. M. Bashelet is in charge of the meat supply for the army. A speculator, M. Berlureau, suggests to M. Bashelet that he disclose to him the price of meat set by the municipal government for the forthcoming closed sales. But M. Bashelet is an honest man. He throws M. Berlureau out of his house for this dishonest suggestion. The same evening M. Bashelet sees the name of his son Henri on the war casualty list. The family is distraught with grief.

SYNOPSIS OF THE PLAY

A few months pass. The portrait of Sergeant Henri hangs in the place of honor in the Bashelet house. The local authorities pay homage to the father of the dead soldier. His rank in the office is raised. He is elected to the presidency of the Society of the Parents of Heroes Who Gave Their Lives for Their Country. He is sent the medal of honor with which his son had been decorated. The breath of glory touches the brow of the modest employee.

The speculator Berlureau, who in the first act failed to involve Bashelet in a shady deal, now uses him as a screen for all his questionable enterprises. Under the banner of the charity organizations of which Bashelet has become an honorable member, Berlureau succeeds in putting over a number of shady deals. Bashelet gets his share from Berlureau's questionable transactions. The financial situation of the Bashelet family is much better now, better than it has ever been before.

Two more years pass. The war has ended. Every small town has its own grave of the unknown soldier. Tomorrow in the local cemetery a solemn ceremony will take place at the grave of Sergeant Henri Bashelet, although Henri's body has never been found. M. Bashelet does not know what grave will be used for this purpose, but he has been told that every unknown soldier is a true son of France, and M. Bashelet has no right to deny to any unknown soldier's grave the name of his son. At first M. Bashelet hesitates, but then he gives in. His psychology and his status have changed considerably during the last two years. Now he is a deputy from the district, a municipal councilor. He receives revenue from the government. He is a shareholder in two or three industries that have sprung up during the war. Now Berlureau is his best friend and his home is no longer that of a modest bourgeois, but a war museum in memory of the local hero, Sergeant Henri Bashelet.

Some changes have taken place in his family. Germaine, Henri's wife, who grieved for her husband for a time, has remarried and she lives away from the family. Tomorrow there will be a meeting to commemorate the anniversary of the war and the ceremony at the grave of the hero. It is late evening in the Bashelet home. Everyone is asleep. The only light is in M. Bashelet's study. At this moment he is rehearsing his speech for tomorrow's ceremony in front of his son's portrait. He is now practically a professional speaker. There is a sudden knock at the door.

"*Entrez!*" M. Bashelet calls, without stopping his rehearsal. He gargles his throat to keep it clear for tomorrow's great event. A strange man stands at the door—pale, in an old army coat and worn-out shoes, with a bundle in his arms. A hoarse, toneless voice speaks, "Father, you don't recognize me? It is I, Henri, your son. I have returned."

"Henri, my boy, you are home!" the shaken father whispers.

A long pause follows. M. Bashelet looks from Henri to the objects around him—at the portrait of the national hero and at the whole museum that is in the memory of Henri Bashelet.

"Now I am ruined!" he exclaims and faints in his son's arms. This is the end of the third act.

The opening of the fourth act finds Bashelet and Berlureau in complete confusion. From their dialogue we learn Henri's story as he told it to them. He had been shell-shocked, had lost his memory, and had been taken captive by the Germans. He had been placed in a hospital for the insane there, and, during these last two years, his memory had gradually returned. Now he is home. It is all very clear. But the announcement of the hero's return will mean the ruin of Bashelet and Berlureau— the loss of their social prestige, honor, and even their financial security. And, besides, how is one to face the mockery and malicious questions? And how about the grave of the unknown soldier, which is now dedicated to M. Henri Bashelet?

Bashelet and Berlureau are trying to persuade Henri that it is better for them all if he conceals his resurrection. Henri himself will not benefit by returning. And what of his poor wife? She belongs to another now. She will be brought to court for bigamy. Germaine enters, shaken by Henri's return. A long dramatic explanation takes place. Of course, she has never ceased to love him, but her new husband is so very rich. She has all she has ever dreamed of now. She is ready to sacrifice everything for Henri, but one must be realistic. And she, too, thinks that it might be a good idea to postpone the announcement of his return. At this moment music is heard and banners are seen through the open windows and the door leading to the balcony. It is the procession on its way to Henri Bashelet's grave. The demonstrators stop under the balcony of M. Bashelet's house. They demand his appearance on the balcony and a few words in memory of his lost son, their hero. The family practically pushes the father to the balcony, and M. Bashelet begins his speech. He is terribly excited and sobs almost sincerely for his son's death, while the son watches from the room with a bitter smile.

In the last act we see the whole cast in Paris in the office of the Deputy of the National Assembly, M. Bashelet. Henri is his secretary. He had agreed to conceal his return and Berlureau has supplied him with a false passport. Life moves forward. The electors present the deputy with an enormous portrait of his son. The Chairman of the Council of Ministers appoints M. Bashelet as one of the Ministers in his new cabinet. Yvonne and Henri are aware of the tragi-comic situation of the family but know of no way out. Thus the Merchants of Glory speculate with everything, even the lives of their own children

HE FIRST PLAY that I was entrusted to direct independently at the Moscow Art Theatre was the play by Pagnol and Nivoix, *Merchants of Glory*. I felt it was beyond my development at this time, as half the cast of this production would consist of the older generation of the theatre—actors such as Vishnevsky, Luzhsky, Khalutina, and Alexandrov. Stanislavsky asked me if I were sure of myself as a director. He said I would have a great number of "actors' rehearsals," as he called them, and he wanted to know if I needed someone of more experience to back me up. He himself would supervise this production.

I asked permission to draw Luzhsky into the work. He was at that time at the peak of his work in all phases of the theatre. Stanislavsky approved my choice.

Definition of the Genre

When I told Stanislavsky my first impression of *Merchants of Glory*, I called the play a satirical-comedy-melodrama. But I also told him that I was afraid of such a cumbersome definition of this *genre*.

"It seems to me," Stanislavsky said, "that your definition of the play is correct. In every good comedy there is always an element of satire. Even the mediocre French comedies of Scribe, not to mention such *chef d'oeuvres* as *Much Woe From Wisdom* and *The Marriage of Figaro*, can have an element of satire. It doesn't have to be political satire.

241

More often, it is satire on a mode of life or a definite trait of a human being. In every instance, satire ennobles the comedy and makes it more significant. I am all for satire in comedy. Of course, one has to know how to direct and act in it. I also see the elements of melodrama in this play. They derive from an old and lasting tradition in French drama. And the combination of these two elements usually guarantees the play's success.

"This *genre* is foreign to Russian drama. It is a pity, because we Russians have a great deal of humor in our life and we have an easily aroused sensibility. Our great classic writers could have created interesting, true-to-life plays in this *genre*."

Stanislavsky talked over with me in detail the distribution of the roles of the play, and he told me the habits of work of the actors he had known for a long time. I, in turn, told him about the young ones whom I knew. He accepted my suggestion that Isaakov, whom I had known from the Third Studio of the Moscow Art Theatre, do the sets. But when two weeks later I brought him the first sketches of Isaakov's sets, Stanislavsky did not accept them.

"Why should you make the modest provincial house of a petty official like Bashelet so large? It looks like a picture gallery. What is Bashelet's job?"

"He is a petty government employee in the meat-supply department for the army."

"Well, you see, even in wartime his salary could not be more than three hundred francs. He could not possibly afford that kind of a house."

"Konstantin Sergeyevich, we were concerned with the third act when he has turned his house into a museum dedicated to his son's memory."

"But this occurs in the third act. What are you going to do with the first and second acts?"

"We will adjust it somehow, Konstantin Sergeyevich. In

this corner we will make a work space for Bashelet himself. Here, a partition for Yvonne . . ."

"Excuse me for interrupting you . . ." Stanislavsky's polite intonation always meant that no argument would be allowed at this point—"You missed the most important aspect of the scene in question. The museum is a surface problem, I would say. Your real problem is to show how the pursuit of glory and betrayal of principles, even though petty bourgeois, has destroyed the honest life of M. Bashelet and his family. This is a big and important inner psychological problem. What means are you planning to use to realize it?"

"Konstantin Sergeyevich, in this case I think it is necessary first to create the family home with exactitude and scenic expressiveness."

"Perfectly correct." This was always his expression when he was satisfied. "Now work on it with your artist."

Social Atmosphere

The day arrived when we were to show Stanislavsky the results of our work with the actors. He saw the first three acts and then said to us: "You have analyzed the play correctly, but you don't feel or understand the 'seed' from which your performance must grow. You are Russian actors and directors, and you are acting and directing this thoroughly French play as if it were Russian. But the whole secret lies in its not being Russian. The logic of the plot, the characters, certain characteristic customs, and the rhythm are not Russian. All I am telling you now and will be telling you during our work about France and the French naturally refers only to the now outdated French bourgeoisie represented by Bashelet. Berlureau is the type of the new bourgeois: initiator, adventurer, speculator, potential industrialist—without the slightest trace of shame or conscience in his dealings, be it an everyday problem or an economic or social one. If it were not for M. Berlureau, M. Bashelet would have remained an honest bourgeois on a small scale. But this is the drama of bourgeois society. The Bashelets cannot escape the influence of the Berlureaus in their midst. They are forced either to be destroyed or to become Berlureaus themselves. I warn you not to apply my description of the French bourgeoisie to all French people. The French people are great—energetic, gay, witty, full of *joie de vivre*—basically a democratic people. They know from their own history that they are carriers of the living spirit of freedom, and they know very well what ideas and events accompanied it. Even in Bashelet's own family, the younger generation represented by Yvonne and Henri do not entirely share M. Bashelet's sense of values. They will search for their own road to life.

"The seed of your future performances must have its root in the specific French bourgeois perception of life, people, and events. All of you, and especially your director and scenic designer, must understand thoroughly the life of the average Frenchman and must know upon what the French character is based.

"First, France is not Paris but the provinces. The old France is preserved only in the provinces, Lyons, Bordeaux, Marseilles. It is there that you can still meet the France of Zola, Balzac, and Flaubert. Perhaps that is the reason why the great writers of the past century placed much of the action of their works in the provinces. Remember *Madame Bovary* and the *Rougon-Marquart* series?

"Two months ago Gorchakov called this play a satire. In what does the satire consist? In your acting today I saw elements of comedy, and once in a while elements of melodrama, but I saw no satire. I am glad of it. An actor should never say to himself that he is a satirical character and therefore he will play in a certain manner.

When an actor plays the character and his relation to the character simultaneously (this is the current style among actors, even in some of our theatres) and also performs all the necessary actions according to the play's development, he is divided in his consciousness, and, in the final analysis, he never can create a character which is clear in its purpose. He will try to do everything that the author directs him to do, all the while winking at the audience. He will constantly fall out of character and won't be able to act truly and vividly. The feeling of satire must be felt by the audience. The more satirical the author's character, the more convincingly must the actor behave, in his stage image, as if he is unaware of the satire. But the director, together with the scenic designer, must create the perfect conditions for revealing the play's satire. They must create a milieu in which the directorial accents and the definitions of the actors' beats are placed in such a way that it will be perfectly clear to the audience that it has witnessed a satirical comedy-melodrama.

"For instance, nothing should strike the audience to that effect in the first scene. At the rise of the curtain, the audience must be impressed with the typical home of a provincial bourgeois of moderate means.

"Every French bourgeois is ambitious to have an apartment not on the top floor and not on the first floor. The first floor is supposed to be damp, and, also, people from the street can peep into your windows. It is not *comme il faut*. The third floor is too high. It is the garret; it is not respectable; it indicates poverty. There remains the second floor. This is perfect, and so it is not called the second floor but *bel étage*. During his many years in the provinces, M. Bashelet has kept his eye on an apartment on the *bel étage*. Perhaps this house has only two stories, but, never mind, he lives on the *bel étage*. And in the attic live the young people—Yvonne, Henri, and Germaine. The main room of the *bel étage* is one with a fireplace and a large table. The gentleman and lady of the house have a rest period by the fireplace. It is the symbol of home. The family gathers around the large table. They eat on this table only on Saturdays and Sundays. The rest of the week the family eat in the kitchen. The kitchen is usually immaculately clean. The stove is washed after each meal and covered with a cloth. The kitchen for the French provincial bourgeois of modest means is the holy of holies and is, in fact, the most livable and coziest room in the house. The fireplace is a kind of family altar; the fire blazes and there are old-fashioned candlesticks on the mantel. There is usually a family legend about the silver candlesticks. Who received them, and where were they received? Usually their history goes far back. '*Oh, c'est mon grandpère qui les a reçu.*' Then the older son inherits them when he gets married. But they always stay in the parents' house while they are alive. Between the candlesticks two framed photographs are usually placed—photographs of the most respected members of the family, *grandmère* and *grandpère*. Of course, on M. Bashelet's mantel there is a photograph of Henri in uniform, taken on the day he left for the front. That is a must. The photograph of the son in uniform is a thing of great value in the Bashelet house.

"The mantel is covered with a velvet cover fringed with small pompons. Near the candlesticks are some tasteless trifles and terracotta statuettes. But someone, sometime ago, presented them to someone, and you will be told a family story about these relics of the petty-bourgeois home. In the flower vase there are last year's maple leaves. 'Aren't they beautiful?' a middle-aged member of the family will tell you, sighing, and then he'll add, 'Autumn is here.' It is certainly a pose, but one must say this while one is still young. (Someday one will be old.) It is so beautiful to feign sadness and submissiveness to fate while looking

at the golden autumn leaves. It is the right thing to do.
It is beautiful to anticipate your fate—of course, in front
of others. But it is all right to go on secretly having an
affair with your son's tutor. No one must know of it.
Otherwise there will be a scandal. In some instances, everyone knows of it, but everyone pretends to know nothing
at all.

"Everything is in its place—the armchairs, the over-
stuffed sofa, and the stitched pillows. God forbid that you
have a green pillow where a yellow one is supposed to be!
The statuettes, books, and pillows must remain in exactly
the same place where they were in the time of *grandmère*
and *grandpère*. And the lamp on the mantelpiece! It might
have been a Roman lamp; then it was changed to a kero-
sene lamp and later to gas; now it has an electric light. It
looks most unusual because of all these changes. It seems
too old-fashioned, but it is treated with such care. It is a
closer member of the family than the old cat or the watch-
dog. The cat and the dog will die, but the lamp has already lived a hundred years and intends to live another
hundred at least.

"And the andirons! Sometimes they are really antique
with a coat of arms on them. Such andirons somehow
testify to a certain intimate connection between the owners
and the ancient feudal aristocracy of France.

" 'Where did you get these andirons?' you are interested
to know. Of course you couldn't have asked a more pleas-
ing question. With a mysterious smile, the head of the
house will say, glancing at the iron crowns which form
the feet of the andirons, 'You know, it has been said that
they belonged to the owner of the Château La Tours. The
Château is on the hill within seven kilometers of our town.
You have passed it. Now, of course, you see only the ruins.
But my great grandmother remembered the last descend-
ant of the owners, and they say that she was not on bad

terms with him . . .' Your narrator modestly refrains
from finishing the thought. These andirons are supposed
to come from the Château. He throws another mysterious
look at them, while you recall that you have seen andirons
at your grandmother's house and also at your aunt's house,
exactly like these. The coat of arms was quite obviously
welded on to them, and you begin to doubt the authenticity
of these, but you dare not say so. They would be just as
offended if you were to say something indecent in the
presence of their young daughter.

"Why am I saying all this to you? In order that you
should get the atmosphere in which the life of the French
bourgeois flows. Their mode of life forms their psychology.
Their mode of life is their ritual which is established once
and for all. No one dares change it.

"Papa rests for half an hour in front of the fireplace, and
everyone walks about on tiptoe—such is the ritual. Mama
went to visit the *curé*. Don't arouse her anger when she
returns from her pious conversation—this is also ritual.
The young people do their work at stated times—the
ritual again. Henri and Yvonne are locked in their rooms.
They are melancholy—ritual. You know they are at the
age when they are melancholy—again ritual. And Henri
and Yvonne must go to their rooms to feel melancholy
when they are not even in the mood. The father will say,
'Henri, I'm sure you want to be alone in your room now.'
And Henri understands that every young man of his age
in the family has done this—again ritual. He may be having a peaceful nap in his room, but the ritual is kept. And
Yvonne, the young daughter, must walk around sad and
languid, no matter how she really feels. The youngsters
have become used to cheating, pretending that they are
doing their homework. No one will bother them then.

"And Mama does not always visit the *curé* if she is not
at home. And papa does not rest by the fireplace but looks

at a risqué magazine which he has borrowed for one evening from his colleague. And everyone, beginning with the young people, knows all this, but everyone has to live up to the ritual because it is *comme il faut*. And feelings— after the first pranks, the first sighs, and the first kisses of love—also become ritual.

"There is sad news from the front. A new list of casualties. You are playing this beat as we Russians feel and suffer these moments: simply, seriously, sincerely, controlling our emotions. But now the list is being read in a French family. And the voice of Germaine trembles a little. Probably this is sincere. Henri is her husband. She still loves him, for they've only been married a short time. Now the list of casualties is read; the name of Henri is not on it. Father Bashelet sighs deeply and raises his eyes to heaven, 'Thank God!' Then he looks down (out of respect for those who are on the list). Then he utters some meaningless phrase, and his hand goes over his eyes unexpectedly. Then he gets up, straightens his coat, gets hold of himself, and quietly leaves the room. It is someone's duty to say, 'Ah, papa! He feels so deeply but he tries to hide his grief from us.'

"There hasn't been a word from Henri now for over two months. In fact, papa very sincerely played the scene according to the best etiquette of French melodrama. And perhaps he did not even get to his study after leaving the dining-room, but instead turned aside for a sudden very important matter."

"Do you mean, Konstantin Sergeyevich, that they put on their feelings?" A surprised and almost frightened question came from one of the young actors.

"No," Stanislavsky calmly answered. "This expression of their feelings is in their flesh and blood. To express them more powerfully in another way is not proper. On the other hand, if he is a little more restrained in his feelings, someone would say, 'Oh, he is a dry, unfeeling man.' No, they sincerely believe that they are suffering, they love, and are jealous. For the French, it is a true expression. For us Russians, it is not quite true. This 'not quite' is the beginning of the satire. This small worm will eat at the edges of the audience's confidence in the sincerity of their feelings. We, the directors, must know how to show this particular moment in the play. But, Luzhsky, you as M. Bashelet should know nothing about the satire. You must plunge as deeply as possible into the atmosphere, the life habits, and all the details of the mode of life and morals. You, as an actor, must get drowned, as we say, during the rehearsals in all these velvets, stitched pillows, napkin rings for the dining-room table, soft embroidered slippers, family photographs, and curtains. Don't be afraid. It is not dangerous. Before the performance, the director will take away all that is superfluous, but an actor will have formed an impression of the stability of this honest, cozy, bourgeois life during this time."

Exaggeration and the Means of Expression

Stanislavsky stopped for a moment, as though he was trying to solve a problem in his thoughts, and then continued: "A rehearsal is your laboratory. It is a chain of experiments. Don't be afraid of exaggerating anything during rehearsals—circumstances, feelings, atmosphere. Seventy-five percent of what we do at rehearsal does not enter the performance. If we could retain a hundredth of everything which we find during rehearsal, then in a hundred rehearsals we would have a splendid performance. But, to our regret, it does not always work out that way. Don't be afraid to tell an actor, 'Rehearse this way today, but I want you to know that you will not play it this way.' An actor who loves to have everything set and fixed during rehearsals is frightened by such direction. 'Why must I rehearse in such a way if I'm not going to do it at the performance?' He revolts surreptitiously and expresses himself to the colleagues who sympathize with him.

" 'Yes, it won't be this way at the performance,' you tell him. 'It will be much better and more expressive.' But one should not go directly to the result without testing and searching for different ways. Most of the rehearsals must be devoted to bold experiments and unexpected experiences. If one wants to follow such a direct *set* method of rehearsal, one can easily do it in twelve rehearsals. That means one rehearsal to a fourth of an act, even allowing an hour and a half for the director to pretend that he's searching.

"Now let's return to the Bashelet family. The first act is very sincere, giving us a picture of honest, simple people and of a small town where everyone knows everyone else. Everyone's life can be seen, even from the *bel étage*. By the way, life is shown more than it is hidden, otherwise the small-town people would have nothing to do. The routine of life is established very solidly. The son of M. Bashelet is at the front, and suddenly—sorrow, the news of the son's death. The family were aware of the probability, but just the same the shock is unexpected. This must be a profoundly dramatic scene, played with a genuine sincerity. This time, without false affectation, M. Bashelet cannot get hold of himself and goes to his room. The women cry. The traditional Saturday dinner is disturbed and the habitual flow of life broken. Between the first and second scenes of the first act a month elapses; is that right?"

"Yes, just a month, Konstantin Sergeyevich."

"Now is the time to prepare your audience for the fact that M. Bashelet's psychology does not remain the same as in the first scene. Luzhsky, you and your director have only a hint of this fact. The director hung the portrait of

Henri on the upstage wall and placed a vase of fresh
flowers in front of it. This is good. When Luzhsky comes
into the room, he casts a glance at the portrait. He does this
also when he leaves. Good, but not enough. The way you
do it, the audience may think that you are simply observing the room to see if everything is in order—for instance,
whether the flowers are fresh in the vase before the portrait.
Only I, who know the play well, understand that with
these glances you are emphasizing your relation to the
portrait. The audience may not get it; then your acting
with the portrait, which, I repeat, is necessary for the
scene, is lost. This is the first step to the future satire. It is
the first sign that the claw of the bird (M. Bashelet) may
get tied up."

"Gorchakov and I wanted to do it more boldly and
sharply, but we were afraid," Luzhsky said.

"That's wrong," Stanislavsky answered. "When you
enter the room, you must stop for one tenth of a second
before the portrait and look at it very sadly. The first time
you do it, the audience will interpret it as a natural attitude on your part. When you stop the second time, the
audience will wonder why the father should show his sorrow that obviously, but when you stop the third time it
will smile and think, 'Oh, the old man puts it on a little
too thick.' If the director can stage it so that, at the moment
of papa's stop in front of the portrait, some of the members
of the family look into the room and then stand still, as
they're already acquainted with this new habit of
Bashelet ('Papa's at Henri's portrait. Don't disturb him!'),
and only Yvonne sees a certain acting in M. Bashelet's conduct and demonstratively crosses to her room to the indignation of the rest of the family—if the director does this,
then the audience will understand that during the past
month the family's life has become based on the cult of
their hero. This is a characteristic touch. It is a trait of the

French bourgeois to have personal family heroes. The authors knew this very well. The English also are noted for this; we Russians, just the opposite. We do not appreciate our family heroes because of our false modesty."

"Isn't there danger of annoying the audience with so many stops in front of the portrait?" Luzhsky asked.

"But the importance lies not in the stop itself but in the psychological reflex that has now developed in M. Bashelet," Stanislavsky replied. "We have to see that he specially enjoys making these stops in front of others. It means that somewhere deep within him lies the actor. Acting is a typical trait in a Frenchman. Besides, you must change your attitude for each stop. Now you have recalled something about Henri. Now you think that the portrait isn't straight and you stop to straighten it, but, in doing this, you linger a little longer than necessary. Now you take the flower from the vase, and for a moment you forget the situation and almost put it in your button hole—as you used to do—but you remember in time and are happy that no one observed you."

"What are you teaching us, Konstantin Sergeyevich? This is a trick," Luzhsky said with feigned horror.

Stanislavsky laughed: "Certainly it is a trick, but it's psychologically justified. M. Bashelet had this habit before the war, before his son's death. This gesture was a muscular reflex, and we all know that muscular memory is the strongest memory. Of course, I don't insist that you do just that. I am only showing you that there is a great variety of attitudes with which M. Bashelet can stop before the portrait, providing that the attitudes are interesting and to the point. You will begin the satirical line of the play with the actions of the character and with the relationship of the character to everything around him but to himself."

I said, "Why, we can do the scene in which the editor

of the local newspaper and the secretary of the Society of Fallen Heroes, Mayor Blancard, come to ask M. Bashelet to accept the presidency of the Society in a most interesting way then. Certainly they all will stop for a moment before Henri's portrait."

"Exactly," Stanislavsky answered. "Let them stand and hold a service in front of the portrait. It will be an excellent mise en scène. Let them all keep their conversation hushed, as if they were in church."

"Will they hold a mourning service?" Luzhsky asked.

"Oh, no, not a mourning service. That is a sad and morbid affair. They are holding a service because they are maneuvering an advantageous deal, and they are praying in their hearts that it will come off, that this old fool Bashelet will not balk. Here is your satire again. It is seen through the mise en scène and through their attitudes and actions, without any need to distort the characters."

I said: "Then in the third scene this room is turned into a museum, dedicated to the memory of Henri Bashelet, according to the author's direction."

"That's right," Stanislavsky replied. "And because this room is an ordinary, rather small room (not a tremendous one such as you originally planned), it will be cluttered when it is turned into the museum. Put two mourning wreaths over the candlesticks. The dining-room table can't be used any more because there is a glass case holding Henri's letters in the middle of the table. In the corner put a mannequin wearing the overcoat of his uniform and his helmet, such as the one in the Czar's palace dressed in the full uniform of Paul I. Henri's war medals are displayed on small pillows under glass and placed on separate small tables or benches. The walls of the room must be covered with Henri's photographs from his early childhood until the day he left for the front. It would be very good to hang some of his weapons on the wall, and a number of palm branches decorated with inscribed colored ribbons."

Luzhsky asked, "Don't you think it might look like buffoonery?"

"If it is tragi-comic buffoonery, then it is good. But I think if each object is carefully displayed in a proper place, not crowded one on top of another, it will give the effect of a very pointed illustration of how the pursuit of glory destroyed the petty-bourgeois coziness, whose basis was so fragile and precarious. We will show how easy and cheap the moral principles which the bourgeoisie are so proud of can be bought. I think that was the authors' idea. The title of the play, *Merchants of Glory*, tells you that."

The Seed of the Character

We fulfilled many of Stanislavsky's instructions on how to approach the acting problems. The next time we showed him our work he said: "Most of the scenes you executed correctly, but you did not overcome your fear of this *genre*. It means that the seed of the play is not planted deeply enough within you. I just saw you play the scene of the meeting between Germaine and her husband Henri after three years of separation—during which time there was the false information concerning his death and Germaine's remarriage. I see in your acting of the scene that you have thought out all the characters' thoughts and situations. You are sincere and true, and you used your temperament to a certain extent. I intentionally say 'to a certain extent,' because I think that this scene should be played with unlimited temperament—and I, as your public, don't see enough of it in your acting. Now why is this? Because, again, you played it from the seed of the Russian character, a Russian feeling of the drama between these two people. You played it simply and deeply, but not effectively or brilliantly—not from the seed of the French character.

"This kind of a scene is a treasure both for actor and audience. People come to see the play for this scene. They weep; they stamp their feet with ecstasy; they throw their umbrellas and canes; they call for the actors and toss flowers on the stage. Now why didn't you grasp the spirit of the French character? Because, as you interpret this scene, it has just one theme: how unhappy we are through no fault of our own. This is a typical theme of an old Russian drama, the old-fashioned Russian theatre. Many works of Russian drama and literature are like this, but, of course, not the best. As I see it, you built the scene along the following beats. First beat: 'It is you. You are alive, Henri.' 'Yes, I am alive and very unhappy.' Second beat: 'I love you,' 'I love you too,' with the undertone of both, 'We are so unhappy.' Third beat: 'What are we to do? We do not belong to each other. What a misfortune!' A timid parting kiss and many tears all through the scene.

"Now how would French actors play this scene? First of all, they would begin the scene with a three second pause—an overture to the scene. First instant: Henri is on the stage. Yvonne has told him that Germaine is coming, that she has betrayed him by marrying another man. Of necessity he turns his back to the audience. Otherwise he won't be able to use that classic turn. In the doorway, on the opposite side of the room, there is heard a stifled exclamation from Germaine, 'Henri!' (This is indicated in the author's directions.) The following scene is executed as precisely as a musical score: Pause. Henri's back is to the audience. ('How can I face her?') Germaine appears at the door, richly dressed, charming. (Her husband is a very wealthy man and there is no reason to dress her as modestly as you did.) She wears a chic little veil. This is important. She leans her hand on the door. Yvonne's frightened face appears behind her for a moment. Again a pause. Germaine looks again at his back. She whispers, *'C'est lui! C'est lui!* Henri!' in a stifled voice. Oh, how skilfully a French actress can put this over, with the most delicate tremor in her voice! Your throat chokes up in spite of yourself.

"Second instant: Sharp classic turn done instantaneously by Henri. Of course, the actor must do this perfectly, with his hand on the window ledge. Then, a loud, masculine, desperate exclamation, 'Germaine!' 'His voice rang through the house.' (This is how Madame Bashelet would describe it to her neighbor, if she were not forced to keep his return a secret.)

"Third instant: What will happen? Both are trembling. You can see this from their hands; otherwise they would not be leaning against the door and the window. All this is classic French school of acting.

"Another moment of hesitation and then they rush across the stage to each other (for this purpose they have to be on opposite sides of the room). He must fling a chair aside, as though by accident. (Of course, it has been placed in his way intentionally.) 'Oh, that gesture!' the old maids in the audience will sigh after the performance. Germaine rushes to him, dropping gloves, scarf, and various other feminine objects. (This is also a must.) Now they cling to each other violently. What temperament! But it is all worked out down to the last detail. They swoon in each other's arms for a moment, without hurting one line of their make-up. Still, you feel that they hug each other so tightly that they almost hurt each other. Germaine nearly faints then, as she slides to the floor. You guess that she wants to beg his forgiveness on her knees, but, of course, he will not allow her to kneel, and he carefully sits her in the armchair. He kneels at her feet and lays his weary head on her lap. This is the final move that crowns this scene. Of course, thunderous applause is expected. If it does not come, all your acting is worth nothing and you will never get such parts again in the French theatre."

And Stanislavsky laughed heartily as he finished describing this style of acting. "These are the first three seconds of their meeting," he continued. "It has to be done instantaneously, adroitly, and precisely as a circus number, accompanied by half-words, half-exclamations, and Yvonne's tear-stained face in the doorway. (Another character must be on stage to react to this overture as the audience should react.) But then Yvonne quietly closes the door. No one will disturb Henri and Germaine now.

"The first beat: Henri quickly gets control of himself, rises from his knees, and sits on the chair which he has previously flung away. It is important to use this chair; this will imply that now he is in complete control. On the way to the chair, he picks up the things Germaine had dropped, acting out his realization that these things had been given her by her new husband. He puts them on her lap, and then he lights a cigarette, silently asking her permission. She assents just as silently."

Stanislavsky brilliantly pantomimes this for both of them, without leaving his seat; his eyes angrily glare at Germaine and then timidly, helplessly, pleadingly, look at Henri. The whole scene was a dialogue without words around the moment of lighting the cigarette.

"A very short pause," he continued, "and then the lines of the play begin. 'You have returned,' 'I was told that you've remarried,' etc. I think there's a whole page of dialogue between them. Henri and Germaine play this beat in a perfectly calm tone and rhythm, as if it were not a husband and wife talking and as if it hadn't been preceded by the three seconds of mad overture. The audience is stunned. These are real people! It had just seen the gust of passion and the outburst of emotion, and now see how calm they are! It's impossible. They cannot keep up this pretense of calmness! But Henri and Germaine continue their conversation in a cool, quiet fashion. And their inner feelings are only revealed by occasional glances at each other (his always angry and hers timid). There is a slight tremor, too, of their fingers. (He crumples the cigarette and she her handkerchief.) The audience is getting impatient. These people, they think, simply have to explode! But the French actors know their audience very well. Just before the audience gets bored, they abruptly move to the second beat.

"Without any psychological preparation and with no transition, Henri jumps from the chair, takes the things from her lap, and flings them away. ('You accepted these things from him! You sold yourself to him!') He tears her veil (that's why she must wear it). He flings her charming hat *behind* the chair, of course. She is petrified. 'You want to kill me, Henri!' 'Yes, I'll kill you!' (A good name for the beat.) He is choking her. He is about to overturn the armchair, when suddenly he lets her go. 'Why don't you resist me?' he says. 'I am happy.' She gives the traditional answer for such a scene. The beat ends.

"The third beat: He returns to his chair, as if in a drunken stupor, and sits half turned away from the audience. His shoulders are shaking—he is sobbing. Oh, horror! He almost killed a human being! Now she rises, approaches him, and smooths back his hair, 'Mon Pauvre!' "

Stanislavsky showed us this scene. He pronounced the French words with an inimitable inflection and cried real tears. And all of us cried with him. But through his tears he said, "The fourth beat now."

Still with tears in his eyes, he began Germaine's lines (the prompter gave him his cues, and Henri answered): he began imperceptibly to interweave Germaine's self-defense through her comforting words, and then her re-proaches to Henri. Stanislavsky improvised:

"She is only a woman. One must understand that. She did not start the war. He should have been smart enough to stay in the rear, or at least have managed to leave her enough to live on, and so make it possible for her to wait for him—all her life if need be. Henri is shocked. ('Oh, God! To whom did I give my love?') And he begins to argue with her. The cues fly from one to the other; their inflections are full of fireworks. This is typical French argumentative dialogue. The phrases and words don't need to be completed. The rhythm, sound, tone, and temperament define the sense of the dialogue. Oh, how they hate each other at this moment! When the argument reaches its highest point, there is an instantaneous pause, and then the concluding phrases, heavy and prolonged, 'Oh, how I love you!' 'And I you, my dearest!' 'Darling!' And now a passionate long embrace."

Stanislavsky held the pause to indicate the length of the embrace, and then he continued, still improvising: " 'Don't call me by that word, Henri! We have no right to love each other. Good-by, Henri.' 'You are right, my darling. We must not love each other. Let us remain friends.' 'Oh, Henri!' 'Oh, Germaine!' 'It has to be. Such is life.' "

Stanislavsky spoke these lines literally in one breath and in rush tempo.

"I improvised the text," he said. "The text of the play is different, but my text is the under-text of any parting scene of a husband and wife or of lovers in this type of French play. All the beats which I explained to you must be played most sincerely. The design of the scene as I out-lined it may be a little extravagant, but the French actor always tries to play every beat as deeply as he can, and only after the scene is finished will he say to the stage manager in the wings, 'I played the scene magnificently, eh? Will you treat me to a dinner at the *bistro* for that?' On the other hand, after such a scene, the Russian actor remains in his dressing-room for another two hours, heart-broken and in tears—only because he pities himself. 'Something like that happened to me,' he says to himself. 'That devil of an author knew how to put it over.' "

The French Theatre

The next day Stanislavsky began to rehearse this scene. He went over separate moments of the design he had out-lined many times, and, in spite of its uncommon nature, he demanded from the actors absolute sincerity in each intonation and movement. He worked hard and persistent-ly with the actors. He was very anxious for us to under-stand the seed of this play by working on this particular scene. We asked him a number of times, "Do all French people react like this? Do they act this way in moments of shock?"

"No," he answered, "of course not. Far from it! But they are accustomed to see themselves react like this on the stage. Every nation has its own idea of art, which includes the theatre. The French people are educated on Corneille, Racine, and Victor Hugo. In comedy it's either the draw-ing-room picaresque type of Sardou, Scribe, and Labiche, or of vaudeville. In operetta, Offenbach and Lecocq. And then there's farce. They have no realistic drama or realistic comedy, except perhaps *The Marriage of Figaro*.

"The theatre of Antoine used foreign plays for the most part, and, although its realistic trend was successful, it was only so because of novelty; therefore, it did not enter into the flesh and blood of the French theatre. This is why contemporary French drama is either drawing-room com-edy or a combination of comedy and melodrama. I know of no serious, profound French play that could be placed next to Ostrovsky, Chekhov, and Gorky. And Molière, who is much loved by the French, is played superficially.

"They are trained from childhood to recite *Le Cid* and *Phèdre* in a pompous manner. In their adolescence they run to see farce and melodrama. The French have many amateur groups. You can rarely find a middle-class French man or woman who has not at some time or other in his youth been part of such a group. This one was told that he had a talent for the stage, but, of course, he had to join his father's business—a pharmacy or some kind of trade or notary office. One must continue in one's father's business. Everyone can't devote himself to the theatre. Also, they have been exposed either to pseudo-classic tragedy or melodrama softened with comedy for three hundred years. Naturally they begin to imitate this in life. There is scarcely a Frenchman who cannot sing operetta couplets for you, or tell you a risqué joke from the most recent farce. They have a special talent for theatrical ceremony. They are the originators of the grave of the unknown soldier. They even decorate nature. Remember Versailles and their chateaux?

"In the past they had a very fine and important literature. But it did not reach outside a limited circle of the intelligentsia, who were mainly located in Paris. They do not read much in the provinces, and they look down on the writer. You can hear them say, 'Balzac? Oh, the one who wrote so much so quickly? I remember something of his. But I can't remember exactly what.' If the author becomes a member of the Academy of Arts and Letters, then, of course, they feel obligated to know about him. They may say, 'Oh, yes! He belongs to my province!'

"The French bourgeois loves to consider himself very honest and virtuous, and often he finds it difficult to combine with his lust for money. In trade he would prefer not to follow the proverb, 'He who does not cheat, does not sell.' But he always does, and with an air of purest virtue. I feel that Luzhsky still does not completely understand the specific traits of Bashelet, the characteristic psychology of a French bourgeois. I have no objection to your being a prude throughout the first scene, Luzhsky. The little talents that so enrich our youth—our dreams and our quest of glory, including the talent of an actor or actress— either are broken or buried so deeply under the stress of earning a living, feeding a family, and educating the children that these duties later become rationalized into a sense of great achievement. All Bashelet's early dreams are overgrown now, as I said before, with a ritual for every hour of the day. Let all this be shown in the first scene. But then his son is killed. One would expect the heart of this genuinely loving father to break, but his son's death brings him suddenly the fame which he had ceased to dream of at thirty. He hears the whispers, 'This is M. Bashelet whose son was killed. See how manly he is. How sturdy his walk! They say that when he is at home he never leaves his son's portrait.'

"On his job his colleagues begin to pay much more attention to him. 'The father of a hero is working in our office.' When, sometimes, he is pointed out to some visiting authority, he becomes aware of his importance. Now he begins to be invited to the mayor's parties. He is visited by youth delegations; his son's former friends come to see him. Henri's medal is sent to him and somebody, by mistake, even congratulated him. For a moment he has the feeling that this is his medal. When no one is around he holds it against his coat. ('What would I look like if I had a medal like this?') Perhaps a minute later he is ashamed of this gesture. But I am absolutely sure that he did it just the same. I don't feel that you are capable of such an action, Luzhsky. You grieve, but that's not enough. Life does not stop for M. Bashelet. Bashelet did not commit suicide;

he did not follow his son to his grave. Quite the opposite! Unexpectedly a new life began for him. Again he came to life. He acquired many new interests and obligations. His son's death turned into the capital which, in his youth, like any other Frenchman, he dreamed of having. This is the subject of the second scene.

"I do not compel you to make a grotesque character out of M. Bashelet. Do it all tactfully and subtly, but do it. If Bashelet isn't as I've described him to you, then there was no purpose in writing this play. And, also, this is a small part of that seed from which the performance as a whole will grow."

Luzhsky interrupted: "I understand you, Konstantin Sergeyevich. I will try to create Bashelet as you see him. But there's so much in me that is disturbed by your direction."

"The fact that you are thoroughly Russian as an actor and a person disturbs you. I have talked so much about France and the French people in a very definite satiric and critical fashion so you would all plunge into the atmosphere of French bourgeois life and feel the specific quality of French bourgeois psychology."

"You mentioned capital, Konstantin Sergeyevich. Do you really think that Bashelet wants to get rich?"

"Passionately, desperately, from the time he was eight years old. He began trying to get rich by selling buttons. But he was told that it wasn't nice and was spanked for it. Bashelet does not come from a merchant family, although they wish they were the successful type. The French love commerce. Remember with what voluptuousness Zola describes a shop in *Le Ventre de Paris*. It is almost an erotic description of the process of selling.

"At fifteen, Bashelet probably repeated his attempt to make money by trying to sell his stamp collection, and undoubtedly he lost on this venture. But the dream of becoming rich never really left him. Money is a symbol of freedom to the French bourgeois. One can do anything with money. The God of the French bourgeois family is stock. Stock offers them the possibility of cutting coupons on capital invested in the soundest enterprises (like the Czar's loans) and of not touching the capital itself during their lifetime, but of using the interest to lead a comfortable life. Stocks are the most important thing in life. The quantity of stock defines the degree of a man's respect from his neighbor. One gives them and leaves them as an inheritance, uses them as security, and even borrows money on them. M. Bashelet had no stocks. But suddenly, after his son's death, he catches the scent of them in the air. And to this is added the aroma of glory. During the last two weeks he has felt actually giddy from the premonition of some very important occurrence in his life. This is for the second scene. It begins with the presentiment and culminates in the certainty that he is beginning a new kind of life.

"The third scene is Bashelet's apotheosis. He is the most important man in the town. He is the conscience of the town. He is its glory. He is the president of the main charity organization and a member of the Commercial Society. His presence gives respectability and assures the population of the town of its honesty. When in doubt whether to invest their money or not, they ask, 'Is M. Bashelet connected with it?' And a number of shares are put in his portfolio. 'Accept it,' they tell him, 'otherwise you cannot be an honorary member. We need you. France needs you. Be a patriot. Your mother country demands this of you.' What sweet, long-hoped-for words! Where had he heard them before? Perhaps many years ago when a theatrical company visited the town and played so magnificently a comedy-melodrama by Scribe or Sardou. 'Tomorrow I have to appear at the grave of my son,' M. Bashelet thinks to himself. 'What pose did the famous actor Duclos take while reciting this monologue?' And here M. Bashelet rehearses his speech for tomorrow before a mirror."

Stanislavsky showed us how Bashelet tried different poses, fixed his tie, swallowed a raw egg to clear his voice, tested his voice at various levels, and at the same time took his shares of stock from the portfolio and placed them behind his son's portrait. "Thieves would never look for them there," Stanislavsky mumbled in an undertone.

"Of course," he said to us after this improvisation, "I know that all this is improvisation, but I am absolutely sure that these were M. Bashelet's thoughts. This is inner monologue that speaks within him, and it is the basis of any role for an actor. When this inner monologue—inaudible to the audience, but observable on the actor's face, in his behavior, and his form of expression—has become part of the actor's consciousness, then the role is ready. I want to inspire and convince you with my improvisations and suggestions to take much more daring steps in the creation of M. Bashelet's character."

Luzhsky replied: "I think that I begin to understand your idea of satire, Konstantin Sergeyevich. It is very difficult for me to do, but I'll try. I must find the inner monologue organically for myself and not force it. It must be logical and integrated as the thought of my character."

"I am very glad that you understand what I'm driving at," Stanislavsky answered. "I know you can do it. M. Bashelet is a very typical French character. Before the end of the third act, M. Bashelet is seriously convinced that he is the hero, not his son. And he's also convinced that his service to his country is much more than his son's. Because of this, his son's return is a terrible shock. First, he thinks his son is an apparition, which he imagines he sees as he rehearses his speech in front of his son's portrait. Then comes the sincere human excitement of a loving father at his son's return: joy, happiness, laughter, and embraces. 'My son, Henri! My little boy!' (Children always remain children in their parents' imagination.) 'My son is home alive!'

"Then, you look at all the things around you—medals, ribbons, and wreaths—and you exclaim in terror just as sincerely, 'Oh, my God! I am lost. I am a beggar again!' And the curtain comes down. Then the conflict begins, the conflict between good and evil in a human being. The audience expects the good to win, but the satire and the great significance of this play lies in the opposite, in evil winning over good. Alas, it is so! And it is most characteristic of bourgeois society and all contemporary Western philosophy, which is basically cynical.

"I was told that this play created a scandal in Paris. Above all else, you see the reward given to M. Bashelet because evil is victorious over good. He is appointed a cabinet member. Of course, it is a scandal for French society. No one can say it is merely a play. There were too many examples in real life. We are putting on this play because the sense of values in it is contrary to our sense of values. We must present it and act it as French satiric comedy, because our spectators must not confuse it with our way of life. Therefore, I ask you to plunge into the design of the play and build your characters to the utmost expressiveness. Follow our method in your acting and work, but get hold of the seed that is alien to our psychology and our outlook on life."

Comedy-Satire

During our rehearsals we tried to follow Stanislavsky's suggestions to the best of our ability. When we showed

him the last act of the play in the office of M. Bashelet,
Deputy, he directed our efforts toward still another more
thorough and precise approach to comedy-satire.

"The set for the last act is poor," he said to Symov, our
set designer. "It is in too good taste. Symov, you told me
that this is a suite in the Tuileries. That is true. But M.
Bashelet hasn't chosen one that is typical out of the thousand rooms of this palace. There must have been many
other parvenu deputies like him in the past, deputies who
changed the rooms to their taste. I don't dispute the architecture of your set, but the *nouveau riche* accepts only two
materials for decorating—marble and bronze. Leave the
configuration as you have it, but the walls must be of
marble and the stucco molding must be simulated bronze.
You ordered an enormous portrait of Henri. This is correct, but when it is carried in it must be covered by canvas
or some other cloth so that it won't become soiled or
scratched. I will tell our prop men right now how to bring
it in. I want all of you actors who are in this scene to follow your intuition as you react to whatever will occur from
now on."

Stanislavsky got up and went on the stage behind the
set. On stage were M. Bashelet's friends: M. Berlureau;
Mayor Blancard, who by now has become a colonel; M.
Richbon, the editor of the local newspaper, much heavier
now and promoted to editor-in-chief of a French tabloid;
Henri, who has agreed to be his father's secretary; and
Yvonne. They have all come to congratulate M. Bashelet
on his new appointment, which he is about to accept from
the Premier of France. He is to be Minister of Social Wel-
fare. Berlureau, the colonel, and the editor have brought
M. Bashelet a present, the oil painting of Henri.

"It is impossible to get it up the stairs, it is so large," an
insignificant-looking second secretary reported to M.
Bashelet. At this point Stanislavsky is heard from the

wings, "Gorchakov, begin the rehearsal. I have everything under control here."

The action on the stage began. The portrait was being squeezed through the doors, and Stanislavsky, who was obviously assuming the role of head mover, gave the orders: "Now, careful, please! Here, this way. That's right. Now look where you are going! Monsieur le Ministre, please move out of the way," he improvised with his usual infectious and triumphant manner. The portrait was completely covered with cloth. Now it was placed in the middle of the stage. Stanislavsky gave the ends of the cloth to several assistants. It is obvious that the portrait will be revealed on his signal, all at once, as a monument is unveiled.

"Hats off before a hero!" Stanislavsky commanded. Everyone obeyed his orders. They took off their hats, holding them just above their heads. Henri saluted ironically. Luzhsky had the most ridiculous expression on his face, a mixture of grief and a pleasant smile, as though saying to himself, "Once more I'm going to see Henri," and even the skeptic Yvonne looked serious at this moment.

Stanislavsky ordered, as if in a circus, "Allez!" The cloth flew off the portrait and . . . Oh, God! The celebration was ruined. The portrait was upside down! (When carrying it in so hurriedly, they must have turned it.) This was why Stanislavsky had gone backstage and whispered to the prop men. And there was Henri standing on his head with his feet up. Everyone on stage was shocked. We in the auditorium laughed loudly and applauded. But Stanislavsky remained on stage with his back to the audience, still in the character of the head mover. He smiled with a triumphant but benign air: "Didn't I do it well for you?" We were applauding his achievement in creating, without text, such a convincing and humorous character. When Yvonne (Stepanova) said her line, "What a masquerade!"

and left the room, it made a marvelous climax to the scene. Everyone came to with a start. Stanislavsky turned to the portrait and, when he noticed his mistake exclaimed, "Oh!" He clasped his head in his hands and ran out, pushing everyone out of his way.

The rehearsal continued. The characters on stage fussed around the portrait, everyone trying to help turn the portrait right side up: the clerks, the colonel, the editor, Berlureau, and even Bashelet himself. Henri stood aside choking with laughter. Suddenly the corner of the portrait struck M. Bashelet's leg. He shrieked, "Oh, the devil!" and involuntarily lifted his foot and stood like a heron. The candlesticks fell off the table; someone accidentally overturned them. A rich drape was torn from the window, and, at this moment, Stanislavsky appeared again at the door. Now he was the head butler with some fantastic aiglets (cords from the drapes) hastily thrown over his shoulders. He announced in a solemn voice with an expression of surprise on his face, "Monsieur Le Deputé, the Premier of France honors you with a visit," and behind Stanislavsky an actor in a top hat who was, according to the play, the Premier, a character without lines, appeared with no less surprised an expression as the curtain fell.

Stanislavsky came to me out of character now and said: "Wait with the curtain, Gorchakov. Mark this mise en scène quickly. Take pencil and paper. Sketch and write. We will all remain on stage. No one must move. Nothing should be touched. Luzhsky, please keep your foot up. M. Bashelet meets the Premier with his foot still up. This is the most delicious touch of the final scene. Gorchakov, learn to take advantage of good accidents on the stage." And Stanislavsky himself remained at the door as the butler, again with a surprised expression on his face, while I feverishly sketched this mise en scène, the finale of the play, *Merchants of Glory*.

Five minutes later, Stanislavsky asked me, "Have you put everything down?" And then he turned to the actors, "Please bear with me a little longer." Then he came down into the auditorium, and checked and corrected my drawing and notations. Then he returned to a discussion of the scene we had shown him before.

"Now you see how much expressiveness you must bring to those moments that decide the turn of events in the play. Yesterday you showed me the fourth scene of the play— the morning after Henri's return home. You began with the scene between the mother and Yvonne. We can say that the problem of the scene is that Henri's rest will not be disturbed. He must have enough sleep. Then Bashelet enters. The women are fine in this scene. But, Gorchakov, you did not find the right rhythm for M. Bashelet's action and his relation to his son's return. M. Bashelet had a sleepless night. He had nightmares of his ruin and downfall— the collapse of his future, his career, and his glory. A French bourgeois can take a lot but not the loss of his fortune. This is why suicides caused by bankruptcy and unsuccessful speculation are so frequent in France. The Russian bankrupt had a completely different psychology. He served his term of imprisonment, shook it off, and was ready for another enterprise. Nobody looked down on him, and his credit was even better than before, because they would say: 'Oh, this man has had experience! I have served a term too and I saved the bulk of my fortune by paying twenty kopecks on a rouble. It's all right. The merchants will deal with him again.' With a Frenchman it is another story. He will wait for ten years for a lucky number in a lottery but once he gets hold of fortune's wheel, he will let it go only with his last breath. To get rich is the sacred dream of the bourgeoisie. Fame? Also not bad to have. But this comes later; first comes the money."

"And how about honor and conscience?" Luzhsky asked.

"One must strike a bargain with one's conscience. Bashelet said in the first act he would never do that."

"That's right," Stanislavsky replied. "He will not allow himself to strike a bargain with his conscience for his personal advantage. But if Berlureau succeeds in convincing him that hiding Henri's return is necessary for others and for his country, he will agree to it. It is only important to find the *way* to bargain with one's conscience. He has been searching all night long for the way but has not been able to find it, and the next morning he comes out of his room looking not clean and fresh as you do, Luzhsky, but like Orgon in *Tartuffe* when he discloses the loss of his fortune. Bashelet is unshaven, unwashed, without a tie, and with his hair uncombed. He feels like King Lear did when he was robbed of everything, and his lips repeat one word, 'Disgrace! Disgrace!' These are the thoughts that feed you, Luzhsky—not the joy of your son's return. The joy is for the mother and Yvonne, those two fine women. You and Germaine have a different set of values. Only then can one understand Berlureau's question, when he hurries to your house after receiving your call. By the way, the dialogue in this scene is written magnificently." And Stanislavsky took the copy of the play and read it to us, making comments as he read.

BERLUREAU: What's the matter with you, my friend?
BASHELET: He has returned. ["Stress the word *he* as strongly as you can," Stanislavsky commented.]
BERLUREAU: (*not understanding*): Who is he?
BASHELET (*pointing to the portrait*): *He!* ["How much despair, exasperation, even hatred can be put in this one short word."]
BERLUREAU (*unbelieving*): He? You must have had too much to drink last night at that party of the

Society of Disconsolate Widows and not enough
sleep afterwards.

BASHELET (*losing his temper*): You're an ass, and an
idiot!

BERLUREAU (*insulted*): I see no reason for you to talk
to me like this.

BASHELET: My son, Henri, he returned last night. He
escaped from a hospital for the insane, but now
he is all right. ["What a rich undertext there is
in 'now he is all right'!"]

Berlureau whistled in answer, and Stanislavsky also
whistled, putting aside the script.

"After that," he continued, "there is a long, long pause.
The two actors playing this scene have a wonderful chance
to use their imaginations. This pause is really a short play
in pantomime. The theme of the pause is: We are caught.
We're all played out. The characters of the pantomime
are two swindlers. Their masks are off. There is no need
to pretend before each other. And they converse in gestures
only.

"The first moment: Berlureau points his finger to the
left, meaning, 'In there?' Bashelet in answer points his
finger at the ceiling, indicating, 'He is up there.'

"Second moment: Berlureau understands. He puts the
palm of his hand against his cheek, meaning, 'Asleep?'
Bashelet answers with an inappropriate gesture, passing
his forefinger across his neck to indicate Henri is shaving.

"Third moment: Berlureau doesn't get it. With his forefinger he repeats the gesture to indicate, 'Oh, he cut his
throat?' Bashelet waves his hand, as though to say, 'No use
trying to talk to a fool like you!' and makes a vague gesture
toward the ceiling.

"Fourth moment: Berlureau again misses the meaning,

and moves his hand around and around his own neck to indicate, 'He hung himself?' Bashelet is about to explain, but the door opens and Henri enters. Both of the swindlers pretend they have been catching flies.

"Now," Stanislavsky said, "the following scene between Bashelet, Berlureau, and Henri is well prepared. Berlureau's question 'Oh, it is you?' is perfectly clear, as is Henri's answer, "Yes, it is I." And it is also clear when Berlureau looks now at the portrait and then says to Henri obnoxiously: 'You know, you don't look at all like yourself. Now stop this comedy and tell us how much we must pay you to get out of here?' It is also natural for M. Bashelet to yell at this point, 'Berlureau, this is my son!' And for Berlureau to yell back, 'Shut up, you idiot! Do you want to ruin yourself with your own hands?'

"And the rest of this scene—so cruel in its cynicism—between the father, the son, and the speculator who sold his soul to the devil long ago is followed by just as sharp and powerful a scene between Germaine and Henri. We have already worked this out. Then there is the touching scene between Yvonne and Henri, and finally the finale of the act. So gradually we approach the end of the play.

"Now let's talk about the appearance of the actors and their external characteristics. The gestures of a French actor are either impetuous, theatrical, or non-existent; he talks only with his eyes and reveals the inner rhythm of his character by a slight movement of his hands. This is a very expressive method. The same applies to their inflections of speech. Their voices are excellently trained, well developed, and most flexible. French actors love to use the loud whisper. They also have a special talent of speaking in a unique toneless voice which jumps from the most colorful to the most restrained inflections. They love the musical phonetics of their language. (Here he pronounced a number of French words, emphasizing the vowels.)

"They love humor, laughter, comedy, light melancholy, and lyricism. All this is the background from which you must create your parts. Now work! Work! I wish you all success. I will see your first dress rehearsal. Good-by until then."

HISTORICAL MELODRAMA

CHAPTER FIVE

THE SISTERS GÉRARD

AN ADAPTATION OF *Two Orphans*
BY Adolphe D'Ennery AND Eugène Cormon

The action of this melodrama takes place in Paris in 1789 on the eve of the French Revolution. Songs are sung on the public square against the King and Queen and the aristocrats, but the

SYNOPSIS OF THE PLAY
King's police work very effectively, suppressing the hungry rioters and every other expression of public unrest. The aristocrats continue in their revels unaware of the forbodings of their imminent fall. At that time, the sisters, Henrietta and Louisa, arrive from the provinces by stagecoach. They are supposed to be met by their Uncle Martain. He had invited them to live with him in Paris, because they have lost their parents. Also, a famous doctor in Paris has promised to restore Louisa's sight.

The stagecoach arrives, but their uncle is not there to meet them. The orphans wait on the square with their baskets and trunks. If they could look into the tavern near the town gate, they would see their Uncle Martain sound asleep in a back room. The police detective Piquar had put sleeping powders in his wine. The Chief of Police, the Marquis de Prael, wants to kidnap Henrietta. He had seen her during the peasant's festival the month before on his estate and had decided to kidnap her upon her arrival in Paris. Piquar had doped her uncle upon his order. Also, Jacques and his gang are having a drunken party in the tavern. Jacques' mother, Aunt Frochard, is a professional

277

beggar who steals children and young girls and then instructs them in her profession. Jacques is very cruel to his mistress, Marianna, who would have left him long ago if she were not so afraid of his knife.

It is night. The two sisters don't know where to turn. Suddenly they are surrounded by men in black capes. They are Piquar's assistants. A cape is thrown over Henrietta's head and she is carried away despite her screaming and fighting. In vain, Louisa cries out her sister's name in the empty square. Nobody answers her call. From the tavern comes the drunken Aunt Frochard. "Who are you looking for my child?" she asks, greatly impressed with Louisa's beauty.

"My sister Henrietta," Louisa says. "She was by my side just a moment ago. What am I to do? Where am I to go? I am blind!"

"Blind?" Aunt Frochard said, pleased. "Come with me, my dear. I'll help you." And she takes Louisa with her.

In the first scene of the second act there is an orgy at the Marquis de Prael's. Count de Lenier, one of the representatives of the high aristocracy, has brought his son Roget. Marquis de Prael brags of his new find, Henrietta. The girl implores the guests to let her go. She tells them her blind sister is alone on the square. But the guests laugh and make fun of her misfortune. Only Roget de Lenier believes Henrietta's story and offers her his help. His father orders Roget to let her alone. But Roget, with a sword in his hand, helps Henrietta escape and then follows her.

Louisa's fate in Aunt Frochard's lair is sad. For a month now, the old woman has forced Louisa to go out singing and asking for alms with her on the street. Aunt Frochard keeps Louisa in rags and hardly feeds her anything so that she will be more appealing and get more alms. The only person who has sympathy for poor Louisa is the violin player, Pierre, who is lame. He is Aunt Frochard's second son. He tries to protect Louisa from Jacques' ugly approaches. He secretly gives her his bread and carries out a constant search for Henrietta.

The first scene of Act III takes place in the Count de Lenier's study. The Count and his wife are discussing their son Roget's behavior. The Count is expressing his fury. He says Roget has abducted some street girl from the Marquis de Prael's. Nobody knows where he keeps her. The Count demands that his wife explain to their son that he is ruining his future. He also wants his wife to find out the girl's address so that she can be gotten out of Paris. The Count sends for Roget and leaves him with his mother.

Roget succeeds in convincing his mother that his father is lying. He begs her to visit Henrietta and see for herself what a fine person the young girl is. Roget reminds his mother how helpful she has always been to those in need. He tells his mother that he knows of her visits to the Bastille to see his tutor Guilbert, who has been imprisoned because of his libertarian ideas. He also confesses that he knows about her love affair with Guilbert. The Countess does not deny it and in turn tells her son that she had a daughter by Guilbert. But because of her fear of her husband, she committed a crime by leaving the baby to the mercy of whoever should find her on the steps of a cathedral. The only sign by which the girl could be traced is the medallion which she put around the baby's neck and inside of which she left a note saying that the girl's name is Louisa. The Countess agrees to visit Henrietta, and Roget gives his mother her address.

The Count has eavesdropped, and having learned her address, he decides to kidnap Henrietta who lives in a small house in a lonely part of Paris. The Countess visits her. She learns from Henrietta that Louisa is not her blood sister and that she was found on the steps of a church. Henrietta has the medallion. At this moment the singing of the blind Louisa is heard from the street. "My sister!" Henrietta cries. "My daughter!" the Countess says. Both run to the balcony. Now it seems that the happy reunion will take place. But there is a policeman at the gate sent by the Count for Henrietta. In spite of the Countess' protests, Henrietta is taken to prison and Louisa is dragged away by Aunt Frochard. The sisters have only time to exchange frantic exclamations.

In prison Henrietta meets Marianna, Jacques' mistress. Marianna would rather be in prison than with Jacques. She arranges for Henrietta to escape, and gives her Aunt Frochard's address. Henrietta appears there. She finds her sister in rags, practically dying of starvation. She demands that her sister be returned to her. But they laugh and Jacques attempts to seduce her. Henrietta in fighting him gets a knife from the table. She is about to stab him when her strength fails. Jacques laughs and rushes at her, but Pierre takes the knife and stabs his brother to death.

The revolution has begun in Paris. The Bastille is taken by the people. The mob bursts into Aunt Frochard's cellar; she tells them Henrietta has murdered her son. Again Henrietta is taken away. In the final scene at the People's Court, all the threads of the complicated intrigue are unwound. Pierre is acquitted, Louisa is restored to Henrietta, Count de Lenier leaves the country. Now nothing can prevent the Countess from accepting her daughter Louisa, and Roget from marrying Henrietta. And soon Louisa's sight will be restored. Pierre dreams of Louisa's love.

I N THE AUTUMN of
1926, Konstantin Stanislavsky suggested to the Senior
Directors of the Moscow Art Theatre that the young directors' group produce a play of their own. As I was studying
and working as a young director in the theatre, I was
naturally very excited. I began to read plays with Markov,
who was in charge of the selection, in order to choose one
to work on. But, to tell the truth, none of those we read
excited us, or seemed to answer the needs of our young
actors.

The time for my consultation with Stanislavsky was
nearing, and I had to give him our choice. Finally, we
thought of a play by Dennery and Cormon, *Two Orphans*.
We reread the play and decided that, with some adaptation, it might be very good material for our production.
Markov said he would like to work on this play with me in
the capacity of régisseur. We also discussed the problem
of casting our young actors, and we decided that the older
parts should be given to the young actors who were capable
of portraying character roles. Then, we gave Stanislavsky
the list of plays we had considered, including *Two
Orphans*.

It took him two days to think it over, and, during those
two days, he discussed everything with us. Finally he said,
"Leave the play *Two Orphans* with me. I remember this
play, but I would like to read it again."

All the next day we waited nervously for his decision,
for by now we were eager to work on *Two Orphans*.

"Well, tell me, what made you choose this melodrama?" Stanislavsky asked us when we met the following morning.

Markov told him why he thought it possible to include a melodrama in the repertoire of the Moscow Art Theatre. He spoke of the necessity of having a variety of styles in the repertoire. He emphasized the noble sources of melodrama that arose during the French Revolution. I, in turn, added some strictly directorial ideas that I had about the play—which, I must confess, were very general. I also spoke of the possibility of turning this melodrama into a realistic-historical play: of the necessity of eliminating from this *genre* its traditional conventions and its pathos. I spoke of my desire to include music. The theme of the play demanded it. We also gave him an approximate distribution of the parts.

The Director's Concept

The genius of Stanislavsky as a director came to life in all its power the moment he began to visualize the different actors of the theatre in the roles of this play. His imagination created the whole performance. The play came alive as he cast it and created the whole production before our eyes. And what a production! Now when some of my students ask me, "What do you mean by the director's concept?" I always remember that day in the big dark room of Stanislavsky's study when he creatively probed all the play's elements.

After he discussed the individual actors for the leading roles, he turned to talk of the play itself: "What you both were saying about your directorial procedure is correct, but I'm afraid it wouldn't be easy for you to realize it. It is even more difficult to free a *genre* from its conventional tradition than to free an actor from his clichés. But try it. It is much better, I think, to give yourself a difficult problem and only half-fulfill it than to restrict yourself to your limitations. In this respect, I strongly disagree with Goëthe, who insisted on the opposite.

"We will talk about a scenic designer a little later when you have a better sense of the play and know what you really need. I don't want to add anything to what Markov has said about his approach to melodrama at this point. When I come to rehearsal and see how it works out, then we'll talk again. Remember one thing, you will have many ideas for this play. Melodrama inspires you as directors, but you must choose only what is pertinent to your purpose in doing the play. You, as a director of our theatre, must direct this play for the great human idea, the idea which is needed today by the people who will come to watch your performance. Test everything that comes to your mind by that idea, and throw away without pity everything that is for effect—everything that will disturb the modest but noble idea. I think this play has one and I think you feel it correctly.

"Work intensely. Don't be afraid of mistakes. But constantly test the logic of your thought as a director, the logic of the theme of the play, and the logic of the behavior of the characters.

"And please don't spend any time during rehearsals on the method. If you see that some of the actors are lagging behind—that some are weak in concentration or in their relationships, or if they cannot express the thought well— have some separate sessions with them and let them have lessons on the side. The melodrama has to be staged in such a way that you and the actors are carried away in rehearsals. Set aside special hours for the lessons. Help an actor to be free in rehearsals. Help him to work in a creative mood, but please don't sit him on the school bench every minute. Even if he's younger than you are, he will never forgive you for that. He came to work in this play, and he's in it to create a part, not to learn or to study the method. Let him use as much initiative as he can. Direct him with the right problems and the right questions but never teach him. When I myself fall into the tone of a teacher (which you all know only too well), I scold myself most severely afterwards.

"Every stage *genre* demands a special approach in the work of the director with the actor. Because you are so young as a director, I like to tell you these things before you begin.

"Explore with the actor to find out how the character lives and what he does in the unusual situations that melodrama presents. Study the life of the human spirit and help your actor to express it in a simple but powerful form. This will educate your actors in developing the characters.

"Melodrama is a complicated *genre*. But a complicated *genre* is always good for actors to work in. In melodrama sincerity of passion must be brought to the highest level. The drama must touch the borderline of comedy lightly and subtly. This is so, because dramatic scenes invariably alternate with comedy in melodrama, otherwise nobody could endure it. The heroes of melodrama are constantly overcoming tremendous difficulties and are constantly suffering. This gives it the flavor of the romantic *genre*. Actors must sense it and live by it. It is not easy. But I repeat, it is most useful. If you find insurmountable difficulties, come to me. That is all for now. I wish you success."

Rehearsal in the Improvised Sets

Three months passed after that meeting with Stanislavsky. We invited the dramatist Massa to help us adapt the melodrama. With him we revised it and gave it a new name, *The Sisters Gérard*. We followed Stanislavsky's suggestions for the most part in the distribution of roles. We worked with the actors with all the enthusiasm that young people have. We analyzed the whole play and prepared to show Stanislavsky the first two acts in a very rough form.

In a large room of the theatre on a sunny day the shades were drawn and the drapes were closed. The lanterns threw yellow and blue light on the boxes and small tables in one corner of the hall. In another corner were steps covered with gray cloth. There was a signboard above the tables made from a carton and on it hung a cardboard sword. Across from the sign a pretzel was cut from the same kind of a carton, gilded and stuck to a stick. On the rear side of the hall a backdrop represented an ancient city in perspective. In front of the backdrop there was something that represented a big arch. Young men in capes and large soft hats that covered half their faces, young girls in full skirts and shawls strolled along the boulevard. Some of them would sit on the benches, a few would disappear and return, seemingly very occupied with something and whispering among themselves. Behind one of the curtains a middle-aged man sat, with the text of the play on his knees, and with a small electric lantern nearby. He was the prompter, who for once did not have his usual place in the center of the stage. A big leather chair and a table near it represented a very important spot. The atmosphere in this hall was filled with that tense excitement so familiar to all theatre people on important rehearsal days.

Stanislavsky was supposed to come to see these two acts of our new work at twelve o'clock. And although students were appointed to meet him in front of the theatre and some even further down the street, suddenly he appeared in the middle of the hall, having entered from the inside of the theatre. He squinted his eyes at the dim lantern light. Stanislavsky was trying to find his way through all those boxes and steps and curtains—our improvised sets.

"He's here!" The word went through the hall.

"I'm not disturbing you, am I? Perhaps you are not ready?" He stood in the middle of the stage. Putting his pince-nez on, he examined our "sets" with curiosity.

"Oh, no, no, how can you say such a thing, Konstantin Sergeyevich! Everything is ready." We directors rushed to him. "Only we expected you to come from the street."

"Oh, I've been here a long time. I was talking with Luzhsky in his study."

"Konstantin Sergeyevich is more nervous than you are," Luzhsky said on cue. "He called me up at ten this morning and told me that we must be here as early as possible to see that you should have everything you need to help you with wardrobe and sets. But it looks as if you got everything you needed."

He couldn't have said anything better to encourage us. (We discovered that Stanislavsky and Luzhsky had been in the theatre for an hour, seeing to it that we got all the necessary props.) We led Stanislavsky and Luzhsky to their places. They were joined by a number of the most important actors of the Moscow Art Theatre. They all asked Stanislavsky for permission to watch our rehearsal. But Stanislavsky answered: "Today I'm only a spectator. I am not the 'boss.' Ask the directors' permission."

Naturally we did not protest. Indeed, we were flattered. It was frightening and flattering at the same time. But we thought that if we failed, it might as well be a complete failure. The number of visitors was soon increased by representatives of all the departments: make-up, wardrobe, lighting, etc. With an audience like this, we didn't have to worry about the kind of attention we would get. When Stanislavsky, giving one more glance at those present, asked seriously, "Can we begin?" the answer of the directors sounded almost calm. For a second the hall was completely dark. The actors took their places very quietly.

The gong sounded. Yellow, blue, and white lanterns were lit and the first act of *The Sisters Gérard* began.

A soft sunset lit the square of the Paris neighborhood. A long line of beggars hugged the window of the bakery where they were waiting for bread. A policeman strolled through the arch. Two men yawned over steins of beer at a table inside the bakery. From the distance the musical sound of a church bell announced evening mass.

Stanislavsky whispered approvingly, "Not bad!" And we all gave a sigh of relief. Everyone in the Moscow Art Theatre knew how important according to Stanislavsky the first impression of a play is.

"If the first moments when the curtain goes up hold your attention," he used to tell us, "it is then easy to watch ten or fifteen minutes of exposition." (And how he always helped us to search for the correct approach in these first few minutes of a performance during the rehearsals, if we directors could not find them ourselves!)

Now came the first pause. The picture was broken by the voice of the baker: "Are you planning to stay here all night? There is no bread. There will be no bread today. Go home." The line of the beggars began to move. It began to be more and more restless. People knew that there was bread but it was hidden for the people who could pay more money. A spy, Piquar, disguised as a street poet, tried to arouse the crowd. The Marquis de Prael and Count de Lenier, draped in their long capes, came into the little café. They sat observing the excitement in the street—so typical of those times. The mob fought the policemen. The policemen beat the spy without realizing that he was a friend. From the square Jacques and his mother approached, accompanied by friends. He met Pierre, who is lame. People began to drink heavily in the café. (This place was one of the low dives of Paris.) It was getting dark.

From the outskirts of the city a stagecoach approached.

Two sisters, Henrietta and Louisa, were left alone on the big square at night in this strange city. Both were very pretty but one of them was blind. A famous Paris doctor, a distant relative of theirs, was supposed to restore Louisa's sight. The girls were orphans—it was not surprising that no one met them here. The spy, Piquar, had deliberately got their uncle drunk and he was sleeping in the café.

There was a plot against the older sister, Henrietta. She had caught the eye of the Marquis de Prael during a feast that was given on his estate, and he had decided to abduct her. The first act ended with the blind Louisa also meeting with misfortune too. She was being abducted by Madame Frochard. The sisters were separated and we could hear Henrietta's voice coming from far away, calling "Louisa! Louisa!"

Lights came on in the hall. And a split-second after this we suddenly heard a muffled cry, "Louisa!" And then we unexpectedly heard an echo still further away, like a sigh, "Louisa!" The audience shivered. Stanislavsky turned to the directors, "Very good. How did you achieve that effect?"

Alas, the directors didn't know. It had been an accident! One of the rooms had a certain type of ceiling that echoed, and, by chance, the last call "Louisa!" had reached this ceiling.

The stagehands began to rearrange the room for the second act. The "audience" surrounded Stanislavsky and discussion began about the melodrama—its impression on the audience, how melodrama used to be played, and how melodrama should be played now.

Playing Melodrama

A quarter of an hour later, Stanislavsky was ready to see the second act of our play. It consisted of three scenes: the first, an orgy scene; the second, in the basement of Aunt Frochard; and the third, in the study of Count de Lenier.

We were worried that, if Stanislavsky didn't like what we would show him today, we wouldn't have an opportunity to show him the scenes of which we were most proud: the meeting between Louisa and Henrietta, the revolt in the Paris suburbs, the destruction of the prisons, the murder of Jacques, and the court scene in which Pierre and Henrietta were the accused. We watched Stanislavsky's face very intently as he looked at our second act, but we didn't think there was anything to worry about, for his face showed his usual interest and attention.

When the second act was over, Stanislavsky turned to the audience and said: "Well now, let me thank you on behalf of myself and the actors, for coming and for being so attentive. With your permission, I would like to remain alone with the youngsters. We are going to have our own very intimate session."

Luzhsky remained, of course. All the actors who had been in these scenes gathered in a circle around Stanislavsky, and, as usual, he began with a question, "Well, is everybody here?"

"I think so, Konstantin Sergeyevich."

Once more he looked at us and smiled, understanding the intensity with which we awaited his judgment. "Well," he began, "I can see the result of a lot of work. It's touching, it's sincere. I even shed a tear or two. You, Stepanova, and you, Molchanova, are really alive in those places where you trust yourselves. In melodrama especially, the actor must believe absolutely in everything that happens, no matter how unbelievable the situation might seem.

"In melodrama the actor must take for granted that everything actually happens as the play indicates. Then and only then will the audience believe it. But if an actor winks at the audience while playing a scene in melodrama

—as though he were saying: 'I'm only doing all these things you see me doing and saying because I'm playing melodrama tonight. Tomorrow I will play in a real drama,' —then the audience will be bored. It won't matter how inventive the actor was in his tricks."

Again there was a short pause. And again he looked at us very attentively. Then he said, "Verbitski, you don't trust yourself at all." Verbitski was playing the spy, Piquar.

"Well, Konstantin Sergeyevich, that's the kind of part it is. I just have no idea what to do with a part like this."

"If I'm not mistaken, you are playing a spy?"

"Yes."

"The part of a spy in melodrama is a most interesting one. He's trying to confuse everyone. He does everything he can to mix things up, because he thinks that he knows better than anyone else."

"Well, everything that you say is very interesting, Konstantin Sergeyevich, but, as far as I can see, there is nothing like that in this part."

"You're wrong. It is you they beat up at the beginning of the play, taking you for a revolutionary."

"Yes, but that somehow doesn't develop into anything."

"Excuse me for interrupting you, Verbitski, but if the author has not made you see that this is the scene where you get the essence of your part, then you don't understand the rules for writing. He has given you this intimation of the character in the very introductory part of your role so as to make sure that the actor, and after him the audience, will see the scene as through a magnifying glass, and so understand the character and all the episodes connected with him. I missed in your interpretation the qualities of an amusing, stupid, self-confident person."

"But he's supposed to be a villain, Konstantin Sergeyevich."

"That's true, but in melodrama one is very often supposed to laugh at the villain. If he is the hero of the play, one despises him and is frightened by him, but if he is a character such as you portray, one laughs at him. I remember very clearly the scenes in which you participated, and I think the directors must work with you separately. If they work with you very carefully, you will understand what you omitted when working on your part."

"I will appreciate that very much, Konstantin Sergeyevich."

"All right, that's that. Now let's go on. Jacques, you are trying very hard to scare me but I wasn't frightened for a moment. I think it's because you are not used to committing crimes or doing all kinds of ugly things—even murder.

"You played your first scene with the blind girl in a most unusual way, Jacques. But in Jacques' life such scenes are an everyday occurrence. Because you yourself think the incident is so horrible, you surround yourself with exaggerated justifications. You are intentionally trying to frighten me and yourself, and, as a result, I don't believe you."

Anders, who played Jacques, said, "But he's not a murderer."

"Not today but maybe tomorrow. I'm not advising you to prepare yourself for murder. Murder is an accidental act or the result of a very special set of circumstances in life. In the latter event, murder has very deep roots in all the elements of the soul and mind. Your hero is not that kind of a man. In the first place, he's lazy. What kind of études did you do for the part?" He turned to the director.

I answered, "Well, in one étude we had Jacques and his gang go from one bar to another, singing songs and annoying passersby, pestering women . . ."

"Well, this kind of exercise is also necessary, but not

at the beginning. An actor must live with his part at least one day of the character's life. Did you give him an étude of Jacques getting up in the morning?"

"No, Konstantin Sergeyevich."

"I would like you to put down this problem and prepare an étude on this idea for me at our next meeting. After that, I will continue to talk to you about your part, Anders. And put down everything we have said now for the record of today's rehearsal so we won't forget it."

"Oh, certainly. I'm doing that now."

"Fine! Well, let's go on. Everything is very sincere, touching, and good in what you are doing, Titova (she was playing Marianna, Jacques' mistress). You don't have to reveal any of your actress' secrets on how, but just how, you achieved what you just showed me. Tell me just one thing: what were you thinking about when Jacques left you alone on the square?"

"I was thinking, Konstantin Sergeyevich, that for the last year whatever I do in the theatre doesn't come off and if I don't do better this time you will throw me out of the Moscow Art Theatre."

Stanislavsky turned to everyone: "Please listen to this attentively. This is a very important statement. It was intuition that put Titova on the right road to work. She didn't imagine herself as a prostitute, but she imagined very vividly what would happen to her as an actress if I threw her out of the theatre. As a result, she gave us an impression of a woman in a most desperate situation. The right intuition gave birth to all her actions. What were you thinking about in the following moments?"

"I didn't care what happened to me afterward."

"That's exactly what I felt when I watched your acting. And I want you all to remember how the right movement and right external actions follow from the correct organic state. Now, Titova, please don't think that when you're rehearsing next time you must remember and repeat mechanically what you did today. If you do that, you will have only the external form. Each time you have to repeat this scene, think only of the personal equivalent that can generate this emotion in you."

"Whenever I think that I would be thrown out of the theatre if I should fail in this role . . ."

"Perfect . . ." A wave of laughter went spontaneously through the hall. Stanislavsky understood the humor of the situation: "We will not throw you out, Titova, but you must always believe in this now, and you must imagine each time in a different way what would happen to you if this really took place."

Stanislavsky again looked at us with a very concentrated expression. "Tell me, please, Puzyreva, why did you put on such a horrible make-up?" Puzyreva was rehearsing the part of Aunt Frochard.

"Well, Konstantin Sergeyevich, Aunt Frochard is a horrible person. She steals children . . ."

"Precisely, but I can't see how you could succeed in tempting any child with a face like that. The moment you appeared on the street, they would run miles away from you. Aunt Frochard must have a very charming, kind face. Nobody must suspect what her occupation is. Everybody must think she is a saint. The only time you see her true face is when she is alone in her own home. I consider it a crude mistake for you to paint on your face the qualities that should come out on it as a result of your action. It should be just the opposite: you must fool your audience. In the beginning, the audience must only suspect that Louisa has fallen into bad company. In the first act of a melodrama the audience should have only a tremor of fear for what will happen. That is what is important. But you took the road of results. One who is mean should have an ugly make-up; one who is kind should be beautiful.

Now I understand why you, Rayevsky, made yourself up as such a good-looking fellow." He addressed the actor who was rehearsing Pierre.

"But, Konstantin Sergeyevich, he is lame—even hunchbacked, according to the author. We thought that, if on top of this, I made him unattractive . . ."

"Now don't try to defend yourself. Your intention was to arouse pity. You wanted to hear me say how sad that such a beautiful boy should be lame."

"How can you say that, Konstantin Sergeyevich!"

"You are not even aware now that this is your secret desire, but when you think over what I have told you, I am sure that you will agree with me. There is another path in art—to show the beautiful through the obstacle. The more obstacles you have, the more brilliantly you can show the smallest drop of beauty. I am talking about the inner world of Pierre. He is a hunchback, lame, with an unattractive face, but he has a kind heart and a talent for music. These two qualities are enough to show the real human being through his unattractive exterior. This is your problem as an actor. The way you are attacking the part you will make yourself seem sweet and sentimental. Those are bad traits for which pseudo-actors were famous in melodrama. A great actor in melodrama would play hide and seek with the theme of the play. He led the audience as far as he could in the opposite direction to his real character. On the other hand, the actors who repeated successful roles in melodrama—actors without the same stature and talent—did not trust themselves and were afraid of the complicated hide-and-seek of the role. They followed the direct path. The villain must look ugly and repulsive; a suffering hero must necessarily be blond and have a golden wig. The fact that our Jacques, the villain in this melodrama, is a handsome and attractive young fellow is good. That's why his behavior will be more repulsive. But I'll come to that again."

"You are magnificent, Mikhailov." Mikhailov was rehearsing the part of Martain, the uncle of the two orphans. "You are the example of how good melodrama should be played. It would be good to end the act with your scene. You were very sincere as usual, Stepanova, but you must have more control over yourself. You are very active on the stage, which is all to the good. But you must also think more, observe more, and listen more. These are also actions, and they are much more powerful actions than those that call for many gestures and too many movements."

"Kniepper-Chekhova is perfectly right in using extreme economy of external movement. Because of this, her dialogue and her action with the words becomes even stronger." Chekhova was rehearsing the Countess de Lenier.

"Ershov is very right in not playing Count de Lenier as a villain in his first appearance. It is very good that he is so reserved in his second scene, but he has not enough dramatic conflict in his dialogue with Chekhova, as his wife. I know that it is very difficult to sit without a move, without even the slightest gesture of the hand, when you are burning inside and only your eyes can express it. But all great actors who played melodrama realized this to perfection. They mastered the art of inner dialogue. Apropos of actors who play melodrama, they are always first-rate actors occupying the highest positions in the company. A mediocre actor cannot play melodrama. In melodrama the actor has to use a great deal of himself, and the mediocre actor without a vivid personality has nothing to add to the role. Authors of melodramas always wrote with a particular actor in mind. Even the best of them are very poor psychologists and writers, but they know to perfection the secret of how to use the stage to influence the audience, because they write for many thousands of spectators and not for a select circle of esthetes."

"But, Konstantin Sergeyevich, they say that melodramas have always been played in poor theatres with bad actors," Chekhova said.

"That's not true. A famous melodrama is only created once. Either it is created at the first performance or it dies that same night. Then nobody ever hears of it again. That is why the birth of a melodrama always depends on the greatest of actors and the most elaborate of productions. The first production is always costly. And when this first production is executed magnificently, then other theatres all over the world copy it. Actors in the different theatres play their roles in imitation of what they have heard of the great actors' performance. The directors imitate all the plans and sets and stage ideas of the great theatre première. You will notice that there are always director's notes and plans in all scripts of melodrama. Pickserecur introduced this. I have a script of his. It is the most typical director's script, in which there are minute instructions, plans, and pictures of the set."

"How are we going to play this melodrama, Konstantin Sergeyevich?" Stepanova asked. "We don't have this great technique."

"You will play it on the plane of sincerity that Mikhailov did today—with a heightened sense of truth and the most complete physical actions. A basic demand of melodrama is that the actors fulfill interestingly and completely the physical actions. That's why I think melodrama is most useful training for a young actor. It develops belief, naïveté, and sincerity of emotion; it helps them to create an unbroken chain of physical actions; and it makes their imaginations work elaborately."

An Improvisation

Stanislavsky thought for a moment, then glanced at our make-shift scenery, and quite unexpectedly gave an order: "Close the drapes at the window. Close all the doors. Put the lights out. Well, it seems to me it's dark enough, isn't it?"

I answered, "Yes, it's quite dark, until our eyes get used to it. . . ."

Stanislavsky got up and went to the furthest corner of the hall. His voice came from the distance to us: "Molchanova, I would like you to come to me now." Molchanova played the blind Louisa.

"Yes, of course, Konstantin Sergeyevich."

For a moment everyone was noisy and gay, but Stanislavsky stopped us very sharply. "I want you to keep absolutely quiet. I want absolute silence. In other words, exactly the same atmosphere that the blind Louisa felt when she was left alone on the square."

We could visualize that helpless girl left alone in a strange city from the tragic deeply serious tone of his voice. There was dead silence in the hall. Molchanova tried to make her way toward Stanislavsky through the many objects which crowded the room. "Excuse me," she said in an odd tone, "it seems to me someone is sitting here. I bumped into somebody." But no one answered her. And because of that, the atmosphere became terrifying. "There is nobody here," she said when she reached the end of the hall. "Konstantin Sergeyevich, have you moved from where you were?" Only silence answered her. Even those of us who were present were stunned. Our attention was so concentrated on Louisa that we hadn't noticed where Stanislavsky had gone. Molchanova continued to wander in the darkness, in the chaos of objects all around her, and her most simple words and exclamations sounded dramatically tense and expressive. And then something unexpected happened. Molchanova suddenly stopped in a corner of the room, sobbing terribly. And then she very timidly said in a very low voice, "Henrietta, Henrietta, where are you?"

We were startled. Her actress' talent had prompted the right attitude toward her sister in the play, and she said the line with such a sense of truth, sincerity, and belief in the circumstances in which she found herself that it made us also believe in them. At the same moment we heard the contented voice of Stanislavsky, and to our great surprise he was sitting next to me. (I was absolutely unaware of when and how he had arrived here.) He said, "Well, that's wonderful! Now you understand what it means to be left alone in complete darkness in that silent square in Paris."

"Yes," Molchanova said, her voice still trembling, from the far end of the hall.

"Put the lights on now," Stanislavsky said, "and come here, Molchanova. Now you know what blindness is like. You were frightened because everything around you was silent, just as silent as Paris seemed to Louisa on that square. Louisa knows the meaning of that silence. It's the kind of situation she has found herself in before. As a rule, the people who can see instinctively dislike blind people. When they encounter a blind person, they always avoid him. This cruelty of our egotism makes us withdraw, because we are afraid the blind person will ask us to do something for him that we don't want to do but which we would be ashamed to refuse. Louisa also knows that around her is an unknown city. Silent though they may be, people are near her. She's used to that. And perhaps there are people watching her from the windows. If it's possible from the director's point of view, I think it would be interesting to have them. An occasional passerby would only emphasize the emptiness of the square. You do not show the emptiness with décor. The egotism of people in the big city is terrible; this is what it is important for us to bring out. This will show Louisa's tragic situation and will emphasize the fact that she is abandoned by her good angel, Henrietta. I am very happy that you, Molchanova, in this improvisation suddenly felt the need to call out your sister's name. It tells me that your performance before me here became for you the reality of the play itself. *This is the real problem of the improvisation.* And now let's analyze the physical and psychological scheme of this improvisation:

1. The improvisation was unexpected, and the situation in which Louisa finds herself in the play is unexpected. You should not prepare yourself for it.
2. You didn't know your way about this room. You bumped into things. You apologized. Your eyes were open. You walked; you weren't 'acting.' You were really looking for me. You did not play at being blind.
3. You were embarrassed to call someone. Your voice sounded stifled and half pleading, and it came staccato.
4. You were frightened because you never knew what would follow. These four elements together constitute blindness. It should be understood as an inner feeling of an individual and not as an external defect."

Molchanova said, "I was told that blindness is usually compensated by an acute ear."

Stanislavsky replied: "Perhaps that is true but the spectator needs only the initial feeling of blindness during the first ten minutes, not all the observations and literature on the subject. The artist must know how to project all the defects of a human being through his inner sensations. Every characteristic trait of any external defect has its own psychology, its own inner reflections, and its own sensations of the surrounding reality. There is very little written about it and very little said, and those who do have physical defects do not like to remind us of them—but the actor must understand them very thoroughly."

Stanislavsky stopped for a few moments and looked at the actors sitting around him. This meant that the particular question was finished for the present.

The Director Demonstrates

"I would like to remind you once more," he continued after a few minutes, "that in melodrama it is extremely important to carry out your physical actions truly, expressively, and interestingly."

Verbitski (Piquar) asked him, "What do you mean by interestingly, Konstantin Sergeyevich?"

Stanislavsky answered: "Carry out your actions in a way the audience does not expect. For example, you are supposed to put Vladimir Mikhailov (Uncle Martain) to sleep. The audience knows this before your scene from the dialogue between the Chief of Police and the Count. By the way, Genia (the Chief of Police), you should have more dignity. You over-emphasize your subordinate position to the Count.

"But he is a count and my superior."

"Yes, but you are the Chief of Police and it is very typical for you to be obnoxious and aggressive. You know so much about everybody that you have a hold even over your superiors. Remember Fouché?"

"I will try, Konstantin Sergeyevich."

"Now let's get back to the point I started to speak about a minute ago, when you must put Uncle Martain to sleep. The scene takes place, as I remember, at a table in the little café."

"That's right," Verbitski (Piquar) said.

"Sit down, please, here, near the director's table. Let's put everything on the table that is supposed to be there: glasses, wine, bread, bologna."

Everything was brought to the table. Then Stanislavsky said, "Vladimir Mikhailov, will you allow me to take your part for a moment? The director will prompt me. All right, let's begin."

Stanislavsky seemed to become smaller practically before our eyes. He looked all huddled over, as if he were cold. He raised his collar and very modestly sat at the edge of the table. Piquar approached the table and said, "Waiting for somebody, old man?" Stanislavsky answered, "Yes, I might say I am."

"The stagecoach hasn't arrived?"

"How do you know I am waiting for the stagecoach?"

Stanislavsky said this with a special quality of suspicion, though there was no indication of it in the script. This unexpected nuance created a very interesting situation, and Piquar, who didn't expect it, stuttered, "Well, yes, well . . . you know everybody is waiting for the stagecoach. Well, I'm waiting and maybe we can drink something together while we're waiting. . . ."

"Why not? I'm all for it." Again the intonation was new to us. It was the intonation of a person who loves to drink.

"Hey, bartender, two mugs of cider." Piquar said. Then he said to Stanislavsky: "Well, who are you waiting for? Your old woman?" At that moment he carefully took a little packet containing sleeping powder from his pocket.

Stanislavsky replied again in a very suspicious tone: "Yes, yes, my old woman and maybe somebody else."

The mugs were brought. Verbitski, as Piquar, was waiting for Stanislavsky to bend down and fix his shoe as the text indicated, because at that moment he was supposed to put the powder into the old man's mug. But Stanislavsky did not bend down, though the prompter was telling him to do so. Verbitski took the mug and said, "Your health!" Stanislavsky answered: "Thank you very much. Thank you very much. Ah, I wish I were younger and stronger."

Verbitski was confused. The powder was in his hand, but the dialogue had to continue. So he said: "Why do you want to be stronger? You seem all right."

"Oh, no, I'm not as strong as I used to be. I feel so sleepy, but it's too early to go to sleep. It must be old age. I will not sleep. I will not sleep!"

Stanislavsky said this in such a wide-awake tone that it was perfectly clear that he wouldn't go to sleep, as the directions indicated he was supposed to. There was no more dialogue between Piquar and the old man, and naturally the scene stopped. Verbitski said, absolutely out of character, "Well, that's all."

Stanislavsky stayed in character, which made us all want to laugh, but of course none of us dared to do so. "What's all?"

"Konstantin Sergeyevich, I have no more words. The scene is finished."

"Why didn't you put me to sleep?"

"Well, you didn't give me a chance to put the powder in the mug, and you didn't drink the wine."

"Suppose the old man didn't drink the wine? What would you do if you were in character?" Stanislavsky asked.

"Well, I imagine I would think of doing it some other way."

"Then why didn't you do something when you saw I wasn't drinking the wine?"

Verbitski replied, "Because in the play it clearly says that he puts the old man to sleep by putting the powder in his mug."

"That remark was in the play because those two actors

who played the scene originally did it so beautifully that it became part of the permanent stage direction in the script," Stanislavsky said. "But in trying to realize this, you did it in a very banal way. The author says you must put this man to sleep. In every theatre the actors should do it in their own way. The tradition of melodrama leaves complete freedom to the actor to carry out the physical actions naturally, keeping them within the logic and the plot of the play. Well, let's play the scene again."

Stanislavsky and Verbitski began the scene again, and Verbitski cleverly began to put the powder into the old man's mug under the pretense of driving a fly away from it, but Stanislavsky pushed the mug off the table without drinking from it at the very last moment, as though by accident. Verbitski said, "Konstantin Sergeyevich, we will never get anywhere if the old man doesn't drink the wine."

Stanislavsky replied: "You think so? Well, it shows me your imagination isn't working too well. All the script says is that you have to put the old man to sleep, but it doesn't say how. The old man can drink or not, whichever he pleases, but you should have a number of ideas as to how to get rid of me."

"Well, to tell you the truth, Konstantin Sergeyevich, I don't know how."

"All right, let's exchange roles. Vladimir Mikhailov, will you sit with me at the table?"

Vladimir replied, "With pleasure."

These two marvelous actors excited our interest beyond words. At the moment when Stanislavsky got up from the table and became the free-and-easy, self-assured Piquar, Vladimir Mikhailov changed into the suspicious, stupid, but touching old man. A greater surprise came to us when they began to improvise the text. The dialogue naturally was started by Stanislavsky, and Vladimir Mikhailov immediately fell into the mood.

Stanislavsky said, "Nice evening, isn't it?"

Mikhailov answered, "Yes, it's all right."

Stanislavsky made as though he were reaching for a little snuffbox, "You want a sniff?" We all understood the tobacco was doped.

Mikhailov said: "No, thank you. I don't use it."

Stanislavsky pretended to sniff it himself, "Perhaps you'd prefer a cigarette?"

"No, thank you, I don't smoke."

Stanislavsky said in an aside: "Oh, this damned old man. It looks as if I'll have to treat him." Then he spoke aloud: "How about a drink? It's my treat."

"Well, it's kind of embarrassing . . . I really don't know . . ."

Stanislavsky said: "Bartender, a couple of glasses." Then he said to the old man, "Waiting for somebody?"

"Oh, nobody special, maybe my niece will come . . ."

The bartender put two mugs on the table. At this moment Stanislavsky took out some change and accidentally dropped it on the floor. Naturally he and the bartender and Mikhailov all bent down to pick it up, and suddenly we saw Stanislavsky raise his hand over the heads of the other two and drop the powder into the old man's mug. We couldn't keep from applauding, and we were also certain that the improvisation had come to an end on this effective point, but we were mistaken. The change was picked up, the money was paid, and Stanislavsky and Mikhailov raised their mugs in a toast. Then, suddenly, the old man looked very suspiciously at the wine, and then at Stanislavsky. We were ready to applaud again Mikailov's talent and spontaneity.

Mikhailov spoke, "With your permission, sir, may I have your mug?"

"What for?"

"Now please, allow me . . ."

"If you wish."

Mikhailov put both mugs together on the table, looked very attentively at them for a moment, and then said: "My mug is fuller than yours. But you're the one treating me, so you must drink mine. That's the custom in this place."

"I never heard of such a custom."

Mikhailov said, "Please, do this for me, otherwise I won't touch my glass." He pushed his mug containing the sleeping powder in front of Stanislavsky.

Stanislavsky said in an aside: "That damned old man! He wants me to poison myself!"

Of course we laughed. By now we had become naïve spectators who were carried away by this game.

Stanislavsky said to the old man, "Thank you, I'll drink to your health." Suddenly he began to sneeze.

Mikhailov was very concerned. "Oh, you have a cold?"

Stanislavsky took a little bottle out of his pocket and poured the content on his handkerchief. "Yes, I'm catching a cold but I have a good remedy." Sneezing more and more, he put the little bottle on the table.

Mikhailov remarked: "Hmm, what a little bottle. . . . May I look at it?" He picked it up.

"If you want to," Stanislavsky answered, sneezing. "Excuse me, I have to leave the table." He went behind Mikhailov, and when the old man picked up the bottle, Stanislavsky put his handkerchief over the old man's face and made a sign to the bartender to come.

Mikhailov now knew that the game was lost, and he began to fall asleep.

Stanislavsky said to the bartender, "Take him to the back room."

Tremendous applause followed.

"Now you understand how you should have acted," Stanislavsky said to Verbitski. Then he turned to Mikhailov: "Thank you for your help. You're a wonderful partner. I hope I didn't hurt you when I pressed the handkerchief to your face."

"No, no. Not at all. Thank you for a wonderful lesson."

"Well, tell me, do you people understand now what I mean when I talk of the logic of the physical action and its significance for melodrama?"

Verbitski answered, "Well, it's understandable, Konstantin Sergeyevich, but if two actors endlessly played out their scene, the performance would never finish."

"I don't think so. All this takes a long time when you are experimenting around in rehearsal. But in the performance the tempo and dialogue are very fast. The good director will keep only the best and eliminate everything that is not essential to the particular drama. It is impossible, I think, to create genuine melodrama without this kind of work. Of course, you don't let your fancy run away with you in this fashion in Ibsen or Dostoevsky. There's no need for it in their work. Gorchakov, I would work out every scene in this manner: for example, Jacques waking up in the morning, the blind girl walking through the streets, etc."

What Is Melodrama?

Stanislavsky continued: "I would like to say a little more about melodrama for the actors in this play. I'm telling you this so that you'll understand the atmosphere in which melodrama as a stage *genre* must be developed and so that you'll know that you must rehearse and play melodrama in a heightened state of excitement. There can be no indifference or coldness in the audience. Everything must be unprecedented and spontaneous so that the audience is electrified and kept in such a mood that one spark can kindle it and can inspire creativity on the stage.

"Melodrama does not tolerate the conventional. Melodrama is life condensed, without unnecessary detail and pause. The director should allow pauses only for a very strong effect and give them to the actor who can hold them convincingly. When the audience watches melodrama, it must be absolutely convinced that whatever it sees on the stage could happen in real life. That is why theatrical convention is impossible in melodrama. If the audience believes that whatever it sees on the stage really happened around it in life, it will be touched and laugh and cry at whatever is going on. Laughter is the reaction of an audience that is moved—that is, if the laughter is called for by a character or situation and not by a trick."

"What about the tricks that are usually used in melodrama?" I asked.

"The audience is only curious about tricks before the curtain goes up. They will comment, 'Let's see what tricks they use tonight.' And then they discuss them again after the curtain comes down. But while the play is going on, the tricks should be so much a part of the play and so well justified that the audience is not aware of them.

"Melodrama must be illusory in the best meaning of the word. I'd like to talk a little more about the matter of truth in melodrama. When you were trying to show me the life of the square, the bar, and particularly of the aristocrats, I felt you missed a great deal. I would like very much to talk with your directors, and then they will work with you actors more on this."

"What do you think of the melodramas of Victor Hugo, Konstantin Sergeyevich?" Kniepper-Chekhova asked.

"I think they are bad. (Don't tell anyone I said so, because they are much in vogue now.) I consider them pseudo-poetic and very affected. They are esthetic but not realistic—with the exception, perhaps, of *Mary Tudor*, a classic melodrama. A classic melodrama always is either realistic or historical. There is a mixture of so many elements in Victor Hugo's melodramas. They may have satisfied his personal esthetic taste, but they didn't satisfy the emotions of the audience. Melodramas usually are created when people are filled with noble and high feelings and they have to express them in some way. That's why your play will be successful, because our audience now, right after the Revolution, has so many beautiful feelings and emotions and likes to see just as noble deeds and strong feelings on the stage. Try not to disappoint them. Well, that's enough for today. Let's plan our future work and, Gorchakov, please take notes.

"First, I want to talk to you directors about the contrast between everyday life and between life and truth in melodrama. That will take us one day. Then you must go through all those études that I mentioned before. You will need about two weeks for this. If you see that you are getting the point while you're doing the études, leave them (don't torture them) and show them to me. If you feel that a certain étude doesn't come off—that you don't get the point we're working for—do it again and again, changing the given circumstances and stimulating your actor's imagination. Then you can go to the rehearsal of the first act on stage. This should be a very careful process. Everything that you achieve in the rehearsal hall must be brought most conscientiously to the stage."

"Perhaps we should work on stage with the curtain down," I said.

"No, that wouldn't be good. It is necessary for you to get accustomed to the stage and to work to achieve the same degree of expressiveness that you had in the rehearsal hall. I would suggest that first you go through all your physical actions without words. You skipped a couple of scenes because you couldn't do them in the hall—for example, the scene of the long bread line and that of the stagecoach's arrival. Treat them like études and I will look at them when they are in an unfinished form. This type of scene needs an exceptional directorial skill. I don't think you have the knowledge for that. Please don't be insulted. Even now, I myself am never sure if I can stage mob scenes as I see them in my imagination. Of course, I know some of the directorial secrets for that kind of scene. I know them and I promise to share them with you. Remind me to do this, not during the rehearsals, but when you and I are walking home together, Gorchakov. When you find how to do all these scenes physically, you can start the text. Please don't whisper. In actual rehearsals on the stage you should speak naturally. Don't whisper and don't shout. Talk as though you are in the actual room that the scenic designer plans for you. That is why I would rather that you have real sets when you work on the stage. I don't like it when directors rehearse in makeshift sets which consist of chairs and tables. Now you'll need two or three weeks to do all this, so let's say I'll see you all again in a month.

"But come to me often and keep me informed how your rehearsals are developing, Gorchakov. I think you live not far from me, and I usually sit in my garden around four o'clock. If I am free there, I would like Chekhova and Ershov also to come to see me. I will tell them how to work on the dialogue with you.

"Don't be upset about spending a whole month on the transfer of the first act from the studio to the stage. You just have to find what's the proper mood for the play on the stage; so far you've only found it in the rehearsal hall. If you find the correct way to work on the stage during the first month, the following work will go much faster, and, if you are working on stage in the right direction, you can leave the last act completely for dress rehearsals.

This always gets marvelous results, if everything has been well prepared for in advance. But the right ending has to be found beforehand. The audience will never forgive you if the performance does not have exactly the right ending. I think it is the great art of a director to know how to end each act. I was taught by a great director, Fedotov. Sometimes, when you have to do a play in a short time, you must begin working on the endings practically from the first rehearsals. Of course, we don't have that problem now."

"What about music?" I asked. "You've said nothing about music."

"Usually music is introduced in melodrama to create a mood for the actor, so as to prepare him for his big emotional scenes. I don't think you need music of that kind or for that purpose. Whenever you use music in this way, you have to have an orchestra, and the audience gets the feeling that the play is actually composed with music. I think this melodrama has a very clever arrangement by which music comes naturally in the scenes of the play that need music to make them more effective. You have music when the sisters are looking for each other, when Mariana is alone on stage, when the Marquises are ridiculing Henrietta, when someone sings on the street. I think you should work on this. I even think that the melodies used are good and sufficiently French in style. Don't complicate them. What do you think, Gorchakov? Do you think that when you use music, you will always be able to justify it in relation to the different scenes?"

"I think so."

"Don't forget to have variety. Sometimes you can bring out the intensity of the dramatic scene by music of a contrasting mood. In a dramatic scene you can have light music—of course, not too light. An experienced composer knows exactly what I mean."

"Well, here is Mr. Oransky, our composer, who has been listening most attentively."

"I think it is very good that you are working with us again, Oransky. The theatre should have its own composer. Music for the dramatic performance is very special music. Well, I'll bid you good-by, and I wish you success."

A choir of enthusiastic voices answered, "Thank you very much, Konstantin Sergeyevich . . . We'll do all you want us to do . . . See you soon . . . Don't forget us . . ."

Dialogue

Stanislavsky kept precisely to the plan of our work. Our next meeting was devoted to the rehearsal of the scene that takes place in the house of Count de Lenier (played by Ershov).

"We will hold the rehearsal in the studio," Stanislavsky said. "It is the most difficult scene in the play because it consists entirely of dialogue that is full of inner emotion and very little external action. Before we begin to rehearse with the actual text, I would like to ask the actors in this scene to answer the following questions: Do you, the father, mother, and son, understand your relationships clearly?"

"Very clearly, Konstantin Sergeyevich."

"Do you understand perfectly the plot of the scene?"

"Yes. We've thought about the scene a great deal and had a long discussion with the director about it.

"Very good. Now tell me, all three of you, are all the inner desires which guide you toward getting what you want in the scene just as convincing to you as to the actual characters of the play?"

"Yes, we as actors want the same things as our characters."

"All right, Chekhova, what do you want in this scene?"

Chekhova (who played the mother) replied: "I want Roget to be pure in soul and body. I do not want him to repeat his father's mistakes or mine. I wish him happiness. I would like to protect him from all the horror that surrounds us."

"Very good. An active problem. Excellent. I believe that you are completely prepared for this rehearsal. But, first, please tell me what moment in this particular scene you consider the strongest, the most important, the most exciting for you."

"When I find out that my son, Roget, knows my past."

"Be more specific. What sentence, what phrase, what thought in the text?"

" 'Roget, you know!' And the phrase that Roget says: 'What tremendous suffering you went through in the name of love.' "

"Wonderful! What is so good is that you consider your partner's text so important. What part of the text expresses the strongest moment for Count de Lenier in this scene?"

Ershov (de Lenier) replied: "Roget's words, 'Here is her address,' and then my words, 'Here is the address,' when I take the piece of paper from the table. Also, 'Here is the address of Henrietta Gérard'—the words of Piquar, the spy, when my attempt to find out her address fails."

"I think you are on the right road. Your problem is precisely in this word 'address'—to find out her address at any price. In this word should be your passion for the girl, your hatred for your wife, and your disgust for your son. Well now, Roget, what is the strongest moment for you in this scene?"

Massalsky (Roget) said: " 'I am proud of my break with you. Arrest me! It will clear me in the eyes of those who blame me for my background.' "

"I am afraid that is a little too declaratory. But I'll leave it up to your conscience to try to find a moment which will excite you more strongly."

"The point where I break with my father. When I declare my break, I want to emphasize not only the political meaning of this declaration, as you call it, but my decision to go to Henrietta, to live with her and for her, and to marry her."

"This is already closer to the purpose. So now you know your main problems. You know what relationships you have to each other and what thoughts and words you use to express them most vividly. Now, as the first exercise for learning how to handle the dialogue, I will ask you to do the following: speak your lines in the order that they are written, but, wherever you find it necessary, substitute for the words and phrases of the text those that express what is really on your mind—what you think in relation to the people to whom you talk. Try to articulate the subtext, as we call it, expressing the most important inter-relationships, thoughts, and problems behind the given text. Tell me, what beats did you establish in this particular scene?"

I answered, "The first beat is the dialogue between Count de Lenier and his wife about Roget's new mistress and the Count's request that Roget leave Paris."

"What name did you give to this beat?"

" 'Insulted Innocence,' " I said. "This ironic title defines the line of the Count's action; he lies about Roget, while he himself is guilty."

"Does this title satisfy the actors in the scene?"

Ershov (de Lenier) said, "It satisfies me completely, because I am pretending to be a most loving father so I can find out where my son has hidden Henrietta during his scene with my wife."

Chekhova (Mme. de Lenier) said, "I am also satisfied, because I feel that my husband's words indicate a certain trace of the truth, but at the same time he is not sincere with me—he is trying to get something out of me without wanting to reveal the whole truth."

"Now let's do that exercise," Stanislavsky replied. "Speak the text of the beat only with your eyes. Don't speak aloud one word, but say your lines to yourself. Do the physical actions as though you were speaking your lines aloud."

The short pause that followed indicated to Stanislavsky that the task wasn't quite clear to the actors.

"Is something not clear?" he asked.

Luzhsky answered, "I think, Konstantin Sergeyevich, what is not clear is how one would know that his partner has finished a sentence if he speaks only to himself."

"He must recognize that from different little signs. The whole question depends on extreme attention to one another. For example, I am sure you all have experienced this: on winter days when your windows are sealed and the voices from the street can't possibly be heard, you have watched with great interest through the glass panes a meeting between a young girl and a middle-aged man across the street. You watch them greet each other, shake hands, ask each other where they are going and how he or she happened to be on this particular corner. This conversation is perfectly clear to you, because it is accompanied by certain gestures, smiles, turning of the head, and movement of the hands. You don't have to hear the first words of this meeting in order to guess them. But you become terribly interested to know what they are talking about in the next stage of the meeting, if only because of the fact that something in their appearance attracts your attention tremendously. It's as though you said to yourself, 'What a pity that it's not spring, when the windows are open and I could be here in the twilight by the window unobserved and could hear so many interesting conversations!' You think these things, and you don't for a moment reproach yourself for eavesdropping. You don't reproach yourself for being so curious that you have a passion to learn about life in every possible way. It is the most natural curiosity—indeed, practically a profession—for an actor and an artist to observe life.

"But now it is winter. You cannot open the window. And you begin to look at the couple with added attention. You don't follow the movement of their lips. You concentrate all your attention on the girl's eyes and those of her companion. And after two or three minutes of very intensive observation, you will be surprised to notice that without hearing the words you understand what they are talking about. The man looks straight into the girl's face, never taking his eyes away from her eyes. Naturally it makes you think that he must have been asking her about something very important to him. And the girl meets his eyes, then looks away to one side, then lowers her head and looks at her muff, and finally she throws a glance up at him somehow from the side and then concentrates her look away from him at something in the distance. The man looks spontaneously in the direction she is looking, but not seeing anything, he looks again at her face and then lowers his eyes and stares at a piece of wood frozen in the snow. The girl becomes aware that he isn't looking at her any more and so turns her eyes to his face for some time, as though trying to memorize his features and to find the answer to a question that concerns her very much. For a second their eyes meet. They look at each other very seriously and then both lower their eyes and look at the steps of the house by which they stand. Once, suddenly, they look at your window so you are frightened. Perhaps they realize you are there! You are glued to the window, but then you realize they are completely unaware that you are watching them. For the last time their eyes meet and both have an expression of bitter reproach. The girl's eye-lashes tremble and she raises her muff to her face as she goes by the man. He watches her go for a few minutes, as though he were having difficulty in deciding whether to follow her or to continue on his way. Now do you need words for that scene? Do you need to add words to this inner dialogue that the couple spoke with their eyes?"

"Konstantin Sergeyevich, are you sure that the audience is observing the actors on the stage just as attentively as you did this unknown couple from your closed window?" Luzhsky asked.

"Absolutely, definitely. In fact, I think that the audience is much more attentive and sensitive to the actor than the actor to the audience. You can hide nothing from the audience—not even the nail polish on your fingernails—if it was not according to the period of the play.

"Trust your eyes and you will guarantee audience attention. Be most aware of each other. Observe each other constantly and you will always guess when one finishes a sentence or completes a thought, although he never speaks it aloud."

In the rapt atmosphere of the whole room, Chekhova looked at her partner and then looked aside with mistrust and wonder. We immediately guessed from the expression of her eyes the first line of her part: "Count, don't you exaggerate the danger? Is Roget's infatuation that deep?"

With the same long and attentive look, Ershov answered her, and in the expression of his eyes we could guess the sentence: "I should ask you that question. You're his mother. It is your responsibility to watch your son's behavior."

At that moment Chekhova raised her eyes to her hus-band, and he, with an exaggerated seriousness, began to look from side to side, obviously saying to himself: "I'm always first to find out about everything. I am telling you this and you doubt me . . ."

It was naturally very easy for us, who knew the text by heart, to understand what Chekhova and Ershov were thinking and it didn't seem to be difficult at all to guess the end of each phrase. The exchange of looks back and forth—"firing glances at each other," as Stanislavsky called it—proceeded easily. Sometimes they added movement of their heads and turns of the body to the expression of the eyes. Stanislavsky did not stop any of these movements nor did he establish any of them. Finally, he asked Massalsky, the third actor in the scene, to join Chekhova and Ershov in their speechless dialogue. It was very interesting to watch them and to see that in some moments of their scene the actors could not contain themselves and keep silent; some words were spoken aloud. I think it was Massalsky who first suddenly screamed out a certain part of his speech. A second after he did this, he threw a frightened look at Stanislavsky, but Stanislavsky just laughed and with a gesture indicated he should go on. But a short while after, Chekhova also started to speak in one of the strongest emotional moments of her scene, and she also looked at Stanislavsky, as if wanting to explain her behavior. But Stanislavsky said to her: "Continue, continue! We will hear explanations later!"

At the end of the scene all three of them began to talk, completely forgetting this was supposed to be speechless dialogue. But how much deeper, more spirited and colorful the end of the scene sounded when the accumulated emotions of the silent dialogue were released. We were waiting with anxiety for Stanislavsky's criticism of the actors for breaking through the silence, but obviously he was completely satisfied.

"It all happened just as I expected," he said. "There are

certain exercises that provoke the actor. This is the kind of exercise that I gave you just now. Actors usually think that all they have to do is to open their mouths and say their words aloud and they are acting. It's not like that at all. You have to earn the right to open your mouth and say the words of the person you are portraying. You must go through serious work for this. You must know the biography of the person you are portraying perfectly. You must answer all those questions that I put to you before the rehearsal, and finally you must 'live through' your correct, precise relationship to the characters in the play, and to the events that occur. You must hold back within yourself your desire to speak the lines; otherwise the words of the dialogue will appear to be glib, as they so often are on the stage.

"So—we have just learned the first rule of dialogue: *limitless attention to your partner*. Everything inside is filled up with the thought and meaning. The tongue is tied up; only the eyes talk.

"Now the second rule. When you hold back, it does not mean to be colorless, or to lack variety of intonation, or to be pale and phlegmatic. As you approached the end of the scene, you intuitively began a lively and passionate discussion. This happened because you were prepared for it by the preceding action of the scene. First, you were silent; then intuitively and in spite of yourselves, you broke into separate words and phrases, and, finally, you began to act the thought of the word. You really talked. The classic pattern of dialogue is: first, silence—which speaks with eyes just as much as with words pronounced aloud—exclamations, separate bursts of words, then phrases that you couldn't possibly hold back, and finally a passionate, active stream of thought—speech. But not all dialogue is written by the author in such open fashion on that scheme. It would be too monotonous if all dialogue in all plays was done in that way. In this particular scene, as you know, your characters speak instantaneously, so that this classic scheme takes place *within*. But I accomplished the concentration of that dialogue and brought it out by forcing you to talk only with your eyes so that you would realize what is taking place inside the character you are playing. But of course before an audience you will speak the text naturally.

"How can you play the scene by speaking aloud and yet preserve the inner scheme of the dialogue? For this purpose we have the second rule: *the use of intonation*. This means intonation of many sorts: strong and weak, colorful and pale, passionate and phlegmatic. Intonation shows a relationship to your partner, to the events of the play, to your own feeling, and to the convictions with which you color your thoughts and words. But you cannot say every word in a phrase with the same strong or weak or passionate or phlegmatic intonation. You must first choose the important word in every sentence and say it in that intonation which you establish for yourself in relation to the thought of that sentence. The important word to emphasize would be the noun (what), then the verb (what to do), and then, following the law of logic and the meaning of the given text, adjectives, adverbs, pronouns, etc. I will ask all the actors in the play to mark in their scripts those words that seem absolutely necessary and important to the meaning of each sentence. Underline them with a pencil. I advise you—in the beginning, I repeat—to pay special attention, first, to the nouns, then the verbs."

Our actors began to do this very seriously. While they were busy with this, Luzhsky took his place near Stanislavsky.

"Don't you think, Konstantin Sergeyevich, that there are other factors in finding the main word in the sentence besides those indications that you gave the actors like the noun and the verb? Don't you think that the actor should know the role very well? And don't you think this includes evaluating the events in the play, the relationship between partners, the given circumstances, and even the specific characteristics of the character for whom one is seeking the important word?"

"Undoubtedly. You cannot do this work mechanically. It can't be separated from the total work on your part, or from the source and the roots of your part."

"It's too bad but very often we do it just the other way around," Luzhsky said. "Many of us, when entrusted with a role, do not think it through thoroughly or study the text. Before we've done this, we have already decided which words are important and what intonations. As one actress said to me, 'I am going to use such an intonation here that everyone will gasp!' I thought to myself, 'I am sure you will have some intonation but who will gasp? Perhaps you, yourself, when I take the part away from you.'"

"As you see, I allow my actors to do this exercise only after two or three months of work on the part. The emphasized words are only tracks on which the logical thought of the character finds the right road to the ear and the heart of the audience. But, of course, when you don't know the thought that you want to express, you can't possibly know which is the important word in a phrase, and you won't know the thoughts you want to express until you know the life and spirit of the given role."

"I agree with you in that order," Luzhsky replied. "You cannot begin working on a part from the text, thinking how to say it correctly. You must give yourself the question: Correct in relation to what?"

Stanislavsky said: "Well, are you actors ready? Have you found the important words?"

"It seems we have," Chekhova answered for everybody.

"Fine," Stanislavsky said. "Now let's do another exercise. I want you to begin your scene again, but you are permitted to use only the words in your parts that you underline. These words should be filled with everything you gathered from your previous exercise: your relationship to each other, all your thoughts and inner actions. Your eyes must do most of the work as before.

Massalsky asked: "In other words, you want us to pronounce only the underlined words and omit the rest?"

"Oh, no, you misunderstood me completely. You say out loud the underlined words, but you say the rest silently to yourself. The amount of time for the pronouncement of the sentence will be the same as before.

"All right, now it's clear," Ershov remarked. "But if I have a very strong desire to say the whole sentence and bring out the underlined words even more strongly, is that permissible?"

"Only in extraordinary cases."

The first word cues which the actors pronounced sounded rather strange, and the eyes of Chekhova and Ershov told us much more than the intonation of the words they exchanged: "Danger? Infatuation?" Chekhova said first. "He wants to get married," answered Ershov. "Is she terrible?" A new question from Chekhova. "Adventuress, greedy, money, clothes," her husband answered.

Because of this scarcity of words, their pauses were full of meaning, and the significance of the pauses was intensified by the expression of their eyes. But even the chopped-up dialogue became more and more expressive and attracted our attention more and more. By the middle of the scene the actors were completely accustomed to this unusual dialogue. The actor's eyes met, and their pauses corresponded to each other, and, as a result, the important words had a more decisive and sharper accent in the beats of the scene. "Dr. Gilbert?" Roget threw an accusation at his mother. "Quiet! Quiet!" his frightened mother answered. "You loved him." "It's a lie!" "I know everything." "No, no!" "Because of me you stayed with my father." "Because of a child." "Sister." "Louisa."

This is how the page of the text looked when I put it down. They only used twenty words from the forty-eight sentences on the page, but their expressions and their pauses told us everything they had skipped. What did burst out was what really was most important.

"If only we could play a scene in this way before an audience," we were thinking, as we realized that the audience must hear the words that we omitted. The audience would see the scene for the first time, while we actors knew it by heart.

They rehearsed the final scene of the act with this particular exercise, as they had rehearsed the previous one, and it sounded full, strong and colorful. It was played with passion as it demanded. And again Stanislavsky was very pleased.

When we had finished, Stanislavsky said: "And now I want to talk about the third rule for dialogue. When you play the scene now, you do it with the rhythm that Apollo bestowed upon you. You do not control the rhythm of the scene; it controls you. That is wrong. An actor must ride the rhythm as an experienced horseman does a wild horse. What rhythm do you think the beginning of the scene has —I mean, what inner rhythm?"

Ershov replied, "Comparative quiet."

Stanislavsky said: "Conduct it for me, please. Let's verify your inner rhythm with your physical action."

Ershov conducted the rhythm with his index finger, as was customary at Stanislavsky rehearsals.

Stanislavsky asked: "Does that rhythm change from the moment Roget comes into the scene? Does the rhythm change for those already playing?"

Massalsky answered, "I think not immediately, but from the very moment when I find out that my father has slandered me."

"Tell me, within the bounds of the rhythm that Ershov just conducted for us, are there any moments when the tempo quickens or diminishes?"

"Definitely," Ershov said. "When I feel that my wife trusts me, my problem becomes less intense. I lessen my effort to convince her. But when I see she doubts my words, I intensify my action and increase my arguments."

"When you increase your arguments and intensify your action, do you speak faster?"

"It seems to me that it does not always work that way. Sometimes, on the contrary, I begin to speak more slowly to convince her."

"Very true," Stanislavsky agreed. "Now I want you all to listen carefully. The scenic rhythm is not the acceleration or diminishing of tempo, but the acceleration or diminishing of the *inner intensity*—the desire to realize the problem and to execute the inner or outer physical action. I want you all to remember this and not to confuse the inner stage rhythm with the outward showing of the rhythm—though very often, in order to discover the inner rhythm, we do use, as we did now, the same method as you use in music.

"Now I would like you three to 'conduct' your rhythm in that scene for the whole dialogue, taking as the basis your relationship to each other, your problems as developed by the plot, your thoughts, and your most important moments and words. I especially emphasize important moments, because the peak moments in the orchestration of your role you will 'conduct' as sharp accents in the orchestration. These are drums and cymbals in the text of your roles."

With utmost concentration, Stanislavsky watched the

three actors conduct the design of their rhythm. We who watched saw that they were again speaking the words to themselves, following all the rules that Stanislavsky had given them today. Again their eyes were talking, again important words would occasionally burst out—sometimes even whole sentences. At the same time, we saw that their relationship, thoughts, and words were completely controlled by their inner problems. Externally they revealed this to Stanislavsky by "conducting" the rhythm with the movement of their hands.

Stanislavsky asked, "What did you learn from this exercise?"

Chekhova answered: "As far as I'm concerned, the exercise compelled me to concentrate more on my thoughts of Roget and on how to make him happy. It made me realize again which beats in that scene are more important to me."

Ershov said, "It may sound very stupid, but it seems to me that my re-evaluation of different moments of my part made my blood sometimes much hotter and sometimes much colder."

Massalsky said, "I can't tell you exactly what I got from that exercise, but I definitely know that I felt much more order and a more definite relationship between the important and less important beats and the problems of my part."

"Your answers satisfy me completely," Stanislavsky said. "They show me that in searching for the rhythm in your dialogue you really were concerned with the inner process that took place and you were not following the rhythm superficially as so often actors do ('Speak faster or slower'). Understanding of the stage rhythm is a very complicated process, as it has many facets, which are, to a certain degree, individual. We will return to working on rhythm again and again until we learn all its specific

aspects. But it is absolutely necessary for the actor to develop in himself the feeling of inner stage rhythm.

"I would like you to do the scene again, following the
text fully, as it is written, but remember those three rules
that we have discovered: first, pay particularly close attention to each other, and develop your attention to such a
degree that you can carry on the dialogue with your eyes
alone; second, have exact knowledge of the relationships,
thoughts, and words in your part which are the more important for the text, and learn how to use intonation to
emphasize important words and, through them, thoughts
and relationships in the dialogue; third, establish the inner
rhythm in the dialogue by evaluating different problems
of the part. I want to warn you that these three rules do
not complete the art of dialogue, but they are the most
important. And as we learn more about the difficult art of
dialogue, we will add many other rules to these basic rules.
Telesheva, from now on I want you to work on these scenes
with the actors. Give me your criticism of the scene that
you have just watched. It's important for me to know in
what direction you would lead the actors."

"I think, Konstantin Sergeyevich, when we rehearse
these scenes without you, we will have to repeat them
using the exercises which you gave us today. When the
actors know the exercises well enough to forget them, then
I feel they will be more relaxed. My criticism of the scene
would be that the actors are still much too self-conscious."

"Very true."

"Then we will try to forget all the preceding phase of
the work and go over and over the scene, concentrating
only on the direct problems of each character. I would like
to discuss with each actor the character he is playing. I
feel that the parts are cast correctly, and I think the three
actors are doing the right thing by beginning to create
their characters *from themselves*. But now I feel the mo-

ment has come when each actor can see what elements of the character he as an actor does not have. For example, Ershov, as we know him, does not have that cruelty or perseverance that is the most definite and characteristic trait of Count de Lenier."

"Superb," Stanislavsky said. "This is the only road to the organic creation of character. Constantly begin from yourself—and then inject the different traits of the character which you as an artist do not have on your palette. Before attacking a new role, each actor must wash off and scratch out cleanly all the colors of the previous role from the palette of his spirit, exactly as a painter washes his palette before he begins a new canvas. Well, now, go ahead and work, and call me once more before final rehearsal if you need me."

The Director's Secrets

One evening when I was walking home with Stanislavsky after rehearsal, I reminded him of his promise to tell me some of the "director's secrets" he had mentioned, especially in relation to the first scene of the first act.

"They are not very complicated secrets," Stanislavsky answered. "The beginning of every act and especially of the first act must be simple and perfectly clear to the audience. The revolt of the hungry Parisians on the eve of the French Revolution serves as the beginning of your play. Aside from the difficulty of portraying in general a revolt of hungry people, you are here touching upon history. You want to show those very same French people who at the end of the play will take the Bastille. This is much too serious and responsible a problem, not only for you as director but for the theatre as a whole. One shouldn't treat history lightly. We have a right to *announce* the news of the taking of the Bastille in that vivid form of which I spoke; but should you think of showing the taking of the Bastille, particularly on the open stage, I would try to talk you out of it, and then, if you would not listen to me, I would forbid it.

"On stage, people must not be shown in an off-hand fashion. To show people necessitates a complex and deep understanding. In addition, you are showing people at the time that their consciousness is ripening for the great historical process which, as we know, is to influence all humanity and affect the history of many countries. The author did not take all this into consideration.

"My advice to you is not to present the first scene of the play as it is written. Don't begin with the revolt. You rob yourself of a much better moment for it later in the play —in the prison. My advice is to create an alarming mood in this first scene. We remember from the history of the period that there was a scarcity of bread in Paris. And because of that just before the revolution bread was hidden from the people. Naturally there were groups of people who always tried to be near the bakery in case bread was brought in or taken out. In your direction of the first scene you have a long line in front of the bakery, and the people in the line tell each other their misfortunes. I find this scene *too static and too obvious*. There is nothing in your scene that arouses the audience's imagination.

"Here is how I advise you to do the scene. Divide your bread line into groups. The actors who are in these groups should live with all the thoughts and relationships that I assume you worked out with them. Spread your groups in different places on the square. Within each group there will be conversation. Within some there will be arguments about certain questions. Establish the movement of people from one group to another and the motives for their changing places. For this kind of grouping you can use certain spots, such as the fountain, café tables, the arch, the pillars, and the statue. Five or six people should come in as the scene begins; some people should leave and then return. All this has to be done without any excitement, rather slowly. The basic physical problem is waiting; perhaps they will bring the bread. The inner action is preparation for the great events and discussion of the situation in the city and of the debate in the National Assembly. Once in a while, in one or another of the groups, someone bursts out with a loud sentence. Choose several phrases, serious and meaningful. Don't let your people declaim, and whatever people say in the group should come as a result of the discussion or arguments they are having. Let them speak mostly with their eyes. The object of their attention should be the bakery, the baker who appears at the window, the policemen walking on the streets, those who do not agree with the majority opinion that things are wrong in Paris. You can find the most interesting action in that scene for the actor who plays the spy. What's his name in the play?"

"Piquar."

"Piquar, yes, that's right. Let him move from one group to another, humming a provocative melody. He comes to one group and sings a provocative stanza under his breath. Then he goes to another group and agrees with whatever they are saying. Then he goes to the third group and argues just to avoid suspicion. Then he rushes to the fourth group in order to hear what they are saying, then very cleverly passes by the policemen and whispers to one of them, telling him who should be watched. I would like you to do that scene just as I have described it. Do you remember that Verbitski (Piquar) asked me, 'How can I show that I am a spy?' I think if you will direct his scene like this he will be happy. What do you think?"

I replied that I was sure he would. "Such precise and colorful actions! Actors love to be given specific physical actions."

Stanislavsky said, "That's true because physical action when it is correct is a bait for the inner action and even the feeling itself. When Verbitski goes through this physical action, I am sure that he will feel the role—he will feel himself being a spy. This is the first beat of the mob scene which begins the play. Add to it sounds: a doleful bell tolling for evening mass, a dog barking in the distance, the sound of coach wheels passing nearby. This beat must last a minute and a half. The second beat will begin with the baker's first cue. He understands very well why the people have gathered on the square; he knows what they are waiting for and, finally, annoyed by more than he can stand, he says: 'You're waiting in vain. There is no bread today. I'm not expecting any.' Aren't those the baker's first words?"

"Approximately, yes, that's the sense."

"Fine. Now get the exact sentence from the play, and, by the way, tell the adapter that I like what he's done very much and those little changes that we bring in here and there are necessary for the construction. They are very slight but essential.

"All right now," he continued, "after the baker's cue there should be a short pause, a reaction of the whole group to his words. Nobody believes him, but only one or two leave the square. How many are in this scene?"

"Eighteen."

"All right, then that's fine. Let two or three leave. This won't hurt the effect and, besides, they should come back into the scene for some reason, and they will have a reason the way I am building the next scene. A very nondescript young man comes into the square, approaches the door of the bakery and knocks stealthily, trying not to be seen or heard by the crowd. But people see him, although they pretend not to. The baker opens the door. He and the young man whisper together and then the young man leaves the square. A complete silence follows his exit. The baker pulls down the curtain at the window. The silence grows more sinister. From the side of the stage where the bakery is, one hears the squeak of a wheelbarrow, the kind you see very often in France. The crowd turns in the direction of the noise. The squeak comes closer and then stops near the back door of the bakery. The people in the crowd exchange glances. Somebody stealthily approaches the baker's door and looks through the keyhole. Then you hear the slam of the back door. The man who was looking through the keyhole rolls a nearby stone to the door, climbs on it, and tries to look over the top of the window curtain."

"How about the police who were in the square?" I asked.

"The police run to the back door to get bread for themselves the moment they hear the wheelbarrow."

Stanislavsky always answered every question. He used to see the scene which he described so clearly, so fully, and so precisely in every detail that he could satisfy every actor involved in the scene and every detail of the production.

"The one who was peeking through the curtain," Stanislavsky continued, "gives the sign to the rest of the crowd and instantly the whole mob is at the bakery door. Somebody attempts to break down the door but it won't give. Nobody will try to break the window. (I would like you to observe that for some reason people don't like to break glass, though it is easier to break than wood. I have been told that even very experienced crooks have a specific fear of the sound of breaking glass.) When they cannot break the door in, one of the crowd picks up an old piece of iron and, with the help of others, breaks the lock, and the whole crowd falls inside the bakery. Now you can make all the noise you wish inside; you can talk all you want but stick to the text of the play. Never talk in general. And use the words of the play which express the reaction, thought, and relationship of the crowd to the current events. This is the end of the second beat.

"The beginning of the third beat: the policemen run in. Count de Lenier arrives. The police prefect rebukes the policemen for not being on the job and commands them to bring order in the crowd. The police run into the bakery. We can't see what goes on inside; we only see, one by one, the various people in the crowd brought out. Slowly they push the rest out. Some of the crowd has succeeded in grabbing loaves of bread. Those who did not, and got only blows from the police, throw violent and angry glances at the Count and the Chief of Police. Soon the whole square is freed of the crowd. The baker bows low to the Count and the Chief of Police and begins to fix the broken lock of his door. The Chief of Police calls Piquar, the spy, and here you begin the first scene of the written play. Do you agree with this design for the first scene of the first act?"

"I think it is magnificent, Konstantin Sergeyevich."

"You understand the real essence of the design. We are not showing the revolt itself but the mood, the atmosphere of Paris in those troubled days preceding the Revolution. It is only a minute, but it's a very colorful episode revealing how people were cheated out of bread. We do not show the arguments between the baker and the line of people, but we are showing a concrete piece of action. The young man who whispers with the baker should tell him, 'The bread wagon will come from a certain small street.'"

I asked, "Don't you think it might be better, Konstantin Sergeyevich, for the baker to tell the crowd there is no bread after the young man has alerted him that the bread is coming?"

"Try it. It might be better. I would advise you to rehearse it both ways and then when I see it with a fresh eye we'll decide which is better."

At this point we were approaching Stanislavsky's home,

and, when we had reached his gate, I asked him hesitatingly how he thought we should handle the scene where the coach arrives. Stanislavsky looked at his watch. "Well, I still have twenty minutes before dinner. Let's go into the garden and we'll sit on the bench and enjoy the fresh air and I'll tell you. That scene is less complicated."

Stanislavsky took his notebook from his pocket and began to draw, or rather reconstruct, the design of the set in our first scene.

"The way you have it," he said, "your stagecoach arrives off-stage and all the passengers appear on the square. You managed the sounds of the approaching coach well, and the ad-libbing of the crowd is all right. The audience expects something very interesting, but from the moment the passengers appear in the square, no matter how well the actors may play the scene, the audience will be disappointed. Here you broke another rule of stage action and of the audience's conception of it. If in the first scene you were trying to show the revolt of the hungry, nakedly, directly, and without hiding anything, in this scene you hide everything off-stage, promising the audience with your off-stage effects something very exciting but in reality bringing them less than you have indicated. In other words, you are cheating the audience."

"Well, I can't possibly imagine . . . how could I bring a stagecoach and horses on stage?" I asked.

"I have no intention of making you bring a big stagecoach and horses on stage. One should fool the audience but only to a certain extent and with taste. Here is what I am suggesting. Behind the arches of the square construct a wooden parapet dividing the higher part of the street from the lower. You must arrange it so that the road on which the stagecoach passes is below the floor of the stage and the coach seems not to arrive but to pass by. In other words, this is only a stop on the route. You absolutely must reveal a small part of the coach, and here is how you can do it. Construct a very small wagon on four wheels that are each of a different size. Fill up the back with empty cartons painted a variety of dark colors. This will give the impression of the baggage which is always in the back of a stagecoach. Now tie it with cord, not too tightly, so that the boxes will move with each move of the wagon. This will give the effect of the coach going over the bumps of the road. On top of the boxes put a cage with two live chickens. The audience will laugh and it will give them the sense of the coach coming in from the country. In front, place a young actor on his knees, dress him in a heavy coat with a hood thrown back—the kind of coat worn as a protection from the dust. Give him a horn and a coachman's whip. The audience can see the baggage and the coachman behind the parapet, and these are the most characteristic details of the coach. From this, the audience will fill out in imagination the whole stagecoach. It will even be convinced that it actually saw the coach on stage.

"I want you to remember this fundamental theatrical rule: establish truly and precisely details that are typical and the audience will have a sense of the whole, because of their special ability to imagine and complete in imagination what you have suggested.

"But the detail must be characteristic and typical of whatever you want the audience to see. That is why naturalism is poisonous to the theatre. Naturalism cheats the audience of its main pleasure and its most important satisfaction, that of creating with the actor and completing in its own imagination what the actor, the director, and the designer suggest with their theatre techniques. Now if your actor who plays the coachman sitting on his knees in the wagon with the uneven wheels, will sway from side to side and blow his horn and stir up the horses with his whip, won't this make a live, active detail which will create the exact illusion of the stagecoach?

"Besides, we have to create a much better scene on stage than the one you showed me in rehearsal. You must have some of your characters, participants in this particular scene, meet the coach, and some of them see people off. This is typical detail of any stagecoach stop. It immediately creates the true feeling of the scene. It would be wonderful if you could persuade a couple of your young actresses to dress like boys and play street urchins, because they, too, are typical enthusiastic observers at the arrival and departure of stagecoaches or trains. Tell these young actresses we will give them a fascinating pantomime. Also, you must have the noise of approaching wheels and the whinnying of the horses. This sound is easy to imitate. I have observed that an audience believes that they see a real animal if they hear the sound; even though they know that there are actually no live animals, they are much intrigued. Someday I would like to ask a good psychologist what the reason is for this. The audience easily believes there is a snake in the box if you bring the box on stage. I have also observed that an audience does not like to see live animals on the stage. It seems to me that this is because the living animals break their attention and emphasize the artificiality of the rest of the stage, including the made-up, dressed-up actors. The whinnying of the horses is absolutely necessary.

"Now let's repeat the scheme of the scene:

"1. On stage the crowd gathers gradually to meet the stagecoach. First come the street urchins. While they wait, they organize some kind of game.

"2. A far-away sound of a horn. Everybody listens. The boys climb on the parapet and look in the direction from which the coach is coming.

"3. The sounds are closer and closer and more varied: stamping of the horses' hoofs, wheels over the cobblestones, the horn again. Those who are meeting the coach crowd closer and closer to the parapet. They try to recognize familiar faces among the passengers, waving with handkerchiefs, hats, and whips. The boys run to meet the coach.

"4. The sounds of the arriving coach grow louder and louder. The murmur of the people grows into exclamations of welcome. The horn is blown fortissimo. The whinnying of horses and the sounds of harness bells; the stagecoach —that is, the luggage and the shoulders and head of the coachman come into view (you will have to pull the wagon by a rope). As usually happens, all those meeting the coach make a general move forward, then go back to one side, forward, and back again." Stanislavsky drew this with arrows in his notebook.

"5. The boys make a lot of noise and then the first arrivals appear from the stagecoach, climbing up the steps that you must build from the lower platform to the stage. Kisses, much general conversation on a high note. The boys offer to carry luggage. Some of the people cry for joy. Someone is looking for a friend he expects and does not find, and he asks the rest of the passengers if he was on the coach. Someone inquires about his mother-in-law, a big fat woman, whether she fell out on the road . . ." Stanislavsky laughed. How wonderful he seemed to me! I looked at his garden and the glassed-in porch of his house, through which I could see the steps leading to the second floor. Now I heard the pleasant tender voice of his wife calling: "Kostya, dinner is ready. Enough for today. They will never have enough of you!"

I greeted Lilina and took leave of Stanislavsky. "Wait a minute," he stopped me. "I haven't given you the last beat of the scene. Among those who arrive and those who are meeting people are the two girls, Henrietta and Louisa, who appear hand in hand. They are happy with the excitement of their arrival. They are not frightened because they are sure their Uncle Martain is here somewhere waiting for them. They are carrying their luggage. I think it would be good if you had many cartons, packages, etc., because they are coming from the country, and, if you have much baggage, you don't need so many people on stage either. When there is a lot of luggage, there seems to be more people than there actually are. Now the coachman blows his horn and the stagecoach moves on. Nobody looks at it except the boys. One of them sits on a suitcase, as if he were riding a horse, paying no attention to anyone else. Only Henrietta turns to the departing stagecoach and waves to the coachman, because he is the last tie to her dear village, the place from which they all have come."

"Kostya!" We heard Lilina's voice again.

"Well, I must go," Stanislavsky said very seriously and then, suddenly: "Perhaps you would like to have dinner with us. Do you students eat enough? How are things with you youngsters these days?"

"Oh, very good, Konstantin Sergeyevich. Luzhsky helps us not only in the theatre but in our personal life," I said. I thanked him for his invitation and tried to hurry away, realizing that I had interrupted his regime.

"Please don't forget that those who have arrived on the coach and those who meet them don't rush off the stage," he said. "They must give Henrietta an opportunity to approach and inquire if anyone knows her Uncle Martain. The square should empty gradually. The last to leave are the boys, who turn again and again to look at the sad-faced girls who wait uncertainly now, seated on their luggage. Finally the lamplighter leaves. He has a little ladder with him. You have a lantern?" he asked me.

"Oh, yes," I answered, trying to get away.

"Kostya, where are you?" Lilina's voice came again from the house.

Stanislavsky continued, "If you will effect the design just as I have told you, there should be great applause when the stagecoach appears." He shook hands with me.

I asked him for the sketch he had made in his notebook, thanked him, and rushed away.

I rehearsed with my actors the scene in front of the bakery and also the arrival of the stagecoach. I described the design of the two scenes as Stanislavsky had given them to me. We rehearsed a number of times most enthusiastically, and then showed the scenes to Stanislavsky. He was very pleased. He praised us, and he was a good prophet, because frequently when we performed *The Sisters Gérard* the audience applauded the arrival of the stagecoach.

The Villain in Melodrama

After a certain length of time, we showed Stanislavsky the third scene on stage. We called this particular scene, "Morning in Aunt Frochard's Cellar." The scene began with Jacques' awakening.

"You have accomplished a lot," Stanislavsky said. "I can see that you worked seriously on the scene, but I don't believe you have a good beginning for it. In your interpretation Jacques does not establish the mood for the scene that follows. And the actor who plays Jacques seems afraid to show what a villain he is. I can also see the director was afraid to establish more active and colorful problems for Jacques. Let me play the part of Jacques with the other actors in the scene. Have Jacques sit in the audience and you, Gorchakov, and you, Telesheva, put down in your notebooks whatever comment you think valuable for the part that you see in my acting."

To our great joy Stanislavsky marched up on the stage. We put the curtain down, and there was intense silence in the orchestra. Two or three minutes passed. When we did the scene, we started it with a short pause. Behind the curtain that divided the living-room from the bedroom, one could hear Jacques snoring. On the high chair in front of the window, Pierre was fixing his violin. There was no one else in the room. Louisa and Aunt Frochard were to come in much later, after the beat we called "Jacques' Awakening."

Can you imagine how astonished we were, when the curtain went up, to see Louisa instead of Pierre sitting in front of the window and looking out with sad eyes? Pierre was sitting in the middle of the room by the table fixing his violin, and under the curtain in front of the bedroom we saw the large dirty bare foot of Jacques. (Stanislavsky had found a white sock somewhere and put it over his shoe, first smearing it with coal.) Naturally our attention was arrested by the hideous foot, and, although at first glance it would seem illogical, even Pierre was trying to hide that horrible-looking foot from view. He even threw a piece of rag over it, but at the moment when Pierre did this, Jacques threw it off and roared angrily. Pierre looked quickly at Louisa and we understood immediately why Stanislavsky put Louisa in the scene. All Jacques' behavior, with Louisa there, was stronger in effect, because it threatened her directly, not hypothetically. All the following action convinced us of this.

Suddenly a shoe came flying from under the curtain and just missed Louisa's chair. "Why aren't my shoes shined?" Jacques' hoarse voice roared.

Louisa jumped from the chair, obviously intending to shine his shoes, but Pierre stopped her with his hand and picked up the shoe and began to shine it.

"Coffee!" Jacques screamed again.

Pierre went to the other side of the room to get the coffee, but there was another shout from Jacques. "I bet you the girl is sitting there doing nothing. I want her to bring me my coffee. Serve me in bed."

Pierre, following the text, said, "She hasn't come back yet." (He took the cup of coffee to Jacques behind the curtain.)

How much this little beat gained in intensity because of Louisa's presence! We were sitting waiting and wondering what would happen to her.

"Where is the cheese? I bet you gave it to your girl," the voice roared again.

In my direction of the scene Jacques and Pierre were already on stage at this point. They had their scene in the "open," as Stanislavsky would call it. But he played the scene using the element of *caché* which made it much more exciting.

"Eh, half-breed, give me my trousers!" Jacques demanded.

"I asked you not to call me names!" Pierre answered abruptly.

Again this dialogue, because Louisa was there, sounded so much sharper than it had before. And as the scene developed, Pierre's situation became more and more unbearable.

"What would you want me to call you, Marquis?"

"Call me anything but half-breed."

"All right. I will call you enamored dove. No, better, enamored rabbit. No, I have a better still, Cupid. Eh, Cupid, help me on with my pants."

At that point the curtain shook violently, making us think that Jacques was sitting on the bed and would appear at any moment half-dressed. Pierre came back and was whispering to Louisa to leave the room and go on the street. But as Louisa got up, she bumped into the chair, and the noise of the chair falling brought Stanislavsky's head out from the curtain. His hair was all messed up and there was a dirty white handkerchief binding it. His shirt was open at the neck. From the way he held the curtain against him, one got the impression he didn't even have the shirt on.

"Ah, the beauty's here!" Jacques roared threateningly, but not without pleasure, sizing her up.

Without a stroke of make-up Stanislavsky's face gave a complete sense of Jacques. Stanislavsky had this art of "making up one's soul" to a great degree.

The following scene between Pierre, Jacques, and the speechless Louisa flowed on following the text. One would think the scene had been written for the three of them.

"Maybe I should make love to that little bird," Stanislavsky said, winking. At the same time putting out his foot beneath the curtain, he commanded Pierre, "Put it on!" and while Pierre struggled to put on his shoe, Jacques continued to make fun of Louisa.

Jacques said: "Devil take her, she's a fresh little piece! It's all right with me that she can't see how handsome I am. She has everything else in place. True, half-breed?" During the conversation, Stanislavsky was pushing his shoe in Pierre's face.

Pierre replied *sotto voce*: "Drunken beast! Control your tongue."

Jacques said loudly for Louisa to hear: "What are you so excited about? Our mother has planned to sell her very soon to the drunken soldiers. Do you begrudge me being first?"

Pierre sprang on him, "Devil!"

Jacques lightly pushed him off: "Oh, you want to play with me? All right, let's play!"

And Stanislavsky arranged it very skilfully so that the two men went behind the curtain, and, obviously, a wild fight began there which we could follow from the movements of the curtain.

Pierre shouted, "You can do anything to me but I will not allow you to touch Louisa."

Jacques was beating him. "Do you want me to break your other leg, you deformed cripple?"

"I won't let you abuse Louisa!"

"I will not even ask your permission."

We heard Pierre's groans, and laughter from Jacques. Both sounds were staccato. The curtain moved in all directions, and from this we got much more of the fight than words could give.

Louisa stood in the middle of that squalid room stretching out her hands imploringly. Her lips whispered: "Don't, don't! Leave him alone!" These words weren't in the text of the play.

"Eh, boys, stop playing!" Aunt Frochard improvised, descending the stairs. From then on, the scene followed the text completely, but suddenly Stanislavsky came from behind the curtain fully dressed, neat as usual, even to his pince-nez. He foresaw the effect it would make on us, because as we applauded spontaneously, he bowed comically.

"Well, Konstantin Sergeyevich, I should like to know when you had time to dress, or even to tie your tie?" Telesheva asked. "You were fighting with Pierre the whole time."

"Pierre," Stanislavsky called, "will you kindly go back behind the curtain and illustrate our fight as though I were there? I'll throw you the cues from here."

And Stanislavsky gave his cues just as he had behind the curtain, while Pierre very convincingly demonstrated two people fighting. Simultaneously, in the orchestra, as he gave his cues, Stanislavsky was going through the action of fixing his tie, pulling down his sleeves, and straightening his coat. In short, he was going through the action that had taken place behind the curtain while he "fought" Pierre. Again we applauded.

Sincerity of Emotion

A few days later, we showed Stanislavsky another scene from the play, which we called, "The House of Henrietta." The set consisted of a small section of a narrow Parisian street: a tall chestnut tree covered the perspective of the street. Three quarters of the stage was occupied by the façade of the two-story house. The house was separated from the street by a small fence with a gate in it. There was an outside staircase that led to the second floor occupied by Henrietta. Following Stanislavsky's suggestion, we had removed the wall of Henrietta's room, and you could see the inside of the room as though you were looking through the window. Henrietta was sitting by the window embroidering.

Stanislavsky saw the scene from beginning to end and then asked us to repeat it. When the curtain went up the second time, he stopped the rehearsal. (He knocked on the table where he sat; this was always his signal to stop.)

"What are you crying about, Henrietta?" he asked the actress.

"I'm not crying," she answered.

"Yes, you are crying. Your whole body expressed world sorrow. I have nothing to look forward to any more. In the first thirty seconds of the scene you cried out the whole part for me. Come on, begin again."

Stepanova decided to sit by the window and hum a song while doing her embroidery, but at the first note, Stanislavsky knocked on the table again.

"What is this, an operetta? What are you suddenly singing about?"

"Well, Konstantin Sergeyevich, what am I to do? I'm not allowed to cry, I'm not allowed to sing . . ."

"Between *forte* and *piano*, there are thousands of in-between notes. Don't sit by the window looking like a seamstress *grisette* from Montmartre. Take off the pretty hair ornament and your coquettish apron. Dust the room and wash the floor. Give Henrietta a pail and a rag."

"But I'm waiting for Roget. I can't look like that . . ."

"Here is the most horrible cliché! In half a minute there must be a love scene and our heroine is all prepared with flowers in her hands and singing a song. Terrible!"

"Konstantin Sergeyevich, in life when you wait for someone, you certainly want to look your best. You would be preparing for the meeting."

"And just at that moment the bell rings and the hero enters, but if you are not ready to meet him and the bell rings, that's where the most interesting action begins. How can you finish dressing? or should you open the door first? . . . or how can you do the thousands of other things that you are planning when you think of his arrival. But the most important thing when you are really expecting someone you love is that you can't waste a second on so-called middle-class 'Gretchen' sentimentality, which our actors so adore in love scenes. Come on, wash your floor, but arouse within yourself the feeling you would have when you do have to do so many things that there is no time for dreaming."

So Henrietta had to start washing the floor. We, the audience, couldn't see her actually washing it because the parapet of the window concealed the floor.

Roget came on. He went upstairs quickly to Henrietta's door.

"Where are you going?" Stanislavsky's voice stopped him.

"I have a rendezvous with Henrietta."

"Well, why aren't you singing the *Toreador Song?* You certainly entered as a leading man. Just try to remember what circumstances preceded your coming to see Henrietta: the arguments between your mother and father . . . suppose you are watched!"

"You are absolutely right, Konstantin Sergeyevich."

And without being asked, Roget, following his own initiative, left the stage. He came back very quickly. This time he walked carefully, looked about before he opened Henrietta's gate, and then quickly went inside and leaned against the wall before he started to climb the stairs.

"What's that? Is Roget a crook? Or Rigoletto trying to get into his own house? All these are clichés. The first time you used the cliché of a leading man, a lover. The second was the cliché of the villain. Both are no good. Try to collect your thoughts. Think what took place during the day. Remember the circumstances. Try it again. Once more."

It wasn't once but ten times more that Roget went in and out, and out and in, until Stanislavsky saw that he was seriously expressing his relation to Henrietta. When finally Stanislavsky was satisfied, we saw Roget come on the stage from the scene before, preoccupied with the conversation that had taken place that morning between his father and himself, not anticipating the love scene. He very cleverly passed by the gate the first time and then carefully, looking around a moment, entered the gate as a man who is familiar with the place. He stopped for a second after opening the gate and then began to climb the stairs.

During this time Henrietta had been washing the floor, so that when Roget carefully knocked at the door we saw the face of a simple natural girl at the window, caught unexpectedly with a kerchief over her hair, a rag in her hand, and her sleeves rolled up. She gave the impression of a country girl working, rather than a seamstress "*grisette*," as Stanislavsky had called her at the beginning of the rehearsal.

The difference between the two images was so strong that we couldn't hold back our exclamations. It was something from real life that we watched, a part of Henrietta's day.

"Now don't change the pose. Don't move. Begin your scene right now. Don't open the door," Stanislavsky said from the auditorium. He had the amazing ability to catch the exact moment of artistic truth and use it to its utmost in the further development of a scene.

The text of the play seemed especially written and perfectly suited for Roget's dialogue which followed, as he stood on the stairs and Henrietta looked at him from the window.

Roget began, "Henrietta!"

"Are you upset about something, Roget?"

"I just quarreled with my father again."

"Because of me. You shouldn't come to see me, Roget."

"You know I can't give up seeing you."

"Let's not talk about it. My landlady objected again. She thinks I'm bad," Henrietta said.

"Because of me? Because I visit you?"

"Yes, we must separate."

"You must leave, that's true. My father is watching us. He was trying to get your address from my mother."

"What? You told your mother about me?"

"Yes, everything. And how much I love you."

Stanislavsky interrupted: "The moment you hit the word *love*, you suddenly begin to sing. If you feel like singing, all right, sing the word *love* with full voice."

"Let me say the sentence again," Roget said.

Stanislavsky replied: "No, why? Sing, please. You have a good voice and a good ear."

"Not good enough to give me the courage to sing."

"Still, I ask you, as a favor, do that exercise. Repeat the whole phrase but sing out the word *love* in any tone or melody you wish."

"But, Konstantin Sergeyevich . . ."

Stanislavsky said very firmly, "I ask you to do the exercise."

Roget said the sentence and tried to sing the word *love*, but it came out very stupidly and falsely.

Stanislavsky said: "Now will you remember that forever and ever. Because as a leading-man type you will have many occasions to play love scenes."

"I will remember."

Stanislavsky: "All right, let's continue the scene now."

The "continuing" didn't go very far, because Stanislavsky worked thoroughly and persistently on every minute element of the actor's skill. One time, the phrase was not quite following the thought; another, the relationship between an actor and his partner was superficial; another, there was not sufficient awareness of the play's circumstances or not clear enough visualization of what the actor was describing; badly executed physical action—even the final kiss between Roget and Henrietta; the rhythm was not held, an intonation was lazy, a gesture illogical. Nothing could be hidden from Stanislavsky. His remarks, the exercises he gave for a necessary illustration, and his demand that they repeat the scene five or ten times included all the actors, no matter how great or how small their prestige or experience. He worked with Kniepper-Chekhova with the same persistence and demanded of her as precise, consistent control of all elements of the actor's skill and of the characteristic traits of the character—details of her analysis of her part, text, rhythm, etc.—as he demanded of the youngest performer in our play.

The dates we had scheduled to show the play in the spring were canceled. Above and beyond the "actors' rehearsals," as Stanislavsky liked to call them, there were also rehearsals for the directors, then rehearsals for production. There were also rehearsals, a great many, for costumes. The costumes of the eighteenth century were Stanislavsky's favorite excuse to teach actors how to wear costumes in general. There were brilliant lecture demonstrations on theatrical costumes of all periods, accompanied by Stanislavsky's personal demonstration of how to wear formal dress, how to wear a hat with a plume, a sword, a cape, how to work with a handkerchief or a fan, or how to take snuff. He took hours in training us how to move and to use a cape as a part of one's dress. The examples and exercises that he gave us we will remember all our life.

After it was decided to show our play in the fall, Stanislavsky invited me to his house.

"As you see, we spent three times as long on that play as I expected. It is because of the *genre*. As I told you before, melodrama is a complicated *genre*, and this means it is difficult. I have a strong feeling that you are upset by our postponement of the play until fall. Naturally, it is very unpleasant for any director, especially a young one, not to stick to the date set. Now take hold of yourself. Don't let it get you down. There will come a day when you will be a supervisor-director and you will have to do the same thing to your young students. Sometimes it is much wiser to postpone the performance than to show it half-ready. Your actors are very young. They are sincere but not experienced. Many scenes in the melodrama must be performed most convincingly. Your young actors lack the technical virtuosity that is necessary; they lack the sureness. I feel that during the summer the inner essence of the play will penetrate and develop in their consciousness. In the fall we will give it another month and a half, spending most of the time on the technique of the physical action which the *genre* of the melodrama demands. I predict a long life for the play after it opens."

The fall came and rehearsals of *The Sisters Gérard* were renewed. I was fortunate to have another opportunity to observe Stanislavsky's regime as he prepared to open the play.

First, we went through the play seated around the table. Then we did scene after scene on the stage, then we looked at the sets separately, and then the costumes and make-up. Then there was a special day for lights and sound effects. Then he put all the scenes together in each act. Next we rehearsed half of the play one day, half the next. Then we had a first run-through, then notes in the foyer which took the whole day, with the corrections made there and then. Then a second run-through. Again notes in the foyer. Then the whole play again around the table. That took two days. Then the third run-through. Notes to each actor individually. Then a whole day of rest for actors, directors, and technicians. Then the first rehearsal with an audience consisting exclusively of "mamas" and "papas." Then notes again and after that the first public performance.

"Now I want you to understand that 'mamas' and 'papas' are the worst, the most unreliable audience," Stanislavsky said to us. "One kind of 'mama' and 'papa,' nobody knows why, expects their child to be some sort of genius. It always expects something extraordinary from the Moscow Art Theatre, and it is always dissatisfied. The other kind, excuse me, is always enthusiastic." God knows what adjective was in his mind for this type of "mama" and "papa."

"The real audience is the one that comes to the fifth or sixth performance, after the excitement of the opening night is over. The first few performances are usually attended by people who come to see the play, because of the prestige of being seen there on the opening night, or because of their social status, or for many other reasons which have no connection with the artists or the performance."

The day of the opening night arrived. We cheered our genius Stanislavsky and our beloved teacher with ovations, and, as usual, his prophecy was right. The play that was born with such difficulty had many years of life in the repertoire of the Moscow Art Theatre.

BIOGRAPHICAL DRAMA

CHAPTER SIX

MOLIÈRE

BY Mikhail A. Bulgakov

The play begins with a prologue: in his dressing-room after the performance, Molière tells his mistress, Madeleine Béjart, who is one of the leading actresses in his company, that he's in love with her sister, Armanda, and wants to marry her. Madeleine is shocked by the unexpected confession of Molière, whom she loves devotedly, and she doesn't have the courage to reveal to him that Armanda is not her sister but her daughter by her first husband. Madeleine tells her secret only to Monsieur Lagrange, Molière's close friend and biographer, who is a leading actor in the company. A poor, stage-struck young man, Moiron, has been hiding in the theatre so he can see the performance without paying, and he overhears Madeleine's conversation with Lagrange. Before leaving the theatre, Molière discovers that Moiron has no place to sleep and takes him home. He quickly learns of Moiron's passion for acting.

SYNOPSIS OF THE PLAY

When the play proper opens, many years have passed. Molière is at the peak of his career as actor and dramatist. His play *Tartuffe* has been completed and has been played before King Louis XIV.

The Church and the Aristocracy feel that *Tartuffe* is a personal insult to them, and the Archbishop of Paris and the Religious Cabal, a reactionary group upholding the feudal order, plot to destroy Molière. The Archbishop calls for Madeleine

351

Béjart to come to confession and extorts from her the fact that Armanda is her daughter. Then the Cabal brings Moiron to the confession. Moiron is now the leading man of Molière's company. Jealous of Molière's love for Armanda, he reveals the conversation he had overheard that night so long ago. The Archbishop informs Louis XIV that Molière is married to his own daughter, concealing the fact that Armanda was the daughter of Madeleine's first husband. Louis then denies Molière his patronage, which is equivalent to outlawing him.

Molière is not young any more. He suffers from a serious heart ailment. Too many blows have struck him simultaneously. Armanda deserts him; Moiron, his favorite student, betrays him. The King believes the Archbishop's denunciation, and *Tartuffe* is taken from his repertoire. The only two friends who stand by him are Lagrange and Bouton, his servant. During a performance of *The Imaginary Invalid* Molière dies on the stage —of a heart attack.

Y LAST WORK under Stanislavsky's supervision was on M. A. Bulgakov's play, *Molière*. Bulgakov submitted this play to the Moscow Art Theatre in 1931, but the actual production started in 1934. The play depicts Molière's private life, his struggle against the Church, and the Court of Louis XIV. It was highly thought of by the Moscow Art Theatre because of the dramatic tension of its plot and its well-delineated characters. Stanislavsky undertook the supervision of the production. Bulgakov and I were appointed as directors. Bulgakov was eager to try his skill as director on his own play.

The Scheme of the Play

As usual, Stanislavsky asked the directors and the scenic designer to work out the plan of production and then come to discuss it with him. But the day before the planned discussion, Stanislavsky telephoned me and asked me to come that very evening. I found him sitting in front of the small table in his study with the inevitable large notebook in hand. On the table was Bulgakov's manuscript.

"Well, how is your work progressing?" He greeted me with his usual question.

I was glad to tell him that the designer had already made a few sketches for him to see, that the actors were thrilled with their roles and impatient to begin rehearsals, and that Bulgakov had a great deal of material on the play's background and the biography of Molière to read to the actors.

"This is all fine and good," Stanislavsky answered, "but how about Molière himself?"

I did not understand his question and asked him what he meant.

"I reread the play again," he said, "and my feeling is that the character of Molière lacks some important characteristics of the real Molière. Bulgakov did not show us Molière's genius, Molière as the great writer of his time, Molière as the predecessor of the great French encyclopedists, philosophers, and thinkers. The plot is very interesting and dramatic. Everything around Molière is brilliantly described. Every act contains a great number of springs that move the action of the play impetuously forward. It has many brilliant situations and fine effects. Molière's personal drama is treated with the correct emphasis, but Molière as a genius-critic of his time is not shown. I consider this a great weakness of the play. I am not sure that the actors can compensate for this failing by their acting. Don't you think that more work should be done with the author on the play before the rehearsals begin?"

"I dread even the thought of it, Konstantin Sergeyevich," I said. "Bulgakov has suffered so much waiting for this production that the slightest remark about the text of the play makes him literally shake with anger. Perhaps, when the rehearsals are under way and he quiets down, we can approach him with the question of some changes."

"As far as I'm concerned, it isn't the text that I'm worrying about, it's the creation of the role of Molière. The rest of the characters are trying to defeat him all through the play, but I have the impression that he is defeated at the very beginning, and their work is to no purpose. There is no place in this play where Molière is shown as the victor in a situation, either as writer or actor. Everything is painted in one black color. I realize that if we were to tell

Bulgakov the truth, he would take the play away from us and we desperately need a new play, so the situation is quite precarious. I asked you to come here to help me find a solution."

"Perhaps, Konstantin Sergeyevich, when you hear the play read aloud by the actors you will change your feeling about it. You yourself have been telling us how important the living inflections are; the actors' expressiveness may make up for the omissions."

"This is fine," he answered after a moment of thought, "but all these things are only means of expressing, only intensifications of the author's conception. What do you think the idea of the play is, to show the victory of the Cabal over Molière?"

"Oh, no, Konstantin Sergeyevich, to show Molière's struggle against the Cabal and his victory over it, and even over Louis XIV."

"This is what you would like to see in the play, Gorchakov. I want it, too, but it is not expressed in the play. Name me at least one scene where you see Molière or his ideas triumphant."

"The scene in which Molière receives permission from Louis XIV to present *Tartuffe*."

"This is Louis' triumph over the Archbishop—the secular power over the ecclesiastic—not the victory for the idea of *Tartuffe*, Molière's masterpiece, against bigotry and hypocrisy. Quite the contrary. In this scene Louis XIV bribes Molière by this very permission to present the play, for, as you know, Molière paid a dear price by being forced to change the ending to glorify the King. There is no scene in Bulgakov's play in which Molière's genius is shown in all its strength."

Stanislavsky was silent, and I had nothing to say. I realized that there were many scenes in the play depicting Molière's tragic life, but there was nothing to show his creative genius, and no scene showing his tremendous influence on the French society of his time.

"This is where the difficulty and complexity of our art lies," Stanislavsky said, breaking the silence. "We all know what ideas should be heard on our contemporary stage, what is correct and necessary, but we have not yet learned how to embody the idea in the scenic image which is put into the plot or action, or how to express the character and behavior of the play's heroes through it. We do not know how to do it—neither we actors, nor directors, nor playwrights. Let us try to help our playwright Bulgakov and ourselves to do this. Begin to rehearse with the actors by emphasizing only the scene of the play and its characters, but don't spend any time on details or finishing touches. Don't work on separate beats.

"Now what do I mean by the scheme of the play? The scheme is the bone outline; it is the skeleton which holds together the inner and outer actions of the play. Rehearse along the lines of its inner and outer action, but don't dress it in the mise en scène and effective forms of expression. Keep the characters on the level of the skeleton outline only; don't cover them with the meat and fat of the juicy actors' images. This will come later. Define the characters only in their basic aspirations and rehearse the play only through its main accents. In this way it is possible to play the entire role of Molière in fifteen minutes and the whole play in forty-five minutes, not counting intermissions. When the author sees this living, acting skeleton—the outline of the main situations—he may see his play's omissions. Let us give him an X-ray of the future performance. It is most useful for testing the material of a play and its characters.

"How must you conduct the rehearsals with this purpose in view? Read the play, talk it over with your actors, and let Bulgakov tell you all he knows and wants to say about his play. Then skip the detailed analysis and study of the text. Select only the leading facts and events. Analyze them thoroughly with the author's help. Create a number of études on the theme of these events and have your actors perform them. Let them improvise the text but keep within the author's thoughts and ideas. Then connect the first étude in relation to the development of the play with the second, then add the third, and so on. Thus, you will have a chain of études. If your choice of the main facts is correct, if you use these as the basis for your études, you will then have the living skeleton of the play.

"To make them follow each other in logical sequence, erect a light series of bridges constructed from the plot. See that the action and relationships of the actors to the main event around which the étude is built develops correctly and logically, and do not stress the question of emotion.

"In the first act, the first event is the King's visit to Molière's theatre and his recognition of Molière's talent; the second, Molière's decision to break with Madeleine and marry Armanda.

"Act Two also has two main events: first, the Archbishop's decision to destroy Molière; second, Molière's eviction of Moiron from his house.

"Act Three: first, Madeleine's confession that Armanda is her daughter; second, the Religious Cabal pronounces Molière an atheist and a criminal.

"Act Four: the King's denial of protection to Molière.

"These are the leading events of Bulgakov's play."

"What about the death scene?" I asked in amazement.

"Honestly speaking," Stanislavsky answered, "the resolution of the drama takes an act and a half. To devote this amount of time to the defeat of the hero who does not even resist his fate is wrong from the point of theatrical construction. It is not right to draw out or to savor the destruction of any human being for an act and a half; particularly is this so in the case of a writer who is a genius, a great thinker, and innovator of his period. I hope that Bulgakov will realize this and change the last act.

"If Molière had been actively fighting in Bulgakov's play, you could play it for ten acts and the audience would watch with great interest, but, as it is, it's just sheer sentimentalism and, judging by his plays, we have no reason to accuse Molière of sentimentalism."

"Konstantin Sergeyevich, you have chosen the facts of the play dealing primarily with Molière, but the rest of the actors will want to have the events of their parts evaluated as crucial to the development of the action," I said, interrupting him.

He answered: "Molière is the most important problem now. Show me these events first, then we will work on the others."

"But Molière doesn't even come into a number of the events you named as crucial," I said, looking through the list he had just given me.

"This is wrong in relationship to the development of the role of Molière, and it is my intention to draw Bulgakov's attention to these gaps in his play."

"In other words, Konstantin Sergeyevich," I said, "the only purpose of this kind of rehearsal is to convince Bulgakov of the necessity for further work on his play."

"Exactly. This is my purpose. But neither the actors nor Bulgakov should be aware of this. As far as the actors are concerned, it is always to their advantage to work on the play's skeleton. If an actor can play a role in fifteen minutes that takes an evening in actual performance, then he knows its red thread and knows how to thread each beat of his role on it as one attaches the pieces of meat to the spit when making shashlik. All you will have left to do is to prepare a delicious sauce from the ingredients (adjustments), and garnish it with the correct flavoring, and the meal is ready."

He laughed. "The comparison is much too appetizing. Do not give it to the actors. It will put them in a prosaic mood. This is my second day on a strict diet, so my imagination is full of delicious food.

"I want to see only you and the scenic designer tomorrow. I would prefer to have our discussion of the directorial concept of the play after the first showing of your rehearsals. I am afraid I will not be able to keep myself from arguing with the author about the defects. He will get upset and refuse to work on it. Begin your rehearsal as I have outlined it for you. Keep in touch with me every day and keep me informed of every detail of the run of rehearsals."

Arguments with the Author

In a few days rehearsals began. I tried to follow Stanislavsky's outline and to keep his instructions. But I did not succeed. My prestige as a director wasn't strong enough to convince the experienced actors to follow this new method, and Bulgakov resisted, claiming that every scene in his play was important. Stanislavsky was ill and so unable to take over the rehearsals. It took us several months before we were ready to show the play to him, and we then improvised mise en scène.

After he had seen the rehearsal, he said: "Good fellows! In spite of all the difficulties, you stuck together and rehearsed to the end. My general impression is favorable, but there is much work to be done. I feel cheated out of something. Perhaps, it is a lack in the play itself. Though I repeat, the play is good and I like it. But I am not completely satisfied. I did not see Molière as a man of great talent."

Bulgakov said, "Perhaps this is because you didn't see the last act."

"I don't think so. I can easily imagine that Molière does not die as an ordinary man. I remember that he died on the stage. But it is not his death that is important, but his struggle for life, for his work, and for his ideas. I must feel the spirit of his genius, and this I didn't get at all. I saw a sick man pushed to the wall. I don't think that one needs flaming monologues to show a genius. Of course not. I would say more: there are minutes when Molière's genius begins to live and then I am all ears, but the very next minute or two the author brings me back to the psychology of an ordinary human being. I, as a spectator, want to know what constitutes the greatness of the man. You are showing me a life, but not an artistic, creative life. Perhaps, you have put in too many brilliant events around Molière, and these tend to hide his genius. They take time and occupy space which you could have given Molière. Did you think of this, Bulgakov?"

"Konstantin Sergeyevich, I say it is impossible to bring out Molière's genius more than I have. As you said yourself monologues will not help and one cannot present his masterpiece, *Tartuffe*, in this play."

"Let us approach Molière from another angle," Stanislavsky replied. "In your play the people around him—his close friends—don't love him enough. They don't worship his talent. Believe me, they should. Imagine then what their reaction would be when they see him cheated and mistreated. There are people around him who understand him and are clearly aware of his struggle, like his wife, Madeleine, M. Lagrange, and M. Bouton."

"Yes, it is true. His genius has to be played up by the actors who are involved with him in the plot."

"And Molière himself has to have an opportunity to show his genius. Your Molière has too much physical action. There is a great need for a scene in which we see him creating. It is important to see him writing and to see him inspired, in despair or in joy or in rage, but not in a physical scuffle as you showed him. Please don't be offended. I exaggerate intentionally. Nevertheless, you depict a great genius as a contentious fellow."

"You are shocked by the scenes in which there is physical fighting," Bulgakov said. "I feel just the opposite. These scenes will hold the audience's attention. The audience must fear for his life."

"I want to focus your attention on Molière. You must help us to build Molière's character. Perhaps I don't make myself clear."

"Oh, I understand you. You expressed yourself very explicitly. I am sorry, but my work as playwright on this play is completed. The play's fate is now in the actors' hands."

"I am not satisfied with Molière just the same," Stanislavsky answered. "Isn't he aware that he gave so much to his society and that he received nothing in return?"

"He was not aware of his importance."

Stanislavsky continued: "I will certainly dispute this. No matter how naïve you take him to be, he certainly knew what a great writer he was, and, if the genius is not aware of his significance for the people around him, then our duty becomes even more urgent to show his greatness. What do we want to achieve in this play? We want to show that he must be loved for his talent, his greatness as a satirist, and his style. I repeat again that we must show how unfair it was that this great man who gave so much to the world received so little in return. I think you show too much of Molière's intimate life and not his great ideas. Did all of you, including the author, ask yourselves what Molière lived for? According to your interpretation, it was only to love Armanda. According to mine, it was to expose without mercy the vices and hypocrisy of his time. He exposed everyone: doctors, charlatans, the Church, misers, ignoramuses, and, in so doing, he antagonized them all. The only protector he had was the King. When the latter rejected him he was completely alone."

"That is a good suggestion. I will write in a few lines to that effect."

"It would be good to add a few thoughts about *Tartuffe* which will emphasize Molière as a satirist. Then the mad anger of the Church against him will be better understood. I am sure that under his outer attitude of respect for the King, Molière was thinking, 'I love you, but you are a real skunk.' "

We all laughed at this unexpected comment.

Stanislavsky went on: "As a spectator, I also want an opportunity to laugh at such thoughts of Molière. He thinks about Moiron, 'You are a crook, a scoundrel, a traitor, a deceiver who lured my wife away from me—but you are a great actor.' "

Even Bulgakov joined us in laughing at his keen wit.

"I would like to see such undercurrents all through this play. Of course if you agree with me, Bulgakov."

"My agreement is not enough. One needs talent to realize this play as you see and hear it, Konstantin Sergeyevich. My intention was to portray the life of a human being."

"Yes, that's right. I see a human being in your play, but this is far from enough. Bulgakov, I want you and all you actors to re-evaluate Molière's relationship to the King, the Archbishop, and to his artist's world, so you can find these added highlights I have been speaking about today and adjust the text accordingly."

"It is much too difficult for me to do this. This play of mine has been under consideration almost five years."

"But in spite of this, it must be done. You have so much

in your play that is right and good, but there are gaps that must be filled. There is no disgrace in making mistakes. They simply must be corrected. Everything points to a successful performance. It seems to me there is little left for the actors and author to add."

"Konstantin Sergeyevich, these improvements have been going on for five years and I'm tired of them."

"I understand and sympathize with you. I have been writing this book"—he indicated his black notebook, which lay on the table—"for over thirty years and sometimes I have the feeling that I've been writing it so long that I myself don't understand it any more. Then I ask my youngest colleagues to read it aloud to me.

"Now we started to work on your play only three months ago. You have already had it read aloud for you. I know that a moment comes when the author ceases to understand his own creation. Perhaps it is cruel of me to be this persistent, but, believe me, it is necessary. All of you will be grateful later on. As far as I am concerned, I will help you all I can, all that my knowledge and physical strength will allow. Bring me any scene tomorrow from your play and in rehearsing it and in working on it with the actors I will try to show you what I expect from you as far as Molière's character is concerned."

"I think this is the best method of working with the author," Bulgakov answered.

"Then all is well. I repeat once more: you have accomplished a great deal; the actors are playing their parts well and many scenes have the right content and the correct form."

Rehearsing the Skeleton of the Play

As often happens in the theatre, the next day the three leading actors, Stanitzin (Molière), Yanshen (Bouton),

and Bolduman (Louis XIV), were ill, and the rehearsal
Stanislavsky had planned for Bulgakov had to be changed
to one which could not be used for the same purpose. And
ten days later, when the actors were ready to rehearse and
we all assembled to begin, a telephone message came from
Bulgakov that he was ill and could not attend this rehearsal
which would have been so important for him. After receiving the message, Stanislavsky thought for a few minutes
and then decided to hold the rehearsal without Bulgakov.
He asked me to put down in minute detail everything that
occurred at this rehearsal.

The scene to be rehearsed was from the third act which
took place in Molière's home. The first beat of this scene
is between Armanda and Moiron rehearsing one of
Molière's plays. Moiron takes advantage of the situation
to lure Armanda into his room. In the second beat, Bouton
returns from the market and to his terror hears the declarations of love from the next room. In the third, Molière
comes home; there is a jealousy scene, and Molière throws
Moiron out of the house. We played this scene for Stanislavsky as we had done it at our first showing for him.

Stanislavsky asked, "Which play of Molière are you
rehearsing?"

Stepanova replied, "This is a scene from the ballet,
Psyche and Cupid."

"In that case, you should go to the ballet to study for
the next three years. Very likely Armanda did go to ballet
school for many years. In those days in dramatic school
they used to teach the students how to dance first, then
how to sing, and only after they had acquired skill in both
were they allowed to act. I am afraid that you, Stepanova,
will not be able to play this scene with an accent on ballet.
Who are you supposed to be during this scene, Livanov?"

"I am supposed to be the faun."

"Maybe, but I don't think that rehearsing the scene

from *Psyche and Cupid* will show the genius of Molière as a writer. Ballet was not the strongest side of his creativity. And if Bulgakov's purpose is to show Molière as a creative artist, he could have given you any brilliant scene from his plays to rehearse. What scene between a man and a woman do you know that you would like to rehearse for this scene?"

Stepanova replied, "I remember a number of scenes from his plays *Georges Dandin* and *Les Precieuses Ridicules*."

I said, "Konstantin Sergeyevich, don't you think that the scene from *Don Juan* between Charlotte and Don Juan would suit this moment of the play?"

"Oh, it's a magnificent scene!" Livanov exclaimed. "I've always dreamed of playing Don Juan! Konstantin Sergeyevich, please let us do it! I remember practically the whole play and I will coach Stepanova and then we will play it for you impromptu."

Stanislavsky laughed. "See how excited you become from the mere suggestion of playing a good scene? That is what I need: to see how just the name of this masterpiece makes you enthusiastic. Now I see the influence of Molière's talent on you. This is the kind of excitement that people had who lived around Molière. I miss it in your production; I miss it as a spectator. I regret very much that Bulgakov is not here now. If he could only see your faces today, he would understand what we want from him."

Livanov asked: "Then it is all right to use the scene for our rehearsal? Stepanova and I will leave you for a moment and I will tell her all about it and we will show it to you."

"There is no need for you to leave us," Stanislavsky answered. "Tell her all you remember about this scene in our presence. Let Moiron get a feeling of being a director, a substitute for Molière. And we will have the picture of one actor being taught by the other, the essence of the rehearsal. Begin the action in the same sets. Stepanova, can you justify why you as Armanda will listen to Moiron as Don Juan in the circumstances given by Bulgakov for this scene?"

"Yes, I can. Today is the opening of the play and I have asked Moiron to go over it with me."

"Pardon me," Stanislavsky said. "According to your play, the declarations of love break through this scene. If the premiere of the play is tonight, can you give time to love affairs this morning?"

Stepanova said seriously, "Oh, yes, I can." The burst of laughter from the auditorium did not embarrass her. "Of course, I can. I wasn't anticipating it. I fought it but it happened so I had to give in to Moiron's desire. It happens in life. Love breaks into the day."

Stanislavsky was very satisfied. "You are perfectly correct. Now begin to rehearse the scene from *Don Juan*. You, Livanov, as director, tell Armanda what she must do in the role of Charlotte. And if some love dialogue breaks into your story, act accordingly."

Stepanova and Livanov started the rehearsal, very much absorbed in the scene. Livanov told Stepanova the gist of the scene very quickly, and he was about to stage it when Stanislavsky interrupted them.

"I am sorry but I must stop you. You are not rehearsing the way you should. Don't rehearse with me but with each other. What you are doing now is to show me the rehearsal's process, but you must really rehearse for the purpose of helping each other. Livanov keeps repeating: 'Keep your head up, lower your hand. That's right. Now one step forward.' Is this the way Molière taught you to act and direct? Is this Molière's great art? Is the great scene from *Don Juan* written about this? And don't tell me, Stepanova, that you need Moiron to help you with such nonsense! Don't you want to become a fine actress?"

"Armanda is already one of the best actresses in Molière's company."

"Just what do you expect to learn from Moiron? To raise or lower your hand? Oh, no, that is not Molière."

"Is it possible that I asked Moiron to correct my acting for the whole scene?"

"Oh! Oh! Now you're caught!—You said is it possible? On the stage you must know definitely and surely what you are doing. This is a very important scene on the stage. True, it is not written yet. Bulgakov, for whom we are preparing this scene, will not know how to write it unless we have a very definite and necessary purpose for it. You have no past for the scene and cannot play without it."

"I think that Armanda reads a great deal, thinks over her roles very carefully, and works hard on her development as an actress."

"This is right only if it has a direct relation to the red thread; if not, then it is superfluous lumber. What is your relationship to Moiron? Is he courting anyone else in the acting company? Do you or don't you need him? Perhaps you want him as a partner for a number of plays, but he casts his eye on another actress, not only because she is a good-looking woman but also because she is talented. In a theatrical company with a fine group of actors this happens. Molière, it is known, had a first-class acting company. Are you aware that you are sharing the same apartment with him, a very good-looking boy of twenty, and that he is your adopted son?"

"I like him very much," Stepanova replied. "I keep him by my side as a page."

"How does his prestige as a talented actor affect you? Do you respect him as an artist? When you appear in Molière's comedies and dramas, you and Moiron are drawn to each other as actors. Your acting talents supplement one another. This feeling is a very special one and I think even more powerful than physical attraction. This unity of talent in partners on stage is of tremendous importance to actors. It gives them a great creative joy. It is stronger than the most passionate kiss. Did you think of that?"

"Not very much, to tell you the truth," Livanov replied. "We only talked over our love attraction."

"One does not contradict the other. Go over the scene again. This time, use the text of Moiron and Armanda as Bulgakov wrote it."

"Oh, what Bulgakov will do to us for this!" Livanov said.

"I will take the responsibility," Stanislavsky answered. "Now begin the scene. Charlotte is afraid of Don Juan. Armanda must play very sincerely. She must completely transform herself into the timid country maid. Her splendid acting impresses Moiron. He caresses her hand, first as Don Juan—but a second later, he has the desire to touch her as Moiron, and then he caresses her for sheer joy of the sensation. There is already love in his second caress. Then Moiron makes her laugh at something. Then he starts to show her how Don Juan would embrace Charlotte, and he embraces Armanda differently. Please rehearse without pseudo-classic pathos. Rehearse honestly, the way we do. If Armanda is a good actress, she acts well. I think that from our point of view Molière created good theatre. In many respects it was realistic and at times it was subtly psychological—for example, in *Tartuffe*, *The Misanthrope*, and *The Miser*. Livanov, weave the love web around your advice to her as a director. And if there is a place where you can hum a tune, do it with talent, so that Armanda can be fascinated and fall into ecstasy at his ability. In every thing you do, the audience must see you two as fine actors. Now go ahead."

This time Stepanova and Livanov played the rehearsal scene with real inspiration and with the mischief of two

talented actors having fun. Stanislavsky watched this impromptu with great delight, while whispering to me, "I
wish Bulgakov could see it!" Suddenly at the height of
their love scene he interrupted them.

"Stop for a moment and listen to me. Do not lose sight
of your characters, but be aware, in the midst of your excitement, of the beauty of Molière's lines. Read together
Don Juan's monologue, inspired by it as actors. It doesn't
matter to me if you do it as Stepanova and Livanov or as
Armanda and Moiron. The monologue was gloriously
written. If you can accomplish this inspiringly, sincerely,
and with real temperament, we will get the sense that
Molière's genius is so powerful that these two young
rascals, about to betray him, cannot help but be captivated
by his talent. If you understand what I expect from you,
continue the scene. Begin from the moment which helps
you get into the scene."

The excitement of all those in the auditorium was
caught by Stepanova and Livanov and infected them.
Livanov began to use the text of Don Juan in his love scene:
"Do you think that I'm such a bad person that I am capable
of cheating you?" He continued the monologue.

> I announce myself the guard of the public morals.
> I'll never say a good word about anyone.
> I'll raise myself into the example of virtue.
> Bigotry is a vice in vogue now
> And all the vogue-vices are always taken for virtue.

Then Stepanova joined him, and Livanov pronounced
the magnificent accusation with great conviction and
ended ad-lib, "The old man is great! Right?" And Stepanova answered with tears in her eyes, "Molière is a genius
always!" "But Moiron is still better," Livanov said, with
all his obnoxiousness, embracing Armanda.

"Impudent boy, you should be spanked! What are you

doing?" Armanda exclaimed, using Bulgakov's text. Both
of them disappeared, then, behind the screen as the play
directed.

Stanislavsky was very satisfied with their performance.
"It is such a pity," he said, "that Bulgakov could not see
you two. Please tell him about it as precisely as you can.
Rehearsing this scene again for him you may not do it so
well. You felt the genius of Molière so strongly that he
forced you two rascals to stop your love pranks. This is the
atmosphere of Molière's home, the aspiring flights of
genius and the sighs of love behind the screen. Please let
us go on with the rehearsal. Bouton enters Molière's room.
He is Molière's devoted servant. Bouton, enter with a
basket of vegetables and fish, as you are returning from
the market. (The French love fish.) Enter without any
suspicion of what may have happened in this room. You
have a letter in your hand, and this justifies your entering
straight from the market, instead of going directly to the
kitchen."

Following Konstantin Sergeyevich's direction, Yanshin
(Bouton) entered the room.

"I will direct you for awhile and you justify whatever
I say to you," Stanislavsky continued. "Translate it into
action. You wanted to put the letter on the table, but you
stumble over some object that our young lovers left behind. Swear to yourself, 'Always disorder! I'm apt to break
my leg some day!' Notice the atmosphere of the rehearsal:
an open script on the floor, Moiron's sword, cape, the overturned armchair. You are about to put the armchair back
in its place when Armanda's scarf and handkerchief attract
your attention. You are thinking, 'Something is not quite
right here.' Turn once more to look at the room. Take off
your wooden shoes, put the basket on the floor and tiptoe
to the screen—servants do that. Listen, eavesdrop, then
carefully start to move away the screen. No one is there!

This is an added effect for the audience. They have just seen the two lovers go behind the screen. Where did they disappear? Now it happens that there is an entrance to Moiron's room behind the screen. You shake your head, thinking, 'It would be better if they were behind the screen.' Go carefully to the door, listen, peep at the keyhole, and decide for yourself what you want to do, but at this moment you hear the outside door slam. You burst out with the lines of your role, 'Oh, my God! I did not lock the door and here he is!' Rush out of the room immediately. You forget to put on your shoes. No time for this. Speak your line, 'He is on the stairs already!' You dash to the door of Moiron's room and knock violently. Instantly Moiron appears. His wig is crooked, his costume awry. Moiron speaks, 'Have you lost your mind?' Bouton, 'He is coming!' And Molière enters.

"You play this scene well, Yanshin. Remember, if you can, the plan as I gave it to you. In case you forget something, consult Gorchakov's notes. Now remain in the character. Stanitzin, we are continuing the rehearsal."

Stanitzin (Molière) stood at the door, anticipating Stanislavsky's direction. Stanitzin appeared at the door and silently observed the room, obviously suspecting nothing, noticing nothing.

Ten years had elapsed since the first act. Molière looked old and tired. Stanitzin rehearsed, of course, without make-up, but A. P. Lensky's remark that one should use make-up on one's soul rather than one's face was applicable to Stanitzin at this moment. Worry and morbid thought were indicated by his heavy walk, one button of his collar open, and a lock of hair falling over his forehead. Everything about him eloquently revealed his disturbed inward condition at that period of his life. He silently approached the table, where he wrote his masterpieces. He sat down lost in thought, then slowly opened his notebook, collected his thoughts, and picked up a pen. Moiron and Armanda peeked out from the door, and from the signs they exchanged behind Molière's back, it was clear that there was no other exit from Moiron's room. Either Bouton had to get Molière out of the room somehow or Armanda had to take the chance and sneak out behind Molière's back. Something fell in Moiron's room. Molière turned quickly. Armanda's dress gleamed for a moment. Bouton gasped in the hall. Molière, still suspecting nothing, went to the door and pulled Bouton out. "What do you want?"

"I forgot my basket."

"Basket?"

And now Molière noticed the wooden shoes and the basket in the middle of the room. At this moment Moiron appeared nonchalantly whistling at the door of his room. Molière glanced at Bouton and then at Moiron and then dashed into Moiron's room. Moiron followed him instantly. We heard Armanda's desperate exclamation, the sound of a slap, and angry shouts from Molière. Moiron flew out of the room, disheveled, with his coat torn, and finally Molière appeared by the door, gasping for breath, with wild eyes. This pause revealed Armanda's betrayal. And it was followed by the scene of explanation between Molière and Moiron. Then Molière threw Moiron out of his house. Next came Molière's repentance scene and his forgiveness of Armanda, who managed to justify herself.

The first two pauses, the entrance of Bouton and Molière, were not worked out by Bulgakov. But Stanislavsky outlined to me a brilliant picture of these pauses in one of our sessions, developing them into a number of extraordinarily interesting actions. I told the actors the design of the two pauses and we tried to execute them as precisely as we could. Yanchin and Stanitzin handled them with skill. Stanislavsky's remarks referred mainly to an analysis of these moments.

"Stanitzin, when you were sitting next to me in the auditorium and watched Livanov and Stepanova doing their scene, you must have noticed their superfluous movements as clearly as you would see your own in the mirror. But when you were on the stage, you repeated their sins. Your movements were much too strained and a number of them were unnecessary. Your entrance into the room when you put your cape on the chair wasn't relaxed enough."

"Yes, I felt the movements were superfluous as soon as I had made them, but I had to go on with the scene."

"It is good that your 'controller' checks it. It means you won't do it again. The pause was well played, but I am sorry that the scene in which you discover Armanda's betrayal is played off-stage. Why does Bulgakov let his actors play the scene off-stage? This is a turning point in Molière's life. I liked the way you, Molière, stared at Moiron. Stare even more directly into his eyes, so you can read the truth. Leo Tolstoy used to look like that at everyone he listened to or talked to. At the end of the scene, look into Armanda's eyes with one thought in your mind: 'Ten years together. Is that possible?' Moiron, begin to shout after he slaps your face. This is a true reaction but don't keep it on one note. You must develop it into a crescendo."

Livanov said, "It doesn't come out somehow."

Everyone laughed.

Stanitzin said: "I am afraid to let myself go in your presence, Konstantin Sergeyevich. Some moments come easily, while I think of some of the others: 'Am I overdoing? Am I cheating?' And I expect you to stop me."

"I imagine I would feel the same in your place. It's only natural. It isn't that you are playing the scene incorrectly. It's just that you must learn to control your temperament better. The scene must begin at freezing temperature. Then go gradually down to forty below. Then return to freezing and rise to eighty above, but in clean-cut fashion.

As it is, you jump from freezing to sixty, and so hot and cold are all mixed up. These changes in the temperature of your temperament must be controlled very skilfully. You must remember that Molière's emotions at this moment are not those of a beast. Moliere is fine, sensitive. Though your pain is deep—for Armanda's and Moiron's treachery hurt you terribly—you must not lose control of your emotions as completely as you do, for you are a highly endowed person, one whose observation and understanding of life are profound. The artist within Molière never leaves him. He observes what the end will be for Moiron, Armanda, and even himself. That is where Molière differs from an ordinary man. The rhythm in which you slapped Moiron's face is the rhythm I would like you to have for the entire scene. Stanitzin, I think that you caught the true spirit of Molière in some scenes today. When you understand exactly what you did at today's rehearsal, you will see that you have discovered the most natural and simple way to his emotions. In my experience I have observed only three cases in which the actor instantly became the character before my eyes, as though he understood suddenly and immediately."

"I am worried about my next scene with the king and the Archbishop," Stanitzin said. "After that, everything becomes easier, because Molière is much more active."

"It is because you lean too far toward the color of insanity in this scene."

"Don't you think that we're making Molière a little too noble?" Stanitzin asked. "With that in view, how can I say in the last act that 'I have flattered and cringed so much in my life'?"

"Flattery is not the dominant quality of Molière's character. What is the most important quality that I must see in this play? That Molière fought and was crushed, not that he flattered the king. In your performance give me this struggle. If you will make the struggle the axis of your character, the rest will come into motion. If in some places we find it necessary to show the nuances of baseness in Molière's character, we can always add them, even at the dress rehearsal. Your scene with Bouton is a very important one. The danger of this scene lies in making a 'little' Molière rather than Jean Baptiste Molière, the writer and artist."

Turning to Livanov, Stanislavsky asked, "Did you feel sincerity in this scene?"

Livanov replied, "I enjoyed some moments tremendously, but some are not yet worked out."

"Do you feel that, even after the little work we did today, we discovered certain things and that much of the play is taking the right turn? We must put it on a solid foundation. I don't start from the flowers but from the roots. My imagination springs from the given circumstances. When you work on your role, you must begin from the root of the character. My theory is to take away the text from the actor and make him work only on actions."

Livanov said: "I tried to work without the text and I found myself developing many more subtle nuances. Often the text hinders rather than helps."

"Now, about the movements. Stepanova, when you repeated the scene you used less movement. I like that. When the tone of the dialogue is correct, you don't want any movement. You must search for the tone until you find the true one. And, after finding it, you must live it over again and again without sparing yourself."

At this moment Stanislavsky noticed that Livanov was asking me something. He stopped and said, "What is he asking you?"

I answered: "He wants to know what you whispered to me while he was rehearsing. If it was something insulting, he would rather hear it from me than from you."

Stanislavsky answered through the general laughter: "No, no! Don't tell him! We said horrible things about him as an actor! Livanov has the curiosity of Moiron. By the way, curiosity is a typical actor's trait and, when he gave it to Moiron, Bulgakov's perception was correct.

"Now about the finale of the scene. It would be better if it ended with Armanda leaving and Molière remaining alone. I would like to see Molière going back to his desk, his hand mechanically lifting the pen. As a spectator, I begin to see the authentic, great Molière in his loneliness. He is alone by the desk with the only two friends that will never betray him, his notebook and his pen. They will preserve his thoughts and emotions for posterity. He sits by his desk thinking for a few more seconds. His face brightens, the gleam of inspiration is in his eyes, his hand rests on the paper; as though of itself the pen moves and his lips whisper immortal verses from *The School for Wives*."

Stanislavsky took the book and read with much bitterness:

> She has no fortune, parents or connections.
> She wrongs my care, my bounty, my affections,
> And yet I love her so, that tho' I doubt her
> The dirty slut, I can't get on without her!
> For shame, you driveller! I rage, I die,
> I strike my face: "Alas, and oh!" I cry.
> I'll go to her although there be no need.
> How looks she now, after so black a deed?
> Oh may my brow be from dishonor free!
> Oh if I must be shamed by Fate's decree
> That fortitude be mine, by Heaven's grace
> With which some people bear their own disgrace!

Then he continued, "Stanitzin, how do you like this ending for the scene?"

"Wonderful! I can play it immediately."

"Fine. Please talk to Bulgakov. Tell him all about our rehearsals. What a shame that he couldn't see it and couldn't live through it with us."

The rehearsals continued, but none of them was as productive as the one I have just described. Bulgakov made some changes, but not the basic ones which Stanislavsky wanted. The character of Molière did not grow from scene to scene. And Bulgakov refused point-blank to use the excerpts from Molière's masterpieces. He was right from his point of view. The difference between his style and Molière's was much too great. Bulgakov's play—its language, its characters, and its situations—could not be combined organically with Molière's plays. Stanislavsky's conception of Molière was rooted in his feeling of the true Molière as he knew and understood him from his works. He could not visualize him apart from his historical role. He was concerned to show Molière, the genius, the philosopher, and the great writer. The rest of Molière's personality was only a background in Stanislavsky's conception. These differences between Bulgakov and Stanislavsky grew deeper and deeper, and I could not bring them together. Also I was impatient and ambitious to have the production ready. I was certain that the actors' performances and our mutual work on the play would hide the defects which Stanislavsky talked about.

With all his patience, persistence, and clarity of purpose, Stanislavsky could not find the expression of his ideas in Bulgakov's text, and so he devoted his work to improving the acting itself. From this angle, rehearsals were extremely important and complete. They taught the actors and directors the Stanislavsky Method in work on the text of the play and on the characters, and in the development of the creative state of being for the actors.

Work with Actors

The scene before the finale takes place in the cellar of Molière's home. In the previous scene Louis XIV has denied Molière his protection, and Duke D'Orsini, instigated by the Cabal, has challenged Molière to a duel and almost succeeded in murdering him. Molière has returned home only to learn that Armanda has abandoned him. He is about to lose his mind. Molière's friends—the actor Lagrange, Bouton, and the remorseful Moiron—fearing for his life, persuade him to hide in the cellar while they guard his house.

Stanislavsky loved to rehearse this scene, but he had to work on it very hard in order to get the sincerity, depth, and power of emotion which it needed. He said, "You have achieved the truth in your acting of the other scenes because you have executed your physical problems correctly. You did not force your emotions. Do you remember my mentioning to you the film that unwinds before the actor's inner eyes when, in character, he has to recall something from his past? Now here you are all assembled in Molière's cellar. You are guarding him. You, Yanshin (Bouton), and you, Gerasimov (Lagrange), must recall how you have come to be here, like rats, in the cellar. Let the film of this theme unwind before your eyes. And live it. Molière is on the verge of losing his mind. It is a very dangerous moment in the role of any actor, because actors love to feign madness. The insane person sees things around him in a different light. It is up to your power of imagination to see a forest full of monsters in place of the cellar. Then ask yourself what you would do—not what you would feel—what physical actions would you perform to save yourself from these monsters? What does it mean to be a madman? Give definite roles to all the objects around you. This chair is a lion, that one a boa constrictor. The closet is a mammoth. Then begin to reason logically: what must I do to save myself from these powerful animals?"

Stanitzin interrupted, "I don't quite understand why I, as Molière, would see my cellar as a jungle inhabited by beasts."

"As long as you are capable of intellectualizing in this manner you are not insane. One who is insane never asks why. He is not capable of questioning. He lacks the capacity to analyze. He sees, hears, and acts but does not reason or ask himself why he sees this here or why he wants to destroy or treasure this broken fork, which at the moment is a magic rod. Your film is unwinding in the wrong direction, and pieces of other films are glued to it. Only rarely do you see familiar bits of your life on this film—separated, disconnected impressions of faces or figures that left especially deep imprints on your memory."

"How right you are! I want to escape the monsters in the cellar, but I still see behind their frightening ugly features the glaring cold eyes of a human being."

"That's better. Now you are closer to the visions of the insane."

Stanitzin started rehearsing: "Madeleine was sitting here, right here on this chair, just now. She is back again with me. Madeleine, save me, save me from him, from this image with the emerald eyes! He is not a king. He is a tyrant! I will destroy him if you only will help me do it, Madeleine."

Yanchin (Bouton) said: "Pull yourself together, master. Our lady Madeleine Béjart passed away three years ago." Then he improvised the following: "There is a monument on her grave. Remember, you ordered a marble statue of Madame Béjart in the role of Donna Anna, and the Archbishop ordered wings attached to it?"

Stanitzin replied: "I protest! I protest! Madeleine was

my guardian angel but she had no wings. She had no wings!"

"She had them but you did not notice them, my master."

"Excuse me for interrupting," Stanislavsky said, "but as far as I remember there is no mention of the monument to Madeleine Béjart in the play."

"No, there isn't in the play, but we've made it our new theme," I replied.

"It could be," Stanitzin said.

Yanchin said, "Bouton and Molière are in such a state that they can imagine anything and I fancy . . ."

"Of course you could invent a new scene for the play," Stanislavsky answered, "and as an exercise of the imagination it is not bad, but it has no direct relation to the moment of the play you are rehearsing. I did not ask you to invent new facts from Molière's past. I am anxious for you to find the right state of being for Molière and his friends precisely at this moment when they are forced into the cellar, hunted down and driven to madness. I suggest that in your imagination you create not just any film but the one which will bring you into the necessary state for these characters in the given scene. Stanitzin, name me all the thoughts, facts, and actions which Bulgakov gives Molière at this moment."

"Protest against the King who showed his fury at me so unjustly. Fear of D'Orsini . . ."

"Fear is neither action nor fact."

"You are right, Konstantin Sergeyevich. Not fear but the need to decide the following question today: whether to appear on the stage in the role of *The Imaginary Invalid* or to leave everything and run away to some province or some remote corner, perhaps over the Alps to Italy."

"Now that is different. These are the thoughts and desires for action which may bring about fear. Continue please."

Stanitzin continued: "I need to complain to Madeleine, when I imagine her sitting here on this chair, that I feel badly, that I am abandoned and persecuted by everyone. Let her advise me how I can save myself. In the past she helped me out of so many difficulties."

"Fine, fine, continue!"

"I need to kill Moiron to avenge all the evil he has brought upon me." •

"This also might be utilized further. Go on."

Stanitzin said: "Away with the King! There were court revolutions before. Let there be a king, but another, a new one."

"Continue!"

"It seems to me that's all. I'm played out."

Stanislavsky laughed: "Good. It is enough for now. Now compose a film following the actions that you have just described. Paint a picture in your imagination of the themes you named. Now it's your turn, Yanchin."

Yanchin started: "Here are the facts: Molière is insane; we will all be executed; Moiron is a traitor. I see a large public square, gallows, crowds, soldiers, the Court on the balconies, and among them D'Orsini and the Cardinal. We are being driven in a wagon, and a tablet hangs around our necks with the inscription, 'Traitors to the King!' By the gallows stands a huge executioner with a fierce face. My action is to awake. All this is a dream. I must save Molière. I must gag him so that he will stop shouting and won't be heard on the street. I must hit Moiron, trample him to death—the scoundrel!"

"Good!" Stanislavsky exclaimed. "It is clean-cut and expressive. Now paint a picture in your imagination corresponding to these actions. Gerasimov, please give us your film."

Gerasimov (Lagrange) presented his film. "Children! Molière and Moiron and Bouton—grown children! They were always like that. Now they meet with misfortune and it is up to me to find the way to save all of us from the revenge of the Cabal. I have been telling them all along not to put on *Tartuffe*. But how can I convince our master? This is now my life's goal. It was his duty, he always said, to fight bigotry, hypocrisy, and petty tyranny. Well, now he pays for it. We are forbidden to play in Paris. Tomorrow night we must leave for the provinces, for Flanders. If I can only persuade the Master. I better let them argue it out among themselves and then I'll take over. There is so much to do. We have to pack all our belongings and get ready for the road."

Stanislavsky continued: "I see that all of you are constructing actions preceding from the concrete facts. This is very important. Only the concrete thought, the specific action, and knowledge of reality make our art powerful, strong, impressive, and, what I consider most important, realistic. That's why I am constantly opposing general fantasies—fantasy for the sake of fantasy—not directed toward disclosing and enriching the facts and circumstances given by the author. Now act. Live the facts you have named. At times I will prompt you with the line of your action. Do not interrupt your acting, and include all my 'prompting' in the line of your behavior."

Stanitzin, Yanchin, and Gerasimov started the scene. Molière's monologue came out very convincingly, even in the most seemingly abstract phrases. ("Rats in a dream. . . . Misfortune. . . . The King lost the battle of his shoe. . . . I have a sore throat. . . . These are events of great importance for whom, for France?") Listening to these phrases, one became fearful for the great man's reason. Bouton hid in the corner of the cellar and stared at his beloved master. He pleaded in a very low voice (which was effective) for his master to be silent, painting the horror of execution with his words. Lagrange sat by the table, deep in thought, and only spoke occasionally to Molière and Bouton. On the table before him were pistols, a sword, a lantern, a large book, and a box of papers. He was inserting some notes in the book.

Stanislavsky was prompting: "Don't illustrate your actions with your hands. Only use words. Act with words. When you see what you are describing, try to make your partner see by making it more vivid. And try to read his understanding in his eyes not in his answers. Only the expression of his eyes convinces you that he is impressed. Don't lose the rhythm which people have when they do not know how much longer they will live—whether it be a night, an hour, or ten minutes. The slightest sound that reaches your ear is in your imagination the shot of a gun. A knock is an explosion. The sound of an unknown voice from the street is catastrophe and death.

"When you talk in detached fashion to yourself, I don't believe you. The highest art for the actor is to listen and to blush because of what he has just heard. Now be careful of your gestures! Please use as few as possible. The one you made now, Lagrange, is too much like an opera singer. The gesture of Venus' hand supporting her bosom is often used by bad opera singers, who do not understand that it is a woman's gesture, not a man's.

"Call Madeleine to you much more simply, Molière— much more simply and realistically. When you say 'dead,' let me see it in your eyes. Talk with your eyes. Use all the animated forms of expression in your text: laughter, tears, quarrels, reproaches, ridicule of one another. Laugh at your sadness. The picture of the scaffold brings you to ecstasy and exaggerated hysterical delight. Please repeat the scene once more."

The actors, inspired by his prompting, repeated it without interruption again and again. Stanitzin, Yanchin, and Gerasimov began to relax, as they became enthusiastic about the problems of their roles. The knowledge that they would repeat it again gave them the rhythm of continuous life and relaxed them from the sense of having to begin and end the scene.

"Now the repentant Moiron enters," Stanislavsky signaled Livanov, "but you continue. Don't interrupt your action even for a second. You are now in that precious state for an actor; you are clearly acting the unbroken line. You have forgotten where the beat begins and you don't know where it will end."

Moiron's scene went well. Livanov, always very sincere, was influenced by Stanislavsky's temperament as a director and unquestioningly followed his instructions with all his actor's fire. Moiron gave his repentance monologue, in which he explained how Louis XIV received him, insulted him by calling him a bad actor, and offered him the job of spy. He played it excellently. Overcome with remorse, Moiron has been drinking, squandering all he had on drinks, even his coat from the theatre wardrobe. Enraged by this confession, Lagrange is ready to kill him. Stanislavsky stopped the scene and asked Stanitzin, "What is your reaction to Moiron's story?"

"I am curious about Moiron as a writer and connoisseur of the human soul, 'What do you feel now? What brought you here?' "

"Correct. Remember, Livanov, never talk without an object. You have one desire, which is to wallow in repentance. 'Judge me!' you are crying in effect to them. Gerasimov, if you turn from Moiron, it's only for a second. You must listen even to his subtext. You want to pour out your anger over Moiron. It is easy to fall into a violent, physical mise en scène, pacing the room, but that's not good. If you are thinking of him as a brazen scoundrel who has the nerve to face you, keep it within yourself and, as you reach the climax of your indignation, let him have it. Don't halt your rhythm or check your temper at this point even for the sick Molière."

Gerasimov asked, "Do I listen to him when he talks about the secret society of the Church?"

Stanislavsky replied: "You are excitable, but the realization of the danger that threatens Molière holds you back. Also, you've never seen Moiron as he is now." Then he turned to Stanitzin. "Are all these parts that compose this scene clear to you?"

"Yes, Konstantin Sergeyevich."

"Now let's go back and work on the previous scene, D'Orsini's attack on Molière. How is your fencing skill?"

Stanitzin replied, "I have studied with M. Ponse himself."

"I suggest that you jump on the table at a certain moment during the scene. I don't understand why it is necessary for you to act like a coward here."

"D'Orsini has insulted me. I challenge him to the duel to defend my honor as a nobleman. Then I have a heart attack. The sword falls out of my hand, but D'Orsini thinks I dropped it intentionally."

Stanislavsky said, "I imagine Bulgakov gave this direction in order to show the persecution of Molière, but it is more important to show that D'Orsini was instigated against him."

Stanitzin asked, "What is more important for our play— to show D'Orsini as a professional murderer who has been instigated against me by the Cabal or to show him as a devoted member of the King's Court?"

"It is more important to show that Molière is being hunted by the Court and the Cabal. But I want Molière to be brave at the beginning of the scene and then to be obviously ill. I have seen a great number of fencing scenes on the stage in France and Italy, but I have never had the feeling that they were really fencing. They have always looked theatrical to me. We must find something to do to make it look real. And Stanitzin, though you are being hunted, say your 'forgive me' only after a bitter fight. Podgorny (D'Orsini), you can show your hatred even by the stick with which you, as a skilful duelist, are beating Molière. It will be very interesting to see that one has a sword, but that a cane is sufficient for the other.

"In your scene, Livanov (Moiron), you did not know that you were to be brought to the King, because you were taken prisoner by the Church. Also, remember that the King is a symbol of justice to you. You trust him completely. And here at last you face justice. The King begins to talk. Listen to his wonderful voice. Don't show your disillusionment immediately. You trust his words. Then comes the moment when, like a slap in the face, Louis calls you a bad actor. From that moment you can trust him no longer.

"The more cheerfulness there is in your line, 'Rejoice, your denunciation is confirmed!' Bolduman, the stronger the slap in the face will seem to be. Livanov, at this moment, let us see your suspicion beginning to form. We must see all the gradations. When the King offers you a reward for your denunciation, you think: 'Is it mockery? Or is it a sincere offer?' And, Bolduman, wait before you say, 'In the theatre? No!' First enjoy Moiron's impatience to know. Then, Livanov, you are lost when you say, 'I, a bad actor?' When you say, 'What am I to do?' you are even more confused. Louis XIV must be completely and sincerely puzzled and surprised when he says, 'What do you want this precarious profession of an actor for?' Offer Moiron the position of a court spy, as though you are offering something very honorable, like a Prime Minister's portfolio. Moiron cannot make it out. 'Does the King laugh at me or is he serious? Your majesty, I a spy?' And only then

does he understand it all. Here's Moiron's line of action:
From great enthusiasm to complete disappointment and
finally to complete rejection of the King.
"Stanitzin, you must work on Molière's appearance.
Your walk is wobbly. I want it much sturdier. Also, the
palm of your hand is not expressive enough. It doesn't live.
You lack that special French deftness. It is certainly a pity
that Bulgakov does not want to include the excerpts from
Molière's masterpieces. But let us use them temporarily at
least. Stanitzin, I think that one of the characteristics of
Molière is his unexpected outbursts of temperament and
his transition to laughter in the strong scenes."

Courage and Faint-heartedness

There were many rehearsals of this character and the
actors benefited tremendously by them. But they could not
change the basic error of Bulgakov's play: he had drawn
Molière on too small a scale. Meanwhile, the sets were
ready, as were the costumes and music. The rehearsals had
been held at Stanislavsky's apartment and also on the
stage. But Stanislavsky still did not give permission for the
dress rehearsal. The actors, the author, the Board of Directors, and I, to whom everyone came for an explanation
of the delay, were all very unhappy. Finally I was forced
to confront Stanislavsky with a direct question: "What am
I to do with the play from now on?"
"Do you think that everything has been done to this
play to make us sure of a fine performance?" he asked me
in return.
"Of course not, Konstantin Sergeyevich. But I have no
strength left to convince Bulgakov to make more changes
or to continue rehearsing with the actors to have them
make up with their skill what is lacking in the play."

"You don't have enough strength, Gorchakov, because you are not completely convinced yourself that the changes are necessary."

"How can you say that? I am thoroughly convinced."

"Why do I, ill as I am, bedridden, have enough strength to persuade you, Bulgakov, and the actors not to rush headlong to the opening?"

What could I answer him? I was silent, and so was he.

"I think, Konstantin Sergeyevich, because you know so much better than all of us together what the performance should be, you will find the strength in yourself to demand continuation of work on the play," I said at last.

"Not because of that alone. It's mainly because I have the courage to admit my mistakes." I did not understand what Stanislavsky meant to say by talking of his mistakes, and he read this in my face. He continued: "I had no right to allow you to start rehearsals until I was confident that the idea of this play was what I considered necessary and right. I made the mistake of falling under Bulgakov's charm. I gave in to the actors' desire and your reasoning. Always remember that the basis for the performance is the play. Until you are sure that the idea of the author is expressed correctly, don't ever start rehearsing! There are many things which can help the author to improve his play—actors, directors, and scenic designers—but nothing can compensate for the author's conception. Bulgakov wrote a play not about the greatness of Molière's ideas nor about his tragic fate, but instead about the personal misfortunes and mishaps of an ordinary writer. The play contains much true human struggle, and this touching material misled us all. The play has brilliant theatrical situations, but they misrepresent Molière. I don't know what to do. I am too ill to come to the theatre. I cannot come to see the production as a whole, but, as far as the inner line is concerned, I do not agree with you, the author, and the actors in many instances. Decide for yourself what to do next."

"What would you do, Konstantin Sergeyevich," I asked, "if you were in my place?"

"I would find some pretext to postpone the production and would try to talk to Bulgakov once more."

"Allow me to follow your second suggestion first and try to have another talk with Bulgakov."

"I wish you good luck. Remember me to your actors. Talk to Bulgakov directly and to the point. Don't be afraid to acknowledge your mistakes. Always have the courage to admit them."

My talk with Bulgakov brought no results. He saw his play on the stage with Williams' brilliant sets and with an excellent company of actors, and Stanislavsky was right in saying that I myself was not strongly convinced that the changes were essential. I reported to Stanislavsky by phone that I had failed to persuade Bulgakov. His answer was very short.

"Release this production on your responsibility. I will not be responsible for this play, as I'm unsure of it and I haven't seen it on the stage. Try to remember what we've said in our frequent discussions about it."

Stanislavsky did not ask me to report to him the result of our dress rehearsal, and he informed the Board of Directors that he could not release the production of *Molière*.

The play opened on February 15, 1936. It closed after seven performances. The two heads of the Moscow Art Theatre, Stanislavsky and Nemirovich-Danchenko, saw that this conception of Molière did not express the personality of a brave, courageous man who was a great writer and satirist. It didn't show the man who expressed the progressive ideas of his time in his work, who fought with an enormous persistence, and who exposed the feudal system of the government. The reaction of the audience convinced them of this. They saw the play was a failure. The background in which Molière was placed in the play belittled his person and made him a vain, mediocre, ordinary man. Besides these mistakes, the characters that stood out were Louis XIV, the Archbishop of Paris, and Duke D'Orsini. There was a fundamental mistake in the concept itself and in its historical authenticity. I was to blame because I disregarded Stanislavsky's persistent warnings. As the director, it was my duty to control my fascination with the external side of the performance—the splendor and power, all those elements which constitute the predominance of external form over content and which inevitably result in formalism.

After the adverse reviews and criticism, Nemirovich-Danchenko and Stanislavsky took *Molière* out of the repertoire. I had my lesson. But it was some time before I realized my mistakes. Also, it took time before I had the courage to admit my mistakes in a letter to Stanislavsky. But he answered at once, as though we had parted only yesterday—as though he had been expecting my letter all along.

> Your analysis of our last work together is correct. Never forget that what keeps the theatre alive is not the brilliant lights, nor the splendor of sets and costumes, nor the effectiveness of the mise en scènes, but the idea of the playwright. Nothing will hide the weakness of the idea of the play. There is no theatrical tinsel that can do it. Never betray the theatre as the most sacred conception in your life. Then you will not have the desire to dress it up in velvet and brocade. If it were only possible to explain this to all who come to take our place . . .